Jane Butel's

SOUTHWESTERN KITCHEN

Also by Jane Butel
and soon to be re-released by Turner Publishing

JANE BUTEL'S TEX-MEX COOKBOOK

HOTTER THAN HELL

JANE BUTEL'S FREEZER COOKBOOK

JANE BUTEL'S QUICK AND EASY SOUTHWESTERN COOKBOOK

FIESTA

FINGER LICKIN' RIB STICKIN', GREAT TASTIN' HOT 'N SPICY BARBECUE

CHILI MADNESS

NEW IN NOVEMBER 2016

JANE BUTEL'S SIMPLY SOUTHWESTERN

Jane Butel's

SOUTHWESTERN KITCHEN

TURNER
PUBLISHING COMPANY

I wish to dedicate this book to all my chile loving friends, students, and family who have always been ready to give inspiration, help with new ideas, and, of course, sample their way through all the recipes.

Turner Publishing Company
Nashville, Tennessee
New York, New York
www.turnerpublishing.com

Copyright © 2016, 1994 by Jane Butel. All rights reserved.

Jane Butel's Southwestern Kitchen

No part of this publication may be reproduced, stored in a retrieval system, or transmitted in any form or by any means, electronic, mechanical, photocopying, recording, scanning, or otherwise, except as permitted under Sections 107 or 108 of the 1976 United States Copyright Act, without either the prior written permission of the Publisher, or authorization through payment of the appropriate per-copy fee to the Copyright Clearance Center, 222 Rosewood Drive, Danvers, MA 01923, (978) 750-8400, fax (978) 750-4744. Requests to the Publisher for permission should be addressed to Turner Publishing Company, 424 Church Street, Suite 2240, Nashville, Tennessee, (615) 255-2665, fax (615) 255-5081, E-mail: submissions@turnerpublishing.com.

Limit of Liability/Disclaimer of Warranty: While the publisher and the author have used their best efforts in preparing this book, they make no representations or warranties with respect to the accuracy or completeness of the contents of this book and specifically disclaim any implied warranties of merchantability or fitness for a particular purpose. No warranty may be created or extended by sales representatives or written sales materials. The advice and strategies contained herein may not be suitable for your situation. You should consult with a professional where appropriate. Neither the publisher nor the author shall be liable for any loss of profit or any other commercial damages, including but not limited to special, incidental, consequential, or other damages.

Cover design: Maddie Cothren
Book design: Mallory Collins

Library of Congress Cataloging-in-Publication Data
Names: Butel, Jane.
Title: Jane Butel's Southwestern kitchen / illustrations by Mark Tucci.
Other titles: Southwestern kitchen
Description: Nashville, Tennessee : Turner Publishing, 2016. | Includes index.
Identifiers: LCCN 2016000710 | ISBN 9781681624600
Subjects: LCSH: Cooking, American--Southwestern style. | LCGFT: Cookbooks.
Classification: LCC TX715.2.S69 B88 2016 | DDC 641.5979--dc23
LC record available at http://lccn.loc.gov/2016000710

9781681624600
Printed in the United States of America
15 14 13 12 11 10 9 8 7 6 5 4 3 2 1

CONTENTS

I wish to thank Marilyn Allen, my literary agent who made all of the business arrangements to republish this book.

———————————————————

INTRODUCTION

Southwestern cooking is considered to be the fastest-growing cuisine in the United States. Whether called Southwestern, New Mexican, Tex-Mex, Cal-Mex, or American-Mexican, this style of cooking earned its position rightfully. Why? Because the foods are distinctive, full of flavor, fun to eat, and reasonable in cost. For the home cook, their preparation is not tricky or difficult, but they may require special attention to some new techniques for those not familiar with Southwestern cooking and ingredients.

I've often taught that it is a cuisine founded on the three Cs—chiles and corn, which are indigenous to this hemisphere, and comino, or cumin, which was brought by the Moors into Spain and by the conquistadors to here. A great deal can be done with the combination of chiles and corn, as there are so many varieties and so many ways to process and prepare both. Both corn and chiles were eaten by the ancestors of today's Native Americans (as were beans and squash, two other important foods in the Southwest).

Southwestern foods have many influences; the strongest are those of the Native Americans and the Spanish conquistadors. Old Mexico and even the Caribbean have contributed ingredients and methods of cooking. The style of cooking is also influenced by the settlers from other parts of Europe who made homes and planted gardens here. Many of the early dishes, such as chili con carne, are still eaten today.

To experience this cuisine at its best, there is no substitute for good-quality ingredients. If good, fresh ingredients are not available, either substitute canned or frozen or wait to make that particular dish. Most of the ingredients freeze very well, and Southwestern cooks keep a supply of seasonal ingredients such as green chiles in their freezers.

Even though there are some excellent Southwestern-style restaurants across the United States, Southwestern foods are always best when prepared at home. Very few restaurants seem able to master the authentic flavors and textures as well as one can at home. With all this in mind, I take great pleasure in sharing with you my experience in making these much-loved foods.

APPETIZERS

The appetizers for Southwestern meals are very special, combining corn, cheese, and chiles with other vegetables, meats, or seafood in unique ways, preparing the palate for the next course. Some are hearty enough to be a light meal. Nachos, quesadillas, and guacamole are Southwestern staples. The variations and combinations of these three are amazing. There are other appetizers, though, such as taquitos, pizzitas, and envueltos, which also rely heavily on tortillas as a base.

Traditional Quesadillas

This is the best way to make quesadillas—it's much easier than using a whole flat tortilla topped with another one. Literally translated, *quesadilla* means "a little detail of cheese." You can vary them using your favorite flavors. Following are four varieties we like. Try these, or create your own from what you have on hand.

About 1 Tablespoon butter, melted
1 (10-inch) soft flour tortilla
1/4 cup mixed shredded Monterey Jack cheese and Cheddar cheese
4 to 6 slices fresh or pickled jalapeño chiles
1 Tablespoon crema*
1 tomato slice, chopped
Sprinkle of crushed caribe chile

Preheat a griddle over medium heat, then lightly brush butter on the griddle over an area the size of half a tortilla. Place the tortilla on the griddle with half of it over the melted butter. Then sprinkle that half with cheeses and dot with jalapeño chile slices. Fold over and brush the top with butter. Fry until the bottom is golden brown, then turn and let the other side become golden.

Place quesadilla on a plate. Cut into wedges. Arrange the wedges of quesadilla, and squirt with crema if desired. Place chopped tomato over the top and sprinkle with caribe.

Makes 1 quesadilla.

*Cremas are made from sour cream thinned with milk to dispense from a squirt bottle and can be flavored with pure red chile powder.

VARIATIONS

Chicken & Pico de Gallo Quesadilla: Add 1/4 cup chopped cooked chicken to filling. Top with an additional Tablespoon of sour cream and 1 Tablespoon of Pico de Gallo (recipe on page 77) or to taste.

Beef & Onion Quesadilla: Add 1/4 cup thinly sliced grilled beef or other cooked beef dish and 1 Tablespoon finely chopped onions to filling.

Chorizo & Black Bean Quesadilla: Add 2 Tablespoons well-drained, fried crumbled chorizo and 2 Tablespoons cooked black beans to the filling.

Shrimp, Avocado & Tomato Quesadilla: Add 4 medium-size shelled cooked shrimp, sliced in half lengthwise, 8 thin avocado slices, and 1 Tablespoon chopped tomato to filling.

Nachos

Nachos are perhaps the most popular snack in Southwestern food. These are especially hearty because of the refried bean layer.

2 corn tortillas, quartered and crisp-fried or baked
Frijoles Refritos (recipe on page 220)
Mixed shredded Monterey Jack cheese and Cheddar cheese
Thinly sliced fresh or pickled jalapeño chiles

Preheat broiler. Place tortilla quarters on a small flameproof serving dish. Top each with a small spoonful of beans, then sprinkle with cheeses and center a slice of jalapeño chile on each. Place under broiler until cheese melts. Serve hot.

Makes 1 serving.

Nachos Grandes

These alone are almost a meal.

4 (6-inch) corn tortillas, crisp-fried or baked
1/2 cup mixed shredded Monterey Jack cheese and Cheddar cheese
Thinly sliced fresh or pickled jalapeño chiles
1/4 cup Guacamole (recipe on page 13)
1/2 cup Frijoles Refritos (recipe on page 220)
2 Tablespoons chopped onion
2 Tablespoons chopped fresh tomato
2 Tablespoons ripe olives
2 Tablespoons sour cream (optional)

To bake tortillas, preheat the oven to 425°F (220°C) and place the tortillas in a single layer, then put a smaller baking pan on top of the tortillas. Bake for about 5 minutes. Remove smaller pan, turn tortillas, and bake 5 or more minutes until crisp. Or use crisp fried tortillas.

Preheat the oven to 450°F (230°C) or preheat broiler. Arrange tortillas in a single layer on a baking sheet. Generously sprinkle cheeses on tortillas. Bake or broil until cheese melts.

Cut each tortilla into four pieces. Arrange them on a round large plate or platter, placing them in an overlapping chain—the point of one slightly overlapping the top of the next. Then sprinkle with jalapeño chile slices. Position a mound of guacamole in the center. Spoon a ring of beans on around the guacamole. Garnish with onion, tomato, and olives. Top with sour cream, if desired.

Makes 2 to 4 servings.

How to Make Perfect Guacamole

Guacamole is one of the most popular appetizers, salads, and toppings. Developed in Old Mexico and Latin America, guacamole's central ingredient is avocado. Avocados are sometimes known as alligator pears; the most popular variety for making guacamole is the Haas. It is black with a knobby skin and buttery yellowish-green interior. The second most popular is the Fuertes, which is the slender-necked, black-freckled avocado with an almost identical interior as the Haas. The other popular avocado on the market is the large bright-green avocado. It has a watery flesh and is sometimes somewhat stringy, so is not ideal for making guacamole.

Since the quality of guacamole is critically dependent on the perfect ripeness of the avocados, it is essential to plan ahead. Perfectly ripened avocados should yield to gentle thumb pressure and the seed sometimes will shake. They should be neither too hard nor too soft. Due to the difficulty of purchasing perfectly ripened avocados, it is generally best to buy avocados at least five days in advance. They should be firm to the touch and have no visible bruises. Ripen the firm ones in a closed paper bag on top of the refrigerator or any warm out-of-the-way place until they yield to thumb pressure. Never ripen them in the sun or heat or try to shortcut the ripening process by microwaving or briefly baking them. The avocados will rebel and turn gray and get hard spots where the heat touches them. They can also develop gray or black strings, which are most disagreeable. If the avocados ripen too fast, refrigerate them until needed. They will generally keep a week or so at optimum ripeness.

The ingredients of guacamole, beyond avocados, vary considerably. The traditional New Mexican ingredients are Spanish onion, fresh garlic, chiles, lime juice, fresh tomato, cilantro, and salt.

Some regions in the country add ingredients such as sour cream, cream cheese, and chopped hard-boiled eggs. Substitutes for the chiles are liquid pepper sauces and salsas. Sometimes lemon juice is used. And of course, various chiles are used, from serranos to jalapeños to green chiles, either fresh, pickled, or canned. In many border states and Mexico, guacamole contains nothing more than avocados, lime, and salt. Then hot salsas are added to suit each diner's palate.

Methods of preparation vary, as do the ways in which guacamole is served. The most flavorful and attractive way to prepare and serve guacamole is to scoop out the flesh into a bowl, coarsely chop it into one-inch squares, using two knives, and add all the previously prepared ingredients at once. The strongest flavors, such as chiles, lime juice, and salt, should be added sparingly. Stir just to combine, then taste and adjust seasonings if needed. This method most approximates the original way guacamole was made, which was to squeeze the avocado with the hands to make large chunks, creating the same result as that by using the two knives.

There are many favorite ways to serve guacamole. The most traditional is with fried tortilla triangles or chips. Other good accompaniments are fresh corn tortillas and vegetable dippers such as jicama, cherry tomatoes, or any preferred raw vegetable. For buffets, it's fun to serve guacamole in a bowl nested into the crown of a large straw sombrero with the accompaniments arranged around the brim.

The best way to save any leftover guacamole is to store it in a tall, narrow container, gently pushing out any air pockets with a spoon or rubber spatula, then closing it tightly with plastic wrap, making sure no air can enter.

Guacamole

Guacamole at its best! For greatest flavor, appearance, and quality, always cut avocados into coarse chunks. Do not mash the avocado or puree it in a food processor. Some like guacamole spicy, while others like it quite mild. Often piquancy is best determined by the other foods you are serving. If some like it hot and others don't, a solution is to serve a side dish of spicy salsa.

> 2 ripe avocados
> 1/2 teaspoon salt
> 1 garlic clove, finely minced
> 1 teaspoon fresh lime juice or to taste
> 1/2 medium-size tomato, chopped
> 1/4 cup finely chopped Spanish onion
> 1 medium-size jalapeño chile, minced
> 2 Tablespoons coarsely chopped fresh cilantro

Halve and pit the avocados; scoop pulp into a bowl. Coarsely chop with two knives. Add salt and garlic, then add lime juice to taste. Fold in tomato, onion, jalapeño chile, and cilantro. Let stand a few minutes before serving to allow flavors to blend. Taste and adjust seasonings.
Makes 2 cups.

Note: Many myths seem to abound about placing an avocado pit in the guacamole to keep it from discoloring or oxidizing. I haven't found that to work. Instead, cover the guacamole well or sprinkle with a few drops of ascorbic-acid mixture, the mixture used to prevent darkening in freezing fruits. Be careful not to add too much of the acid, as it can be slightly sweet.

VARIATION
Guacamole Dressing: Combine 1/2 cup guacamole, 1 1/2 cups extra-virgin olive oil, and 1/2 cup red wine vinegar or balsamic vinegar.

Taquitos with a Trio of Dippers

Taquitos are sometimes called flautas ("flutes") and are served with salsa, sour cream, and guacamole for dipping. If possible, use the two- to three-inch corn tortillas. If desired, you can freeze uncooked taquitos in a rigid, sealed container up to two months or cooked taquitos up to four months. To serve cooked frozen taquitos, heat on a baking sheet in a 425°F (220°C) oven until hot, about five minutes.

24 small corn tortillas
About 1 1/2 cups cooked meat filling such as beef, pork, or chicken taco fillings*
Vegetable oil for frying
Salsa
Sour cream
Guacamole (recipe on page 13)

Soften tortillas by placing each one briefly on an ungreased hot griddle until soft and pliable. Working with one tortilla at a time, place a narrow row of filling along the center of a tortilla, roll tightly, and secure with a wooden pick.

Heat about 1/4 inch of oil over medium-high heat in a large heavy skillet. (Deep fat does not work; the fillings will fall out.) Fry the taquitos, turning to brown evenly. Drain well on paper towels. Serve with salsa, along with sour cream and guacamole.

Makes 24 taquitos.

*To flavor filling, use cooked meat, which could be leftover, and mix with a clove of minced fresh garlic, 2 Tablespoons of appropriate stock, such as chicken with chicken (which could be made with bouillon), and 1 Tablespoon of minced onion. Taste and adjust seasoning.

Envueltos (Chicken-Stuffed Soft Tortillas)

Like an envelope, the folded-over soft tortilla makes an ideal covering for the chicken. Sometimes these are called soft tacos.

    6 corn tortillas
    1 cup shredded cooked chicken breast
    Salt to taste
    2 Tablespoons coarsely chopped fresh cilantro
    1 garlic clove, minced
    3 green chiles, parched, peeled (see page 340), and chopped,
        or 1 (4-ounce) can chopped green chiles
    1/2 cup sour cream
    1 teaspoon pickled jalapeño chile juice or more as desired
    1 cup shredded lettuce
    1 large fresh tomato, cut into wedges
    1 avocado, peeled and cut into long slivers

Preheat oven to 350°F (175°C). Warm the tortillas in the microwave or briefly on a hot ungreased griddle. Combine chicken, salt, cilantro, and garlic. When tortillas are warm, place one or more on each plate. Spoon one-sixth of the chicken down the center of each tortilla. Spoon one-sixth of the green chiles on top of chicken. Roll each tortilla around the stuffing and place it seam side down to hold it together. Place plates in the oven to heat a few minutes. Combine the sour cream with the jalapeño juice, making it as hot as desired by adding juice to taste. Place some sour cream on top of each stuffed tortilla. Garnish with lettuce, tomato, and avocado slivers.
Makes 3 to 6 servings.

VARIATION
Omit pickled jalapeño chile juice and sour cream; instead, serve a spicy salsa on the side.

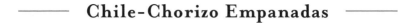

Chile-Chorizo Empanadas

Empanadas have been a favorite snack for centuries throughout the Spanish-speaking world. They are a great way to stretch morsels of meats, cheeses, and vegetables. Baked empanadas always have a short pastry crust and deep-fried empanadas have a bread-dough crust. Empanadas can be frozen up to two months unbaked and up to four months baked. Freeze in layers between waxed paper, wrapped tightly in foil. Reheat at 400°F (205°C) for fifteen minutes.

> 1 pound chorizo
> 2 green chiles, parched, peeled (see page 340), and chopped,
>   or 1 (4-ounce) can chopped green chiles
> 2/3 cup sour cream
> **Pastry for 2 (9-inch) double-crust pies or empanada pastry (recipe on page 279)**

Preheat oven to 400°F (205°C). Put sausage in a skillet over medium heat. Cook, stirring to break up meat, until browned; drain. Place sausage in a bowl and add green chiles and enough sour cream to make a thick, relatively dry filling that holds together.

On a floured board, roll out the pastry and, using a 4-inch cutter, cut into rounds. Spoon a little filling in the center of each pastry round, fold in half, moisten the edges with a drop of water, and seal edges with a fork or flute them. Place on a baking sheet and bake 15 minutes or until golden.

Makes about 48 appetizers.

VARIATION
Use fruit pie filling instead of the sausage mixture.

Chile con Queso

Literally translated, this is chile with cheese, and it is the Southwest's most popular hot dip. Serve warm with tortilla chips. Chile con queso may be poured into a rigid container and frozen up to four months.

1/3 cup vegetable oil
1/2 cup finely chopped onion or 3 green onions with tops, chopped
1 garlic clove, finely minced
1 Tablespoon all-purpose flour
3/4 cup evaporated milk
1 medium-size tomato, chopped
1 pound processed cheese food, cut into 1-inch cubes
1/2 cup mixed shredded Monterey Jack cheese and Cheddar cheese
3 Tablespoons finely minced jalapeño chile

Heat oil in a heavy saucepan over medium-low heat. Add onion and garlic and sweat until onions are softened. Stir in flour. Gradually stir in evaporated milk and cook, stirring, until mixture thickens slightly. Add tomato, cheeses, and jalapeño chiles. Cook, stirring, until thick and smooth, about 5 minutes.
Makes 2 cups.

Note: Keep warm in a chafing dish over hot water, a fondue pot, or a crockpot on the lowest setting. Leftover Chile con Queso is excellent spooned over crisp tortillas for instant nachos, or over hamburgers, under steaks, or in omelets.

Carne con Queso

1 Tablespoon vegetable oil
1/2 cup chopped onion
1 pound processed American cheese
1 cup Red Chile Sauce with ground beef variation(recipe on page 84)
1/4 cup chopped or sliced pickled jalapeño chiles

Heat oil in a large saucepan. Add onion and cook until softened. Add cheese, Red Chile Sauce, and jalapeño chiles. Cook, stirring, until cheese is melted. Serve warm in a chafing dish, a fondue pot, or a dish set over a candle warmer. Provide corn chips for dipping.
Makes 2 cups or 6 to 8 servings.

Queso Flameado

Popularized in San Antonio, this is a Mexican version of Swiss fondue.

12 to 18 ounces mild Cheddar cheese or Monterey Jack cheese or a combination
1 pound chorizo, fried, drained, and crumbled
2 fresh jalapeño chiles, thinly sliced (optional)
18 flour tortillas, warmed

Slice cheese fairly thin or shred it. Place in a heavy skillet that will double as a serving dish. Melt cheese over low heat, stirring constantly. Add crumbled chorizo in a line down the center of the cheeses. If using the jalapeño chiles, arrange slices at right angles to the line of chorizo. Serve immediately with folded tortillas. To eat, dunk pieces of tortilla into the melted cheese and top with some chorizo and chiles, as desired.
Makes 6 servings.

VARIATION
If not garnishing with chiles, serve with chopped fresh jalapeño chiles and fresh salsa.

Pickled Posole

This lightly spiced, corn-based snack is special anytime—anywhere. No one can guess what it is! You can serve it in salads or create main-dish seafood or chicken salads. Serve laced with salsa-based dressing.

    1/2 pound dried posole
    1/4 cup fresh lime juice
    2 teaspoons salt
    1/4 cup virgin olive oil
    3 garlic cloves, minced
    1 1/2 fresh or dried bay leaves
    2 leaves Mexican sage, chopped, or 1/2 teaspoon dried leaf sage
    1/2 teaspoon ground or crushed Mexican oregano
    2 teaspoons ground cumin
    2 Tablespoons ground mild chile
    1 large Spanish onion, thinly sliced, separated into rings
    1/2 fresh or canned jalapeño chile, finely chopped
    1/2 cup vinegar
    1/4 cup chopped fresh cilantro, divided
    4 leaf lettuce leaves

Rinse and sort the posole; place in a heavy pot. Cover with water and boil, stirring occasionally, until tender, about 3 hours. Do not season until kernels have softened. Cool to room temperature and drain. Sprinkle with the lime juice and the salt.

While the posole is cooking, place oil, garlic, bay leaves, sage, oregano, cumin, ground chile, onion, jalapeño chile, and vinegar in a food processor or blender and process until combined. Pour over the cooled posole and stir well, using a gentle folding motion without breaking the posole kernels. Add 2 Tablespoons of the cilantro and stir again. Marinate in the refrigerator, stirring occasionally, at least 4 hours or overnight.

Arrange in a shallow rectangular bowl, tucking lettuce leaves into each corner. Garnish with the remaining 2 Tablespoons of chopped cilantro. Serve with a small bowl of wooden picks.

Makes 8 cups.

Vegetable Coulis

This puree adds a colorful note as an underliner and an artful signature to complement Southwestern dishes. Use a single vegetable or a combination of vegetables. Season to taste with chiles, cilantro, lime juice, or lemon juice.

1 Tablespoon light olive oil
4 cups prepared vegetables, such as chopped green, red, or yellow bell
 peppers or fresh tomatoes, peeled, seeded, and coarsely chopped
Fresh minced jalapeño chile or serrano chile
Fresh cilantro (optional)
Fresh lime juice or lemon juice
Ground chile
Salt and freshly ground black pepper to taste

Heat oil in a heavy skillet over medium heat. Add vegetables, cover, and cook about 5 minutes or until softened. Add the fresh minced chile and cilantro, if using. Cook about 1 minute. Pour mixture into a food processor or blender and process until pureed. Season to taste with lime or lemon juice, ground chile, salt, and pepper. If too moist, pour back into skillet and cook, stirring, over medium-high heat until thick. To serve, spoon some on each plate and top with desired appetizer or entrée.

Makes 4 cups puree.

Note: Sour cream or mayonnaise mixtures flavored with salsa, herbs, and chiles can be used to decorate the coulis or the plate, using any desired design, such as a swiggle or zigzag.

Grilled Squash Blossoms on Salsa Vinaigrette

Oh so showy, but quick and easy. Just remember that the blossoms are highly perishable. I like these much better than the batter-dipped blossoms. These are very available in the summer; in winter months only very special suppliers of out-of-season produce will have them.

    12 fresh squash blossoms from zucchini or summer squash—either with
        (female) or without (male) the little squash attached
    6 ounces chèvre cheese or cream cheese, softened
    1/2 teaspoon ground Mexican oregano
    1/4 teaspoon crushed pequin quebrado chile
    1 recipe Salsa Vinaigrette (recipe on page 73)

Lay out blossoms on a baking sheet. Preheat broiler. Mix cheese, oregano, and crushed chile. Stuff each blossom with about 1 Tablespoon of the cheese mixture. Place blossoms under the broiler and cook only until the cheese begins to bubble. Do not brown. To serve, spoon some vinaigrette on each plate and top with 2 or 3 warm blossoms.
Makes 4 to 6 servings.

Pizzitas

A Southwestern version of the Italian snack food, these "pizzas" are rather similar to a tostado. Amounts of ingredients vary depending on the number of tortillas.

    Corn or flour tortillas, crisp-fried
    Fried, crumbled chorizo, Italian sausage, or pork sausage
    Stewed chicken, pork, or chile beef
    Very thinly sliced onions
    Frijoles Refritos (recipe on page 220), or cooked pinto beans
    Green chiles, cut into strips, or jalapeño chile slices
    Chile con Queso (recipe on page 17), shredded Monterey Jack cheese, or Cheddar cheese
    Creamy Salsa Verde (recipe on page 82), Salsa Roja (recipe on
        page 82), or Salsa Fresca (recipe on page 78)

Preheat oven to 300°F (150°C) oven. Place tortillas on a baking sheet. Bake 5 minutes or until warmed. Increase oven temperature to 450°F (230°C). Top warm tortillas with a combination of some of the remaining ingredients. If desired, add a second layer. Bake about 5 minutes or until heated through.

Calabacita Bites in Crispy Blue Corn Bread Coating

Make these either a few minutes before serving or, preferably, set a small deep-fryer near your serving table.

> 1/4 cup all-purpose flour
> 3 Tablespoons blue cornmeal
> 1/4 teaspoon baking powder
> Dash of salt
> 1 large egg, slightly beaten
> 2 Tablespoons milk
> 3 zucchini, each about 1 inch in diameter and 5 inches long
> 1 quart vegetable oil
> Fresh Garden Salsa (recipe on page 79) or salsa of your choice

Combine flour, cornmeal, baking powder, and salt in a shallow bowl. Add egg and milk and mix well. (This batter will hold, refrigerated, up to 6 hours.)

Cut zucchini into 2-inch-long pieces. To cook, heat oil to 375°F (190°C). Using long bamboo skewers, pierce each piece of zucchini and dip into the batter, then fry until light golden. Drain well on paper towels. Serve warm on the skewers with salsa.

Makes 6 servings.

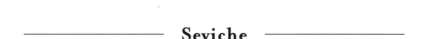

Seviche

This is very fresh raw seafood or fish that "cooks" in its own marinade. For an attractive first course, serve it in wine glasses with a crisp tortilla triangle speared into the top.

1 1/4 pounds fresh bay scallops, shelled raw shrimp, or cod fillets
    cut into 1 1/2-inch pieces, or any combination
Juice of 5 or 6 limes
3 or 4 fresh green chiles, parched, peeled (see page 340), and chopped
1/4 cup olive oil
1 Tablespoon chopped fresh cilantro
1/8 teaspoon ground Mexican oregano
Salt and freshly ground black pepper to taste
1 avocado, ripe but firm, cut into thin wedges
3/4 cup thinly sliced red onion or 4 green onions, quartered
    lengthwise and cut into 1 1/2-inch pieces
1 tomato, cut into wedges
Fried tortilla triangles*

Place seafood in a shallow glass dish and pour lime juice over it. Marinate in the refrigerator 4 hours, turning occasionally.

Combine green chiles, olive oil, cilantro, oregano, salt, and pepper. Pour over the seafood mixture and mix gently. Add avocado wedges, onion, and tomato wedges. Stir very gently to coat with marinade, being careful not to break the avocado or tomato wedges. Cover and refrigerate 1 to 2 hours. Serve in a wine glass with a spear of a deep-fried tortilla triangle.

Makes 8 servings.

* Make by cutting a tortilla into a triangle the full length of a tortilla and deep frying in 375°F (190°C) vegetable oil.

VARIATION

Any leftovers can be drained and combined with cooked pasta or tossed with your favorite vegetables and dressing.

Smoked Trout

Trout are so delicately flavored they make delicious appetizers when smoked. And, if you like to fish and catch a great number, smoking is a wonderful method for preserving them for future meals from the freezer.

Handful of mesquite or other wood chips
4 small trout, ready to cook
Salt
Freshly ground black pepper
Lime wedges

Preheat oven to 425°F (220°C). Turn a roasting pan into an inside smoker: Sprinkle bottom of pan with a handful of mesquite or wood chips. Place a rack over the chips. Put the roaster on stove over medium-high heat. When the chips begin to smoke,* place cleaned fish on rack, sprinkle with salt and pepper, and cover. Place roaster in the oven. Roast 25 minutes, or until fish just begins to flake when pierced with a fork. Serve with lime wedges.
Makes 8 servings.

* If you have a smoke detector in your kitchen, the smoke from the chips may set it off!
Note: Will freeze for up to 8 months.

Carnitas

These are a very popular snack in Old Mexico and are very easy to make. They are great served with a fresh salsa for dipping. Freeze, tightly wrapped, up to two months.

2 pounds fresh boneless pork, with at least 1/4 inch of fat and/or skin left on
3 garlic cloves, finely minced
1/2 teaspoon salt
2 teaspoons ground, pure hot chile or to taste
1/2 cup fresh orange juice
Water

Cut pork into bite-size cubes or into strips about 2 1/2 inches by 1 inch. Place pork in a heavy skillet; add garlic, salt, ground chile, orange juice, and about 1/2 inch of water. Bring to a boil over high heat; then reduce heat and simmer, stirring occasionally, until all the water has evaporated. Increase heat a little and cook the meat until it is well browned and crisp. Serve warm.
Makes 6 to 8 servings.

Note: Pork shoulder is the best cut for this; it is not necessary to use an expensive one. A small amount of fat is left on because it will fry crisp and give a wonderful flavor and texture. You can prepare the meat ahead and warm the pieces on a baking sheet just prior to serving.

Beef Jerky

This is a nice snack for hiking or camping or, when cut into bite-size pieces, it is excellent as a cocktail snack. Originally, the chile was added to the "jerked" beef to prolong freshness while the meat hung from high branches to dry. Jerky, or dried chile meat when reconstituted, was probably this country's original convenience food.

> **2 pounds beef flank steak, excess fat removed, sliced about**
> **1/8 inch thick, with the grain of the meat**
> **1/4 cup dry red wine or red wine vinegar**
> **2 Tablespoons white wine vinegar**
> **1 garlic clove, well mashed**
> **1 teaspoon ground hot or mild chile**
> **1/2 teaspoon salt**

Place flank steak in a bowl. Combine red wine vinegar, white wine vinegar, garlic, ground chile, and salt in a separate small bowl. Pour marinade over steak and stir to coat. Marinate 1 hour. Gently squeeze excess marinade off each piece of meat.

Preheat oven to 200°F (95°C). Lay each slice of steak across oven rack. Bake 6 hours or until very dry. Store in an airtight container in the refrigerator.

Makes 8 to 12 servings, as a snack.

Note: Do not attempt this recipe unless your oven will maintain a low temperature. Jerky can also be made in a food dehydrator.

Soups & Stews

From hearty and hot to cool and light—we've created a collection of both old and new soups and stews, with something for every occasion. Perhaps the stew with the most mystical properties is the Albuquerque posole, a dish that is served at all feast days, important celebrations, and New Year's Day. Of special note are the chilis—everything from the traditional chili con carne or Bowl o' Red to new chilis with black beans and chicken, and even a vegetarian version.

Our creamed vegetable soups featuring corn and squash are excellent to start a more formal Southwest dinner in cold weather, whereas the gazpachos or cilantro-cucumber are soothing in the summer.

Pueblo Posole

This is the festival food traditionally served at New Mexican Native American or Pueblo celebrations. According to their belief, eating posole brings legendary good luck, hence it is enjoyed by most New Mexicans, particularly for the holidays. Posole is the chicken noodle soup of Mexico—known for its healthful properties and refers to the dish as well as the main ingredient. In Mexico, they like to serve posole garnished with thinly sliced radishes, shredded cabbage, cilantro sprigs, lime wedges, and cubed avocado. Posole is made from lime-treated corn kernels and is the mother process for all corn products made from masa such as tortillas.

> 1 pound dried posole
> About 1 quart water
> 2 pounds pork shoulder, cut into small cubes
> 2 garlic cloves, finely chopped
> 1/4 to 1/3 cup crushed caribe chile
> 2 Tablespoons ground cumin, divided
> 1 Tablespoon salt

Cook posole in unsalted water over medium-low heat, stirring occasionally, until soft, about 2 hours. (It will never soften in salted water.) Add water as needed. Meanwhile, in a heavy skillet, cook pork in its own fat until very brown. Add a little water to deglaze pan, and combine with the posole.

Add the garlic, chile, 1 Tablespoon cumin, and salt, and stew until posole and pork are very tender and flavors blend, at least 2 hours or up to 6 hours, depending on desired texture. Add the remaining 1 Tablespoon cumin, then taste and adjust seasonings.

Makes 8 to 12 servings.

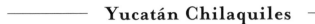

Yucatán Chilaquiles

I taught a comparative weeklong cooking class at the Melia Mayan Hotel in Cozumel, and when vacationing there to plan the school, I was very fond of their chilaquiles and requested the recipe. These were a breakfast staple on their buffet line. The chef gladly gave me the recipe that follows. You can use this as a basic and substitute other meats or tofu and other salsas.

    2 1/4 pounds chicken breasts
    1 quart chicken stock
    20 tortillas
    1 quart vegetable oil (optional)
    Salsa Rachero Yucatán Style (recipe follows)
    1 pint sour cream
    3/4 cup Queso Blanco
    Jalapeño chiles, thinly sliced

Simmer chicken in chicken stock in a large saucepan until tender, about 20 minutes. Remove chicken from stock, reserving stock for another use. Cool chicken slightly, then skin, bone, and shred the meat. Meanwhile, prepare Salsa Ranchero Yucatán Style.

Preheat oven to 350°F (175°C). Cut the tortillas in sixths, making triangles. Use tortilla triangles baked at 425°F (220°C) in a double layer on a baking sheet until crisp, about 12 to 15 minutes, stirring every 5 minutes, or heat oil in a large saucepan to 375°F (190°C). Add the triangles in batches and fry until crisp. Remove with a slotted spoon as they are cooked and drain on paper towels. Place the fried tortillas in a casserole dish and top with shredded chicken. Then cover with the salsa. Top with dollops of sour cream and cheese.

Bake about 15 minutes to blend the flavors evenly and heat through. Serve with jalapeño chiles. *Makes 6 to 8 servings.*

Salsa Ranchero Yucatán Style
    1 1/2 pounds (4 to 6) tomatoes, peeled
    1 Tablespoon vegetable oil
    6 garlic cloves, minced
    1/2 cup chopped onion
    2 Tablespoons fresh cilantro, coarsely chopped
    2 Tablespoons epazote leaves (optional)
    1/4 cup chicken stock
    1 Tablespoon Worcestershire sauce
    Salt to taste

Place tomatoes in a blender or food processor and process until pureed. Heat oil in a deep skillet. Add garlic and cook until it sizzles; then add onion, cilantro, epazote, chicken stock, Worcestershire, and salt. Cook about 5 minutes. Taste and adjust seasoning, then keep the salsa warm until needed.

Black Bean Soup

This is a very popular soup in the Southwest and can be the basis for lots of variations. For instance, serve with a companion soup, as described in the note following the recipe.

  5 cups chicken broth
  4 to 5 cups water
  3 cups dried black beans, sorted and rinsed
  2 meaty ham hocks
  5 garlic cloves, minced
  2 1/2 teaspoons salt
  1 cup diced onion
  1 and 1/2 Tablespoon ground cumin, divided
  2 Tablespoons ground hot chile
  1/4 cup pickled jalapeño chile juice or to taste
  Sour cream
  Minced green onions
  Crushed caribe chile

Combine the chicken broth and 4 cups of water in a large pot and add the beans, ham hocks, garlic, salt, onion, 1/2 Tablespoon cumin, and ground chile. Cook, adding more water if necessary, until the beans are tender; they should be soft when mashed against the side of a pan. Stir in the pickled jalapeño chile juice to taste. Add the remaining 1 Tablespoon cumin, then taste and adjust seasonings if necessary.

Spoon soup into soup bowls. Garnish with a dollop of sour cream, green onions, and a sprinkle of crushed caribe chile.

Makes 6 to 8 servings.

VARIATION

A Tablespoon of sherry or rum is delicious poured over the top of the soup just before serving.

Note: Sometimes in restaurants you may see this soup served in the same bowl with another soup such as the Spicy Butternut Squash Soup (recipe on page 32) or the Mexican-Style Cream of Corn Soup (recipe on page 31). To do this, use a wide soup bowl and ladle both soups into opposite sides of the bowl at the same time.

Mexican-Style Cream of Corn Soup

Warm and soothing, this is the perfect soup for a cold day.

2 Tablespoons butter
1/2 cup finely chopped onion
2 1/2 cups cooked whole-kernel corn, divided
5 cups chicken stock, divided
2 green chiles, parched, peeled (see page 340), and chopped
Salt and freshly ground black pepper to taste
1 cup whipping cream

Melt butter in a small saucepan. Add onion and sauté until softened. Place 2 cups of the corn, the onion, and 1 cup of the stock in a blender or food processor; process until pureed.

Combine remaining 4 cups stock, green chiles, and the puree in a saucepan. Season with salt and pepper and cook, stirring occasionally, over low heat 10 minutes. Whisk cream into soup and bring soup almost to a boil. Ladle soup into soup bowls and garnish with the remaining 1/2 cup of corn.

Makes 4 to 6 servings.

VARIATION

Whip 1/2 cup whipping cream with 1/8 teaspoon salt until stiff. Place a dollop of cream on each bowl of soup and sprinkle with ground red chile.

Spicy Butternut Squash Soup

Rich with spices, this is a hearty soup.

- 1/3 cup dry sherry
- 1 Tablespoon olive oil
- 1/2 cup chopped onion
- 6 garlic cloves, minced
- 1 Tablespoon grated ginger root
- 2 cups vegetable broth
- 4 cups cubed butternut squash
- 1 Tablespoon lime juice
- 1/2 teaspoon ground coriander
- 1/2 teaspoon grated nutmeg
- 1/4 teaspoon ground cumin
- 1/4 teaspoon ground pequin chile
- 1 Tablespoon grated lime peel

Heat sherry and oil in a large soup pot over medium-high heat. Add onion, garlic, and ginger root; cook, stirring frequently to prevent browning, for 10 minutes. If vegetables stick, add a small amount of broth.

Add remaining broth and squash. Bring to a boil. Reduce heat, cover, and simmer 25 minutes or until squash is tender. Let cool 10 minutes. Pour soup mixture, in batches if necessary, into a blender or food processor. Process until pureed. Return soup to pan. Stir in lime juice, coriander, nutmeg, cumin, and pequin chile. Heat until hot. Ladle into soup bowls. Garnish with lime peel.

Makes 4 to 6 servings.

VARIATION
Cook in a pressure cooker 8 minutes.

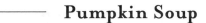

Pumpkin Soup

I've enjoyed making this soup with Halloween pumpkins. Native American in origin, it is very easy to make and dramatic to serve, especially in a well-cleaned, warmed whole pumpkin.

1 (3-pound) pumpkin
2 Tablespoons unsalted butter
1 large potato, cut into 1/2-inch cubes
1 cup chopped onion
3 cups chicken stock
3 cups water
1/3 cup low-fat evaporated milk
Salt and white pepper
Freshly grated nutmeg

Preheat oven to 350°F (175°C). Halve pumpkin, remove seeds, and scrape out any stringy material. Place on a baking sheet. Bake about 30 minutes or until fork-tender. Cool, cut into chunks, and remove the skin.

In a deep soup pot, melt the butter over medium-low heat and cook the potato and onion until onions are softened. Add chicken stock and water to the pot and simmer until potato is tender. Add pumpkin and evaporated milk.

Process or blend the soup a little at a time, pureeing it well. Return puree to the soup pot over medium heat. Add salt, pepper, and grated nutmeg to taste. Stir and serve.

Makes 4 to 6 servings.

Cream of Roasted Red Pepper Soup

The flavor of this soup is wonderful and fresh; it is also low in calories.

3 medium-size red bell peppers
1 teaspoon dried whole thyme leaves
1/4 teaspoon salt
1/4 teaspoon freshly ground black pepper
2 garlic cloves, minced
1 teaspoon olive oil
1 1/2 cups water, divided
1 Tablespoon butter
1 Tablespoon all-purpose flour
5 Tablespoons low-fat sour cream, divided

Preheat broiler. Cut bell peppers in half lengthwise; remove and discard seeds and membranes. Place peppers skin side up on a baking sheet and flatten with the palm of your hand. Broil peppers 3 inches from heat 10 minutes or until they are blackened and charred. Place peppers in a bowl of ice water and chill 5 minutes. Remove from water; peel and discard skins. Combine the peppers, thyme, salt, black pepper, garlic, oil, and 1 cup of the water in a blender or food processor. Process until pureed and set aside.

Melt butter in a medium saucepan over medium heat. Stir in flour and cook 1 minute, stirring constantly. Gradually add reserved pepper puree and the remaining 1/2 cup water, stirring well. Cook 10 minutes, stirring constantly, until thickened and bubbly. Remove from heat and stir in 3 Tablespoons of the sour cream. Spoon 1/2 cup soup into each of 6 individual soup bowls. Top each serving with remaining sour cream and serve immediately.

Makes 6 servings.

Sopa de Ajo (Garlic Soup with Tortilla Strips)

My uncle Harry, who lived in Mexico, loved cooking Mexican specialties. He got this recipe from an Acapulco chef. We've always loved it.

2 Tablespoons olive oil
4 garlic cloves, coarsely chopped
4 corn tortillas, cut into 6 wedges each, or 1 cup broken corn chips
1 quart rich beef stock
2 Tablespoons chopped green chile or to taste
2 teaspoons pure ground mild chile, divided
2 corn tortillas, cut into 1/4-inch strips and crisp-fried
1 cup shredded Monterey Jack cheese
1 jalapeño chile, thinly sliced

Heat oil in a 3-quart saucepan with a tight-fitting lid. Add garlic and cook briefly. Add tortilla pieces and fry, crushing with the back of a wooden spoon. When tortilla pieces are lightly browned, add beef stock, green chile, and 1 teaspoon of the ground chile. Simmer 10 minutes.

To serve, ladle into soup bowls, then sprinkle each serving with one-fourth of the tortilla strips and top each with 1/4 cup of the shredded cheese. Heat briefly in a hot 450°F (230°C) oven or under a low broiler temperature until cheese melts. Top each bowl with jalapeño chile slices.

Makes 4 servings.

Avocado Velvet Soup

Serve this refreshing chilled soup at a summer lunch or as the first course for a special dinner.

   2 cups chicken broth
   3/4 cup nonfat yogurt
   3 fully ripe avocados (preferably Haas)
   1 teaspoon lime juice
   1 teaspoon salt
   2 Tablespoons chopped onion
   1 teaspoon crushed caribe chile
   1 lime, thinly sliced

In a medium saucepan, bring chicken broth to a boil; stir in yogurt and remove from the heat. Peel the avocados and remove seeds.

Combine stock mixture, avocados, lime juice, salt, onion, and caribe chile in a blender or food processor; process until pureed. Refrigerate until thoroughly chilled. Garnish with thinly sliced lime.

Makes 4 to 6 servings.

Cilantro-Cucumber Soup

The perfect combination of hot and cold; the cucumber and yogurt are cooling, but the caribe chile adds a touch of heat.

1 Tablespoon unsalted butter
1 medium-size cucumber, peeled, seeded, and chopped
2 Tablespoons sliced green onions with tops
1 1/4 cups skim milk
1 teaspoon whole cilantro leaves
1/2 cup plain low-fat yogurt
Thin cucumber slices (optional)
1 teaspoon crushed caribe chile
Fresh cilantro sprigs

Melt butter in a small saucepan; add cucumber and green onion and cook until vegetables are tender. Add the milk and cilantro leaves. Simmer 5 minutes over medium heat, stirring constantly, until flavors are blended. Pour mixture into a blender and process until pureed.

Stir yogurt into cucumber mixture, cover, and refrigerate 2 hours. Garnish with cucumber slices, if using, caribe chile, and cilantro sprigs.

Makes 2 servings.

White Grape Gazpacho

My Mexican aunt's family used to have this simple, cool, and light soup as a first course on hot summer Sundays.

  4 bread slices
  2 Tablespoons white wine vinegar
  1/4 cup blanched almonds
  2 medium-size garlic cloves
  4 cups ice water
  2/3 cup olive oil
  1 bunch white seedless grapes

Remove crusts from bread; tear white part of bread into pieces and place in a bowl. Add vinegar, let soak into bread, and then squeeze.

Grind almonds, bread, garlic, ice water, and oil in a blender or food processor until almonds are ground as fine as possible. Pour into a bowl, cover, and refrigerate until well chilled. Serve very cold, garnished with 7 or 8 grapes per serving.

Makes 4 to 5 servings.

Mexican Gazpacho in a Goblet

Summer is especially meant for chilled soup first courses. Gazpacho is a classic dish and is especially nice served in sherbet glasses on the patio preceding a spicy Mexican or Spanish dinner. There are many versions of this Spanish specialty, but this one is easy, yet very traditional.

1 cup tomato juice
2 Tablespoons red wine vinegar
Few drops hot pepper sauce or finely minced hot chile to taste
1 garlic clove, minced
1/2 teaspoon salt or to taste
Freshly ground black pepper
1 medium-size onion, finely chopped
4 large very ripe tomatoes, peeled and chopped
1 large cucumber, peeled and chopped
1 large green bell pepper, chopped
16 or more romaine lettuce leaves
8 to 16 ice cubes
16 slices of dry French bread (optional)

Combine tomato juice, vinegar, hot pepper sauce, garlic, salt, and black pepper in a large bowl. Add onion, tomatoes, cucumber, and bell pepper. Stir gently to combine. Taste and adjust seasonings.

Cover and refrigerate 1 hour before serving. To serve, line stemmed glasses with lettuce leaves and place an ice cube in the bottom of each glass. Add soup and bread, if using, in layers and serve with long-handled spoons.

Makes 8 large or 16 small servings.

Note: Serving with the bread is traditionally Spanish, but can be omitted.

Easy Gazpacho, Río Grande Style

A friend, Katie Rust, made this delicious gazpacho for an Albuquerque fund-raiser years ago.

1 large sweet onion, chopped
2 medium-size cucumbers, peeled and chopped
4 large or 6 medium-size tomatoes, peeled and chopped (reserve juice)
1 garlic clove
1 (4-ounce) can pimientos, drained and chopped
3 cups chicken broth
1/4 cup red wine vinegar
2 Tablespoons olive oil (optional)
1 teaspoon sugar
2 teaspoons salt or to taste
Ice cubes
Toppers: minced garlic, croutons, diced unpeeled cucumber, chopped parsley, sliced green onions, diced green bell pepper, peeled chopped tomatoes

Process onion, cucumbers, tomatoes, garlic, and pimientos in a blender until fairly smooth, or put through a food chopper using fine blade. Add chicken broth, vinegar, oil, if using, sugar, and salt.

Mix well and chill thoroughly. When ready to serve, place an ice cube in each soup bowl. Ladle soup into bowls. Offer small bowls holding 3 or 4 of the toppers.

Makes 6 servings.

Bowl o' Red with Fixin's and Mixin's

Chili, without a doubt, is the most controversial of all American foods. The controversy rages over beans or not, ground beef versus cubed or no beef at all, red or green chiles, and the issues go on and on—the focus of numerous competitions and national organizations. No other food has gained the same level of glory with all the competitions and the organizations behind it. For years, there's even been a major push to name chili our national food. Enthusiasts—known as chiliheads—flock to countless contests, support numerous restaurants, and keep the cooking and consumption of chili at an all-time high.

Often labeled "bowl o' red," the original brew has but a few simple ingredients and was popularized well over a hundred years ago. Because of the simplicity of its preparation, its stick-to-the-ribs propensity, and its long-keeping quality, chili gained early fame as our country was expanding westward.

And it was in the West that chili originated. Probably the cowboys first learned the secret of sprinkling chili on the red meat, known as jerky, from the Native Americans. Red chiles are an abundant source of vitamins A and C, and act as an antioxidant, thus preserving foods that possess a high percentage of chiles.

You'll note that the dish is spelled *chili*, but the name of the spicy pods that are its most important ingredient is spelled *chile*, which is the Spanish spelling.

Besides chiles, beef is the traditional main ingredient, plus onions, garlic, cumin, and a touch of salt. With the large proportion of chiles, salt becomes less important, as chiles, especially coupled with an acid, replace the desire for salt, an important fact for those needing to reduce their salt intake.

The differences in proportion as well as the variety of ingredients are endless. There are lots of strong feelings and lore about how various ingredients got into the recipes. My grandfather, who was a railroad executive out among the cowboys, was emphatic that the only reason chili got cluttered up with beans and tomatoes was to extend the dish. This was because most of the cowboys lived on chili the entire run of the cattle drive. As they ran low on supplies, beans were added to make it thicker, and as the chili became less red, tomatoes were added, since there was no chile to be found. This watered-down version of the real thing is still popular in many places.

Chili's popularity has been well earned. It was the right taste as well as convenience at the right time. Some have even conjectured that chili was this country's, if not the world's, first convenience food—due to the ease of preparation when jerky is used as the base, as it often was by the early settlers and Gold Rush prospectors.

During the Civil War, chili powder was developed for the convenience of the marching armies of the South. In the jails, chili was very popular as the standard fare, getting its label as the Soup of the Devil and causing the school board of San Antonio, Texas, to prevent its being served to school children to keep them from being tainted.

Serving chili is no simple feat—at least in our house! We always serve it with "fixin's and mixin's," which are chopped Spanish onion, a coarsely shredded mixture of Monterey Jack and Cheddar cheeses, pickled jalapeño slices, and sour cream, along with fresh lime wedges dressed up with a fine dusting of ground mild chile on the cut edge. Really hot chilis are served with ponies of tequila on the side.

Cooked pinto beans are served as an accompaniment. Also, we like to have Posole as an additional or alternative side dish served under the chili. For bread, we are particularly fond of Blue Corn Skillet Bread or buttered flour or corn tortillas. And some people insist on corn chips.

Bowl o' Red

The influence behind this recipe came from my maternal grandfather, who when working with the Santa Fe Railroad learned how to prepare it from the "cookies," or trail cooks. It has won numerous chili cook-offs and is one of the really true original chilis.

2 Tablespoons lard, butter, bacon drippings, or rendered beef fat
1 large onion, coarsely chopped
3 pounds lean beef, cut into 1/2-inch cubes
3 medium-size garlic cloves, finely chopped
1/4 cup ground pure, red hot New Mexican chile or to taste
1/4 cup ground pure, red mild New Mexican chile
1 Tablespoon ground cumin, divided
About 3 cups water
1 1/2 teaspoons salt or to taste

Heat lard in a large heavy pot over medium heat. Add onion and cook until softened. Remove from heat.

Add beef, garlic, ground chiles, and half of the cumin to pot. Break up any lumps. Stir in the water and salt. Return to heat. Bring to a boil, then reduce heat and simmer, uncovered, 2 1/2 to 3 hours, stirring occasionally, until the meat is very tender and the flavors are well blended. Add more water if necessary. Taste and add the rest of the cumin; adjust seasonings.

Makes 6 servings.

Corrales Chili

The Spanish brought pork to the New World, and it became a favorite in New Mexico for combining with the pure, full-flavored chiles.

4 pounds pork shoulder, fat and bone removed, cut into 1/2-inch cubes, reserving fat
3 garlic cloves, finely chopped
1 1/2 teaspoons salt
3/4 cup ground mild chile or part ground hot chile
1 1/2 Tablespoons ground cumin, divided
1/2 teaspoon dried leaf Mexican oregano
3 cups chicken broth
4 cups cooked pinto beans or 2 (16-ounce) cans pinto beans, served on the side

Heat pork fat in a heavy skillet over medium-high heat until melted. Add the pork cubes a few at a time, stirring to brown evenly. Add garlic and salt, stirring well. Remove from the heat and stir in the ground chile, half of the cumin, and oregano, coating the meat evenly with the spices. (If you are using a combination of mild and hot chiles, do not add the hot chile yet.) Add a small amount of the broth and stir well.

Return to the heat, add a bit more broth, and stir. Continue to add broth, a little at a time, stirring, until the liquid is smooth. Simmer, uncovered, about 1 hour, stirring occasionally. Taste, adding the rest of the cumin, and adjust seasonings, adding ground hot chile to taste at this point. To add, remove the pot from the heat, sprinkle the chile over the top, and stir well. Serve the chili with a bowl of pinto beans on the side.

Makes 6 to 8 servings.

Devil's Brew

This chili is for serious-minded fire-eaters; it has a well-balanced flavor but a very hot temper! It will freeze well for up to a year.

2 Tablespoons bacon fat or lard
3 pounds lean beef chuck, cut into 1/2-inch cubes
2/3 cup ground pure, hot red chile
3 Tablespoons ground cumin, divided
1/2 teaspoon freshly ground black pepper
2 large onions, coarsely chopped
3 garlic cloves, minced
Water
1/4 cup crushed caribe chile
1 teaspoon dried leaf or ground Mexican oregano leaves soaked in 1/4 cup warm beer
1 Tablespoon cider vinegar
1 1/2 cups beef broth, divided
3 mild or hot green chiles, parched, peeled (see page 340), and chopped,
    or 1 (4-ounce) can chopped green chiles, drained
1 large tomato, chopped
1 Tablespoon masa harina

Heat fat in a large heavy pot. Remove from heat and stir in beef, ground chile, 1 1/2 Tablespoons cumin, pepper, onion, and garlic. Add enough water to barely cover the meat. Bring to a boil, then reduce heat and simmer, uncovered, 30 to 40 minutes, adding more water as needed.

Stir in crushed chile, oregano-beer mixture, vinegar, 1 cup of the beef broth, the green chiles, and the tomato. Simmer, uncovered, 30 minutes, stirring often. Dissolve masa harina in the remaining beef broth. Stir it into the chili along with the remaining 1 1/2 Tablespoons of the cumin and simmer, stirring, 15 to 20 minutes.

Makes 6 to 8 servings.

Chesapeake Bay Chili

This Eastern chili contains beans and tomatoes and is mild mannered.

1 Tablespoon bacon drippings
1 large onion, chopped
3 pounds lean beef, chopped or coarsely ground
1/4 cup ground mild chile
2 to 4 Tablespoons ground pure, hot red chile
2 Tablespoons ground cumin, divided
3 garlic cloves, chopped
1 Tablespoon Worcestershire sauce
2 cups water
1 (8-ounce) can tomato sauce
2 teaspoons salt
1 (16-ounce) can pinto beans, undrained
Crushed pequin chile to taste (optional)

Heat bacon drippings in a large heavy pot. Add onion and beef. Cook, stirring occasionally, until browned. Add the ground chiles, 1 Tablespoon cumin, garlic, and Worcestershire, and cook about 2 minutes.

Add water, tomato sauce, and salt, and cook, uncovered, about 45 minutes. Add beans and cook 10 minutes or longer. Taste, adding the remaining 1 Tablespoon of the cumin, and adjust seasonings. Add pequin chile to taste if a hotter flavor is desired.

Makes 6 to 8 servings.

Kansas City Chili

Robust and particularly crowd pleasing to novices at chili samplings!

    3 pounds lean beef chuck, coarsely ground
    2 pounds lean ground beef
    2 large onions, diced
    5 garlic cloves, minced
    1/4 cup ground pure, mild red chile
    1 1/2 Tablespoons ground cumin, divided
    2 (28-ounce) cans peeled whole tomatoes
    2 (15-ounce) cans tomato sauce
    3 cups water
    1 1/2 Tablespoons salt
    2 (16-ounce) cans pinto beans, drained (optional)

Brown beef, onions, and garlic in a large heavy pot, stirring frequently. Add ground chile and 3/4 Tablespoon of the cumin. Stir in the tomatoes (breaking them up with a fork), tomato sauce, water, and salt. Mix thoroughly. Simmer, covered, about 2 hours or until meat is very tender. Taste, adding the remaining 3/4 Tablespoon of the cumin, and adjust seasonings. If adding beans, add to chili about 30 minutes before serving.

Makes 10 to 12 servings.

Black Bean & Chicken Chili

A great way to serve black beans and for using leftover chicken or turkey, this chili is quick too, especially if you have the black beans already cooked.

    1 1/2 cups cooked black beans or 2 (15-ounce) cans
    About 2 cups chicken broth
    1 medium-size onion, chopped
    1/2 green bell pepper, diced into 1/2-inch pieces
    1/2 red bell pepper, diced into 1/2-inch pieces
    1 garlic clove, finely chopped
    2 teaspoons ground cumin, divided
    1 teaspoon salt
    1/2 cup ground pure, hot red chile
    3 cups chopped, cooked chicken
    1 Tablespoon lime juice
    1 Tablespoon tequila (optional)

Combine black beans, chicken broth, onion, bell peppers, garlic, 1 teaspoon cumin, salt, ground chile, and chopped chicken in a large pot. Cook until vegetables are tender and flavors blend, about 10 minutes.

Taste, adding the remaining 1 teaspoon of the cumin, and adjust seasonings. Add more broth if necessary. Just before serving, pour a little lime juice and tequila over the top of each serving, if desired.

Makes 4 servings.

Bean & Bulgur Chili

This chili is full flavored and very versatile. Try wrapping some in a flour tortilla for a veggie burrito.

2 Tablespoons olive oil
2 cups coarsely chopped onions
4 medium-size garlic cloves, minced
3 celery stalks, coarsely chopped
3 carrots, coarsely chopped
1 (28-ounce) can tomatoes, coarsely chopped, with juice
1 Tablespoon fresh lemon juice
1/4 cup ground pure, hot red chile
1/4 cup ground pure, mild red chile
1 Tablespoon ground cumin, divided
Freshly ground black pepper
1/2 teaspoon ground Mexican oregano
1 1/2 cups green bell pepper, chopped
1 cup tomato juice
1/2 cup bulgur
2 (15-ounce) cans kidney beans, drained
2 teaspoons salt

Heat oil in a large heavy pot over medium heat. Add onions and garlic and cook until the onions are softened. Add celery, carrots, tomatoes, lemon juice, ground chiles, 1/2 Tablespoon of the cumin, black pepper, and oregano to the onions and cook, covered, until the vegetables are nearly tender, 10 to 15 minutes. Add the bell peppers and cook 10 minutes.

Meanwhile, bring the tomato juice to a boil in a small saucepan and stir in bulgur. Remove from heat, cover, and let stand 10 minutes.

Add kidney beans and salt to the vegetables, then add the bulgur mixture. Stir thoroughly and simmer 30 minutes over low heat. The chili will be thick; add water as needed and stir occasionally to keep from sticking. Taste, adding the remaining 1/2 Tablespoon of the cumin, and adjust seasoning before serving.

Makes 6 to 8 servings.

Bernalillo Beef Stew

This savory combination of local vegetables and meat over rice is typically New Mexican. Simple to prepare, it is especially delicious when complemented with flour or corn tortillas for sopping up the juice. The stew can be frozen for up to eight months.

3 Tablespoons butter, lard, or bacon drippings
2 1/2 pounds beef stew meat, cut into 1 1/2-inch cubes
1/4 cup all-purpose flour
1 large onion, coarsely chopped
2 garlic cloves, minced
3 large tomatoes, peeled and chopped
Water
4 green chiles, parched, peeled (see page 340), and chopped
2 teaspoons cilantro or parsley, minced
Salt and freshly ground black pepper
3 medium-size carrots, zucchini, or green beans or a combination of the three
4 cups cooked rice

Melt butter in a large heavy skillet. Lightly coat stew meat with flour. Add beef cubes to the skillet a few at a time and cook, stirring, to brown on all sides. Add onion and garlic to the beef and cook, stirring occasionally, until onion begins to soften. Add tomatoes, 1 cup of water, green chiles, cilantro, salt, and pepper. Cover and simmer until beef is tender, about 1 hour, adding a little more water if needed.

Add carrots, zucchini, or green beans and simmer, covered, about 15 minutes, or until they are tender but not falling apart. Serve hot over the rice.

Makes 4 to 6 servings.

Calabacitas Guisadas (Hearty Zucchini Stew)

This New Mexican combination of beef and zucchini is an excellent choice for guests or for a family dinner. I always remember how well Jo Huber made it for our many happy outings with the Albuquerque Pilot Club. She and her husband, Joe, were quite famous for preparing it as soon as the summer green chile harvest began. As with the other native chile stews, it is served with steaming, buttered flour tortillas. Appropriate as either a side dish or a main course, this can be frozen for up to eight months.

1/4 cup butter, margarine, or bacon drippings
2 1/2 pounds beef round steak, sliced into thin strips about 2 inches long
1 medium-size onion, thinly sliced and separated into rings
2 garlic cloves, minced
4 medium-size zucchini, sliced 3/8 inch thick
8 to 12 green chiles, parched, peeled (see page 340), and chopped (1 cup)
1 1/2 cups corn kernels, fresh or frozen
1 teaspoon salt
1/4 teaspoon ground cumin
3/4 cup shredded Cheddar cheese

Melt butter over medium-high heat in a large heavy skillet. Add beef slices a few at a time, stirring to brown well. Remove to a plate as they brown.

Add onion, garlic, and zucchini to same skillet; cook, stirring occasionally, until zucchini is crisp-tender. Stir in the browned beef, green chiles, corn, salt, and cumin, and cook 5 minutes. Stir in shredded cheese and serve as soon as the cheese has melted.

Makes 6 to 8 servings.

Pueblo Green Chile Stew

Senator Joe Montoya from New Mexico was famous for this stew. He won the Capitol Chili Cook-Off more than once with this recipe. Absolutely critical: you must serve flour tortillas on the side for scooping up the great sauce. The stew may be frozen for up to three months.

2 pounds boneless pork, cut into 1-inch cubes
3 Tablespoons all-purpose flour
2 Tablespoons butter, lard, or bacon drippings
1 cup chopped onion
2 garlic cloves, minced
3 cups canned or fresh chopped peeled tomatoes
1 teaspoon salt
1/2 teaspoon ground Mexican oregano
1/4 teaspoon ground cumin
20 fresh green chiles, parched, peeled (see page 340), and
    coarsely chopped into ½-inch-wide pieces

Lightly coat pork cubes with flour. Melt butter in a large heavy skillet or saucepan. Add pork cubes a few at a time, stirring to brown well. Push to the side of the pot. Add onion and garlic and cook until onion is soft. Stir in the browned meat.

Add tomatoes, then salt, oregano, and cumin. Cover and simmer 1 hour, stirring occasionally and adding water as needed. Add the green chiles. Simmer 30 minutes or longer, adding a little more water if necessary, until flavors are well blended. Taste and adjust seasonings.

Makes 4 servings.

Feijoada (Brazilian Black Bean & Sausage Stew)

I first sampled this in Rio de Janeiro and grew to really like it. Sometimes I add a lacing of sherry or rum to each serving.

> 3 cups dried black beans, sorted, rinsed, and soaked overnight
> 1 (2-pound) smoked beef tongue
> 2 quarts water
> 1 pound hot sausages
> 1/4 pound slab bacon
> 1 (1-pound) piece corned beef
> 1 Tablespoon vegetable oil
> 2 garlic cloves, minced
> 1 teaspoon ground pure, hot red chile
> 1 cup strong coffee
> Salt and freshly ground black pepper
> 1 lime, thinly sliced
> 1/2 cup chopped sweet onion or green onions (optional)
> 1/2 cup shredded Monterey Jack cheese or sour cream (optional)

Drain the beans. Add tongue, beans, and enough water to cover by 2 inches to a large pot. Boil 10 minutes. Reduce heat, cover, and simmer 1 hour. Prick sausages with a fork; leave bacon in one piece. Add sausages, bacon, and corned beef to beans and tongue. Simmer until tender, 1 to 2 hours, stirring occasionally and adding water as needed.

Heat oil in a small skillet. Add garlic and cook until golden. Remove from heat and stir in chile powder. Add 1 1/2 cups of the cooked beans to garlic and mash thoroughly. Return to the pot. Add coffee, salt, and pepper. Simmer 15 minutes.

To serve, remove meats from beans. Peel and slice tongue and cut other meats into uniform pieces. Arrange on a platter to serve along with the beans. Serve beans in bowls. Garnish with fresh lime slices. Add chopped onion and shredded cheese, if desired.

Makes 6 to 8 servings.

Note: This can be frozen for up to 2 months. To serve, thaw in the refrigerator overnight and heat until simmering, about 30 minutes over medium heat.

Salads & Salad Dressing

The types of greens are perhaps a bit limited in the Southwest, but the variations of side-dish salads and entrée salads are not. Citrus, beans, jicama, and cabbage are treated to exciting combinations with the tart accent of creatively combined dressings.

Some of the salads, like the taco and hot seafood salad in this chapter, are definitely main dishes, whereas others, such as the pinto bean salad or Hot Green Beans with New Potatoes and Salsa Vinaigrette, double as both vegetable and salad.

Red Grapefruit, Watercress & Jicama Salad

Jicama is a large root vegetable from Mexico. After peeling, the almost sweet, crisp interior can be cut into strips for salads, appetizers, or snacks. Wonderful with seafood, this light and tangy salad is also good with broiled or baked poultry dishes.

> 1/2 cup jicama, cut into 1/2-inch cubes
> Juice of 1 lime
> Crushed caribe chile
> Salt
> Tangy Garlic Dressing (recipe follows)
> 6 cups watercress leaves, rinsed and dried
> 1 cup red grapefruit sections, chilled

Arrange jicama in a single layer in a glass or stainless steel pan. Squeeze lime juice over jicama, then sprinkle with the chile and salt. Marinate 30 minutes. Meanwhile, prepare dressing and set aside. Just before serving, drain jicama and combine with the watercress, grapefruit sections, and dressing.

Makes 4 servings.

Tangy Garlic Dressing

> 2 Tablespoons extra-virgin olive oil
> 1 Tablespoon vegetable oil
> 2 garlic cloves, minced
> 2 Tablespoons balsamic vinegar
> 1 teaspoon Dijon mustard

Mix olive oil, vegetable oil, garlic, balsamic vinegar, and mustard together and whisk until blended.

Jicama & Grapefruit Salad with Raspberry Vinaigrette

This salad is a variation of the salad above and is a composed salad as opposed to a tossed one.

> Raspberry Vinaigrette (recipe follows)
> 8 red or green lettuce leaves
> 2 large pink grapefruit, cut into sections
> 2 cups jicama, cut into thin strips

Prepare the vinaigrette. Place 2 lettuce leaves on each of 4 chilled salad plates. Arrange grapefruit sections in a pinwheel pattern, then scatter jicama strips on top of grapefruit. Drizzle with vinaigrette.

Makes 4 servings.

Raspberry Vinaigrette

> 1/2 cup walnut oil
> 1/4 cup raspberry vinegar
> 1 teaspoon Dijon mustard
> 1/2 teaspoon sugar
> Freshly ground black pepper

Whisk the oil, vinegar, mustard, sugar, and pepper together in a small bowl until slightly thickened.

Caesar Salad Originale

When the recipe for Caesar salad was originally developed in Tijuana, the dressing was stabilized with a coddled egg. The egg has been omitted from this version.

2 heads romaine lettuce
3/4 cup extra-virgin Spanish olive oil, divided
3 garlic cloves, divided, 1 crushed and 2 minced
2 cups diced firm white bread, preferably homemade
1/4 cup red wine vinegar
2 Tablespoons fresh lemon juice
1 teaspoon Worcestershire sauce
1 teaspoon freshly ground black pepper
4 to 6 oil-packed anchovy fillets, minced (or 1 teaspoon or taste of anchovy paste)
1/2 to 3/4 cup freshly grated Parmesan cheese
Crushed red pepper flakes

Separate lettuce into individual leaves, rinse, and dry. Wrap in a towel and chill until ready to serve.

Heat 1/4 cup of the oil and the crushed garlic clove in a skillet over medium heat. Add the bread cubes and sauté until the croutons are delicately browned and crisp. Add additional oil if necessary. Remove the garlic and drain the croutons on paper towels. (This can be done ahead of time.)

In a salad bowl whisk together remaining 1/2 cup oil, minced garlic, vinegar, lemon juice, Worcestershire, and black pepper. Add anchovies to taste, starting with 3 or 4 anchovies. Whisk until well blended.

Break greens into bite-size pieces. Toss greens with the dressing and top with 1/4 of the croutons. Let each guest add Parmesan cheese, crushed red pepper, and additional croutons to taste.

Makes 4 servings.

VARIATION

California-Style Caesar Salad: Arrange one-half of each head of lettuce on a chilled salad plate. Sprinkle lettuce with croutons, crushed pepper, dressing, and grated Parmesan cheese.

Hearts of Palm Salad with Salsa Vinaigrette

1 cup Salsa Vinaigrette (recipe on page 73)
1 cup hearts of palm, sliced
1 large head romaine lettuce
Freshly ground black pepper
3 Tablespoons toasted sesame seeds
24 cherry tomatoes, halved
1/2 cup pitted ripe olives, halved crosswise
3 green onions, chopped
1 recipe Guacamole (recipe on page 13)
1 cup corn chips

One day ahead, prepare vinaigrette, place in a bowl, add hearts of palm, and refrigerate. Toss with a spoon occasionally.

To make the salad, rinse and dry lettuce and tear it into bite-size pieces; place in a large serving bowl. Sprinkle lettuce with pepper and sesame seeds. Add the hearts of palm with vinaigrette, tomato halves, two-thirds of the sliced olives, and the green onions and toss together. Spoon guacamole in the center of the salad and sprinkle remaining olives around guacamole. Top the salad with the corn chips and serve.

Makes 4 to 6 servings.

Mexican Potato Salad

This has been a favorite Fourth of July salad. The recipe can be doubled, tripled, or even quadrupled, depending on the number of guests.

6 cups diced unpeeled potatoes
1/2 teaspoon salt
1/4 cup butter, thinly sliced
1 1/4 cups finely diced celery
3 Tablespoons chopped onion
1 1/2 Tablespoons finely diced red bell pepper
1 1/2 Tablespoons finely diced green bell pepper
1 hard-boiled large egg, chopped
3 Tablespoons spicy salsa
3 Tablespoons cider vinegar
2 Tablespoons extra-virgin Spanish olive oil
1 1/2 teaspoons salt
1/4 teaspoon freshly ground black pepper

Cook potatoes with the salt in a saucepan of boiling water to cover until tender. Drain, return to the saucepan, and stir butter into hot potatoes. In a medium bowl combine celery, onion, bell peppers, egg, salsa, vinegar, oil, salt, and black pepper. Add to potato mixture and toss to combine. Cover and refrigerate to blend flavors.

Makes 6 servings.

Ensalada de Frutas Frescas (Fresh Fruit Salad)

This fruit salad is especially nice with spicy entrées such as moles.

8 red lettuce leaves, rinsed and dried
1 avocado, cut lengthwise into thin slices
2 bananas, sliced diagonally
1 medium-size cucumber, peeled and diced
1 navel orange, peel and pith removed, sliced crosswise
Spicy Walnut Raspberry Dressing (recipe follows)

Line 4 plates with lettuce. Arrange avocado slices on lettuce, top with bananas, then with cucumber. Garnish salads with orange slices.

Spoon dressing over fruit 10 minutes before serving.
Makes 4 servings.

Spicy Walnut Raspberry Dressing
2 Tablespoons walnut oil
2 teaspoons raspberry vinegar
2 teaspoons lime juice
1/4 to 1/2 teaspoon crushed caribe chile

Whisk together oil, vinegar, lime juice, and caribe chile in a small bowl until thickened.

Fajita Salad

This is a popular and trendy main-dish salad that can be served either in a deep-fried edible salad bowl made from a flour tortilla (see frying instructions page 341) or in a glass or wooden bowl.

  1 serving of Chicken Fajitas (recipe on page 107), Beef Fajitas (recipe on page
      158), or Shrimp Fajitas (recipe on page 129), or any combination
  1 1/2 cups mixed salad greens, washed and dried
  1 tostado (see page 341), made from a 14- to 16-inch flour tortilla (optional)
  3 strips each red, green, and yellow bell peppers
  3 radishes, thinly sliced
  1/4 cup diced tomato
  1/4 avocado, peeled and cut into thin slices (optional)
  1/4 recipe Pico de Gallo variation of Salsa Vinaigrette recipe (recipe on page 73)

Grill or pan-sear chicken, beef, or shrimp. Meanwhile, place mixed greens in bottom of the tostado or salad bowl. Top with chicken or other meat, bell pepper strips, radish slices, diced tomato, and avocado slices, if using. Drizzle with the dressing and serve with a sharp knife and fork.

Makes 1 serving.

Marinated Coleslaw Mexicana

Great to keep on hand at all times, this slaw can be used as an accompaniment to Southwestern main dishes and added to burritos, tacos, and tostados. It's ideal to take along on picnics.

  1/2 medium-size cabbage, chopped or shredded
  1/2 teaspoon salt
  1/2 cup vegetable oil
  1/2 cup vinegar
  1/3 cup sugar
  1/4 to 1/2 teaspoon crushed caribe chile (optional)

Place cabbage in a large heatproof bowl and season with salt. Combine oil, vinegar, and sugar in a saucepan. Bring to a boil, stirring to dissolve sugar. Pour hot dressing over the cabbage, toss to combine, and marinate at room temperature 1 hour or in the refrigerator 3 hours. Stir in chile to taste, if desired.

Makes about 8 cups.

Taco Salad

This is an attractive, delicious, and filling buffet salad. You can either add the crisp corn chips to the salad or place the salad in a deep-fried tortilla bowl. For convenience in entertaining, prepare the meat topping ahead of time and reheat before assembling the salad.

1 pound lean ground beef
1 onion, chopped
1 garlic clove, minced
1 Tablespoon ground pure, mild red chile or to taste
1/4 teaspoon ground Mexican oregano
3 Tablespoons red wine vinegar
3 Tablespoons vegetable oil
1/2 cup water
2 cups cooked pinto beans, drained [1 (15-ounce) can or freshly cooked]
Salt to taste
1 1/2 quarts mixed salad greens, washed, dried, and torn into bite-size pieces
1 1/2 cups shredded mixed Monterey Jack cheese and Cheddar cheese
4 green onions, sliced
2 medium-size tomatoes, cut into wedges
1 avocado, peeled, pitted, and cut into thin slices
1/3 cup sliced pitted ripe olives
1/2 pound corn chips or broken taco shells
Salsa of your choice

Cook beef, onion, and garlic in a large skillet over medium heat, stirring to break up beef, until the meat is browned. Add ground chile, oregano, vinegar, oil, water, beans, and salt to taste. Simmer about 20 minutes to blend flavors.

To assemble the salad, place salad greens in a large serving bowl. Top with the warm beef mixture, cheese, green onions, and tomatoes. Arrange avocado slices and ripe olives over the top. Coarsely crush corn chips and sprinkle on top.

Makes 6 servings.

VARIATION
Place salad briefly in a hot oven or under the broiler to melt the cheese.

Hot Seafood Salad en Tostado

This seafood salad recipe got its influence from mainlanders who were somewhat short of fresh fish—hence the inclusion of chicken breast in a seafood salad. You can substitute firm-fleshed fish, such as red snapper, if you prefer.

2 Tablespoons unsalted butter
1/2 pound skinless, boneless chicken breast, cubed
20 medium-size shrimp, shelled and deveined
1/2 pound king crab legs, cracked, peeled, and cut up
1 large tomato, diced
4 green onions, sliced
2 celery stalks, diced
1 jalapeño chile, minced
1 avocado, sliced, then diced, reserving 4 slices for garnish
4 (12-inch or larger) deep-fried tortilla bowls (page 341)
Juice of 1 lime
1/2 cup shredded mixed Monterey Jack and Cheddar cheeses
12 ripe olives (optional)

Preheat oven to 450°F (230°C). In a large, deep skillet, melt butter, then add the chicken cubes and brown lightly, stirring constantly, 3 or 4 minutes. Add shrimp and cook, stirring, until pink, 4 or 5 more minutes. Add crab, tomato, green onions, celery, jalapeño chile, and avocado cubes and cook, stirring gently to avoid mashing avocado, just to warm the ingredients.

Meanwhile, warm the tortilla bowls and divide the salad ingredients among them. Sprinkle each with one-fourth of the cheese, then place in the oven until the cheese melts. Top each salad with an avocado slice and olives, if using.

Makes 4 servings.

Hot Green Beans with New Potatoes & Salsa Vinaigrette

A pair of spring's favorite vegetables make a refreshing change when dressed with salsa vinaigrette. You can vary the vegetables if you like.

8 small new red potatoes, well scrubbed and with a 1/2-inch belt of skin removed
1 1/2 pounds fresh small green beans, rinsed, strings and tips removed
1 cup water
1/2 teaspoon salt
1 recipe Salsa Vinaigrette (recipe on page 73)
8 whole red lettuce leaves
8 thin strips of red bell pepper

Place new potatoes, green beans, and water in a heavy saucepan. Cover and steam about 5 minutes over medium-low heat, or until potatoes are just tender, not mushy. Peek once or twice to be sure the water has not evaporated. When vegetables are done, drain off any excess liquid and allow them to dry for about 5 minutes.

Toss vegetables with Salsa Vinaigrette and keep tossing every 15 minutes or so until the vegetables have absorbed most of the liquid. Refrigerate for about an hour. Arrange lettuce leaves on salad plates, spoon salad onto lettuce, and garnish with bell pepper strips.

Makes 6 to 8 servings.

Mexicali Salad

Oranges and onions drizzled with a sweet-sour dressing have long been popular for serving with Spanish- or Mexican-influenced dishes.

    1 large head romaine lettuce, coarsely chopped
    3 oranges, peel and pith removed, cut into segments
    4 paper-thin slices red onion, separated into rings
    1/4 cup toasted slivered almonds
    3/4 cup white wine vinegar
    3/4 cup vegetable oil
    2 Tablespoons honey
    1/2 teaspoon poppy seeds
    1/2 teaspoon celery seeds
    Freshly ground black pepper
    1 cup pitted ripe olives, drained and chopped

Divide lettuce among 4 chilled salad plates, then top with the orange segments, onion rings, and almonds. Combine vinegar, oil, honey, poppy seeds, celery seeds, and pepper in a bowl and beat with a whisk until slightly thickened. Drizzle some of the dressing over each salad. Sprinkle olives over salads.

Makes 4 servings.

Frijoles Slaw

This is especially attractive as a salad. It is also a delicious ingredient in burritos.

    2 cups cooked pinto beans, well drained [1 (15-ounce) can or freshly cooked]
    3 1/2 cups shredded white cabbage
    1 large carrot, cut into thin strips with a vegetable peeler
    1/2 cup minced Spanish onion
    1/2 cup mayonnaise
    1/2 cup plain nonfat yogurt
    1/4 cup Fresh Garden Salsa (recipe on page 79), divided
    16 large romaine or leaf lettuce leaves, rinsed, drained, and chilled

At least 2 hours or up to 1 day before serving, combine beans, cabbage, carrot, and onion in a large bowl. Mix together mayonnaise, yogurt, and 2 Tablespoons of the salsa in a small bowl. Add the dressing to the vegetables and toss until the vegetables are well coated. Taste and adjust seasonings.

To serve, place 2 lettuce leaves on each chilled plate. Top with the slaw and a small amount of salsa. *Makes 8 servings.*

Sweet Onion–Bean Salad

Serve this as the main dish for lunch or as a side dish for a hearty meal. Crusty squares of hot buttered corn bread are a tasty accompaniment.

   2 cups cooked pinto beans, drained [1 (15-ounce) can or freshly cooked]
   4 hard-boiled large eggs, chopped
   1 cup Monterey Jack cheese, diced into 1/2 inch cubes
   1/4 cup sweet onion rings
   Red Chile Vinaigrette (recipe follows)
   4 to 6 Bibb lettuce leaves
   4 to 6 parsley sprigs

Mix together beans, eggs, cheese, and onion rings in a medium bowl. Cover and refrigerate for flavors to blend.

Pour vinaigrette over the bean mixture. Mix well. Serve in lettuce cups, garnished with parsley. *Makes 4 to 6 servings.*

Red Chile Vinaigrette
   2 Tablespoons vegetable oil
   1 Tablespoon cider vinegar
   1 Tablespoon ground hot red chile
   1 teaspoon prepared mustard
   1/4 teaspoon salt
   1/4 teaspoon freshly ground black pepper

Whisk together oil, vinegar, ground chile, mustard, salt, and pepper in a small bowl until slightly thickened.

Ensalada Guaymas (Shrimp Salad, Guaymas Style)

A refreshing and elegant salad. Garlic and chiles combine with shrimp and peas to make a delectably spiced first course or luncheon entrée. Warmed hard crusty Bolillos (recipe on page 255) or wheat tortillas are a delicious accompaniment.

1 1/2 pounds fresh shrimp, shelled and deveined
1 (10-ounce) package frozen green peas or 1 1/2 cups fresh green peas
1 green onion, very thinly sliced, tops included
2 Tablespoons thin pimiento strips
3/4 cup mayonnaise
1 garlic clove, minced
2 green chiles, parched, peeled (see page 340), and finely chopped, or 1/4 cup canned
      chopped green chiles, or 1 canned jalapeño chile, very finely chopped
1 Tablespoon coarsely chopped cilantro or parsley (optional)
Lettuce leaves or avocado halves
Lime wedges

Cook shrimp in boiling salted water 3 or 4 minutes or until pink; drain and cool. Cook peas until tender but still slightly firm; drain and cool. Combine shrimp, peas, green onion, and pimiento in a medium bowl. Cover and refrigerate until chilled.

Mix together mayonnaise, garlic, green chiles, and cilantro, if using. Gently combine with the chilled shrimp and peas. Serve the shrimp salad on lettuce leaves or in avocado halves garnished with lime wedges.

Makes 4 to 6 servings.

Ensalada de Navidad (Christmas Salad)

This salad is a great holiday buffet or dinner salad as it combines the colors of Christmas and it can be made ahead. For a buffet, serve it on a large platter.

> 3 small heads Belgian endive
> 1 small head Boston or red leaf lettuce
> 2 large red bell peppers, cut into a very thin julienne
> 1 recipe Salsa Vinaigrette (recipe on page 73)

Rinse endive and cut into halves lengthwise. Cut off and discard about 1 inch of the root end. Slice each half into 1/4-inch-wide strips. Rinse and pat dry the lettuce leaves.

To serve, place the lettuce leaves on chilled plates and evenly divide the endive and bell peppers over them, then drizzle the vinaigrette over all. Or serve buffet style on a lettuce-lined platter.

Makes 6 servings.

VARIATION

If Belgian endive is not available, 3 cups green bell peppers, jicama, or snow-white mushroom slivers can be used instead.

Nopalito Salad

The cactus paddle (leaf) provides an entirely different flavor in this salad. Fresh cactus paddles, or nopales, are sometimes available in supermarkets. Nopalitos—diced or slivered nopales—are generally available canned.

8 lettuce leaves
1 cup sliced fresh nopales* or canned nopalitos
2 tomatoes, cut into wedges
1 medium-size red onion, thinly sliced and separated into rings
Salsa Vinaigrette (recipe on page 73)

Arrange 2 lettuce leaves on each of 4 serving plates. Arrange cactus slices alternately with tomato wedges on the lettuce. Sprinkle with a few onion rings. Top with vinaigrette.
Makes 4 servings.

*For fresh cactus paddles, parch as for green chiles (see page 340) until the skin blisters, then chill before peeling. Steam 5 minutes or until the cactus is tender. Cut into thin slices.

Herb Lime Vinaigrette

I created this dressing for a Southwestern restaurant we had in New York City called the Pecos River Cafe. It is light and fresh tasting.

1/4 cup fresh lime juice
1/2 cup extra-virgin olive oil
2 Tablespoons chopped cilantro (optional)
1 teaspoon chopped fresh basil or 1/2 teaspoon dried basil, crushed
1 teaspoon chopped fresh dill or 1/2 teaspoon dried dill weed
1/2 teaspoon salt

Combine lime juice, oil, cilantro, basil, dill, and salt in a blender or mini food processor and process until well blended.
Makes about 3/4 cup.

Corrales Chicken Salad

A rather simple chicken and rice salad that can be embellished with steamed or raw broccoli, carrots, zucchini, or any other vegetable. Pine nuts, pecans, or walnuts are also good.

3/4 cup uncooked white rice
2 cups chicken broth
4 cups cooked chicken, well seasoned, cut into cubes
2/3 cup Salsa Vinaigrette (recipe on page 73)
1/2 cup Pepper Jack cheese, diced
1/3 cup chopped green chiles parched, peeled (see page 340), and seeded
16 lettuce leaves
1 avocado, cut into thin strips
Juice of 1 lime
1 small tomato, chopped

Cook rice in chicken broth in a medium saucepan over low heat until tender; cool. Combine cooked rice and chicken cubes in a bowl. Add vinaigrette, cheese, and green chiles and mix. Taste and adjust seasonings, if needed.

Serve salad on a bed of lettuce. Sprinkle avocado slices with lime juice and add as garnish. Top with a little chopped tomato.

Makes 6 to 8 servings.

Ensalada de Tres Frijoles y Aguacate
(Three Bean Salad with Avocado)

Very rich and hearty enough for a vegetarian main dish.

2 cups cooked black beans or 1 (15-ounce) can, drained
2 cups cooked pinto or kidney beans or 1 (15-ounce) can, drained
2 cups cooked chickpeas or 1 (15-ounce) can, drained
1 medium-size onion, thinly sliced and separated into rings
1 medium-size tomato, halved and seeds gently squeezed out, chopped
1/2 cup olive oil
1/4 cup sherry wine vinegar
1 teaspoon prepared mustard
1 teaspoon sugar
1/2 teaspoon ground Mexican oregano
1/2 teaspoon salt
Freshly ground black pepper
1 to 2 teaspoons finely minced jalapeño chiles (optional)
3 to 4 avocados
Lettuce leaves (optional)

Place black beans, pinto beans, chickpeas, onion, and tomato in a bowl. Whisk together oil, vinegar, mustard, sugar, oregano, salt, pepper, and jalapeño chiles, if using. Pour over the bean mixture and toss to combine. Cover and marinate in the refrigerator several hours or overnight.

To assemble individual salads, cut the avocados in half and remove the pits and peel. Place lettuce leaves, if using, on each plate, top with an avocado half, and spoon bean mixture into avocados.

Makes 6 to 8 servings.

VARIATION
Add 1 cup cubed Monterey Jack cheese to the bean mixture. Serve bean salad in lettuce cups if avocados are not in season.

Guadalajara Salad

A corn-and-pepper salad that goes well with most any main dish; in addition, it eliminates the need for a vegetable dish.

2 cups cooked fresh whole-kernel corn or frozen whole-kernel corn, thawed
1/4 cup diced red bell pepper
1/4 cup diced green bell pepper
4 green onions, minced
1/2 cup Creamy Salsa Verde (recipe on page 82)
Crushed caribe chile

Toss corn with bell peppers and green onions in a medium bowl. Add salsa verde and toss to combine. Lightly sprinkle with crushed chile.
Makes 4 servings.

Texas Piccalilli Corn Salad

Corn relish has long been popular in Texas and the Midwest, and it goes well with fiery dishes. Piccalilli is popular in the Midwest and Southwest as a relish made from cabbage, bell peppers, onions, and whatever is still in the garden at frost time.

2 cups cooked whole-kernel corn or 1 (12-ounce) can whole-kernel corn, drained
1/4 cup piccalilli (pickled vegetable relish)
1/2 cup diced celery
1 Tablespoon sugar*
1 teaspoon salt*
2 Tablespoons wine vinegar*
6 Tablespoons vegetable oil*
2 quarts shredded salad greens

Combine corn, piccalilli, and celery in a medium bowl. Dissolve sugar and salt in vinegar in a small jar with a tight-fitting lid. Add oil, cover, and shake until thickened. Pour over the corn mixture. Cover and refrigerate several hours, stirring occasionally. Add to salad greens and toss lightly to mix.
Makes 6 servings.

*If preferred, dissolve sugar and salt in vinegar in a nonreactive bowl and whisk together. Add oil and whisk to combine well.

Chimichurri Dressing

The Argentinean parsley salsa makes a crisp, clean, delightful salad dressing base. Use on any combination of greens and vegetables.

    2 Tablespoons Chimichurri Salsa (recipe on page 81)
    1 teaspoon prepared mustard
    2 Tablespoons red wine vinegar
    3 Tablespoons extra-virgin olive oil

Place salsa in a measuring cup or small bowl and whisk or beat with a fork. Add the mustard and vinegar, then the oil, and beat until thickened. Chill slightly, then serve immediately.
Makes enough dressing for a salad for four.

Salsa Vinaigrette

Don't ever toss out leftover fresh salsa. One of my favorite ways to use it is to make this salad dressing.

    1 teaspoon Dijon mustard
    1/4 cup red wine vinegar
    1 cup extra-virgin Spanish olive oil
    1/4 cup Salsa Fresca (recipe on page 78)

Combine mustard, vinegar, and oil in a small bowl. Whisk together thoroughly. Add salsa to mixture and whisk until well blended.
Makes 1 1/2 cups.

VARIATION
Use Pico de Gallo (recipe on page 77) instead of Salsa Fresca.

Fresh Salsa & Other Southwestern Favorites

The most popular table condiment in America is now salsa—and no wonder. It is flavorful, versatile, and offers endless possibilities. *Salsa* is actually the Spanish word for sauce, but the name has become synonymous with the tomato-based, chile-laden sauce sold by endless manufacturers in the supermarkets. You needn't be limited to these ingredients. The only requirement for a fresh salsa is that you combine a juicy vegetable or fruit with chiles and onions. You can even add juice or vinegar to make it if the chosen fruit is not juicy enough. Garlic and cilantro are popular additions. Salsas are best when freshly made and allowed to set for at least 15 minutes before serving.

In addition to the fresh salsas, this chapter also includes some of the traditional cooked sauces that are used for egg dishes, enchiladas, burritos, and other Southwestern favorites, as well as those barbecue sauces for which the Southwest is famous.

Golden Salsa

I developed this salsa to accompany grilled swordfish and the Citrus Turkey Breast in Champagne Vinegar Marinade on page 101. It is both beautiful and delicious.

1 cup finely chopped cantaloupe
1 cup finely diced Vidalia or other sweet onion
2 jalapeño chiles or to taste, minced
6 Tablespoons fresh orange juice
1/4 cup coarsely chopped cilantro

Mix cantaloupe, onion, jalapeño chiles, orange juice, and cilantro well in a medium bowl. Taste and adjust seasonings, adding more jalapeño chile, if desired. Serve with Grilled Swordfish (recipe on page 119).

Makes 3 cups.

Seckel Pear & Tomatillo Salsa

I created this one evening in Woodstock, New York, to go over grilled catfish. I used home-grown tomatillos, and they were wonderful with the mellow crunch of the tiny Seckel pears!

1 cup chopped unpeeled Seckel pears (6 to 8 pears)
1 cup chopped fresh tomatillos
1 cup chopped red onion
1 habanero chile or chipotle chile or to taste, minced (or 1/2 teaspoon ground chipotle)
Juice of 1/2 lime
2 Tablespoons coarsely chopped cilantro or to taste

Combine pears, tomatillos, onion, chile, lime juice, and cilantro in a medium bowl, cover, and marinate 15 minutes. Serve as desired, adjusting seasonings to taste.

Makes 3 cups.

Salsa Tequila

A splash of tequila makes all the difference in this robust salsa; it has a way of mellowing the searing nature of terrifically hot foods. I like this sauce on seafood, chicken, and any kind of chops—pork, veal, or lamb.

1/2 cup diced tomato
1/2 cup finely chopped white or red onion
4 jalapeño chiles or to taste, finely minced (remove seeds and ribs from chiles for a milder salsa)
1/4 cup tequila
1 garlic clove, minced
1/2 teaspoon salt or to taste

Combine tomato, onion, jalapeño chiles, tequila, clove, and salt and let stand at least 30 minutes at room temperature.

Makes 1 1/2 cups.

Pico de Gallo

This salsa is so hot that it will "make you jump as high as the top of a cock's comb"—the literal translation of this dish's name. The salsa originated in northern Mexico and was originally made with chipotle chiles. I have found that fresh jalapeño chiles with a pinch of pequin chile substitute quite well if chipotles are unavailable. This salsa is a staple with fajitas.

3 chipotle chiles (or 1 1/2 teaspoons chipotle powder) or fresh jalapeño chiles, finely chopped
1 large tomato, coarsely chopped
2 garlic cloves, minced
1/2 teaspoon salt
1/2 teaspoon pequin chile or to taste (omit if using chipotle chile)
3 Tablespoons coarsely chopped cilantro
1/4 cup fresh lime juice

Combine chiles, tomato, garlic, salt, pequin chile, cilantro, and lime juice in a medium bowl, cover, and marinate at least 1 hour to develop natural juices before serving.

Makes 1 1/2 cups.

Cold Salsa Verde

An Old Mexican favorite that is good over almost any meat or tortilla dish. Don't substitute unripe green tomatoes, because they lack the subtle, sweet taste of the tomatillos.

1 cup quartered, cooked fresh tomatillos
2/3 cup coarsely chopped onion
1 Tablespoon cilantro
1 jalapeño chile or serrano chile, chopped
1/2 teaspoon salt (optional)

To cook the tomatillos, bring to a boil in about an inch of water in a saucepan. Add the hulled tomatillos, quartered. Cook until tender, about 5 minutes. Reserve the cooking liquid. Add the tomatillos to a blender or food processor and process until coarsely chopped. Add onion, cilantro, chile, and salt and process to combine. Taste and, if necessary, adjust seasonings.
Makes about 2 cups.

Salsa Fresca

This refreshing salsa can be as mild or as hot as you like, depending on the chiles used. This is the political salsa of Mexico and probably the most popular. Families learned after one of the many revolutions that if they had a bowl of this salsa on the table at mealtime, they would not be killed by the Federales, the Mexican Federal Militia. The story is that after a narrow victory, the majority politically in charge wanted to diminish their opposition, due to a narrow victory. So they summoned the Federales to execute on site any family at mealtime that did not have food on the table replicating the colors of the Mexican flag—red, green, and white. This salsa became quite popular as the word got out as it was "life-saving."

Any leftovers of this sauce can be added to guacamole, chile con queso, or added to a vinaigrette salad dressing or can be frozen up to four months for later use in cooked dishes.

1 large tomato, finely chopped
1/2 cup finely chopped onion or 2 green onions, including tops, chopped
4 green chiles, parched, peeled (see page 340), and chopped, or 1 (4-ounce) can
    chopped green chiles, or 2 to 4 fresh jalapeño chiles, finely minced
1 garlic clove, finely minced
1/2 teaspoon salt
1/2 cup coarsely chopped cilantro (optional)

Combine tomato, onion, green chiles, garlic, salt, and cilantro, if using, in a medium bowl; marinate at least 15 minutes. Leftovers can be covered and refrigerated up to 3 days.
Makes 1 1/2 to 2 cups.

VARIATION
Black Bean Salsa: Add 3/4 cup cooked black beans.

Fresh Garden Salsa

The best of the best. This is packed with spicy flavor and was created when I was on contract to recreate the menu for Del Taco, a chain of fast-food Southwestern restaurants.

2 cups canned tomatoes, drained and roughly chopped
6 Tablespoons fresh tomato, finely diced
2 Tablespoons red wine vinegar
2 teaspoons Spanish onion, minced
2 Tablespoons fresh lime juice
2 teaspoons flat-leaf parsley, minced
1 heaping teaspoon sea salt
1 garlic clove, minced
1/4 cup water
1 Tablespoon pickled jalapeño chile juice
2 Tablespoons minced fresh chives
1 teaspoon serrano chile, finely minced
1/4 cup diced canned green chiles
6 Tablespoons finely chopped green bell pepper
1/4 teaspoon sugar
Pinch of ground oregano
Pinch of ground cumin

In a ceramic or glass bowl combine tomatoes, vinegar, onion, lime juice, parsley, salt, garlic, water, jalapeño chile juice, chives, serrano chile, green chiles, bell pepper, sugar, oregano, and cumin. Mix well, cover, and let marinate at least 30 minutes. Serve at room temperature.
Makes 3 1/4 cups.

Chiltomate

A wonderful Mayan salsa, this is equally terrific served with tostadas or as a sauce with meats, poultry, and fish dishes.

    4 medium-size tomatoes
    2 medium-size onions
    1 habanero, serrano, or jalapeño chile, minced*
    3 garlic cloves, minced
    1/2 cup fresh lemon juice
    1 bunch cilantro, coarsely chopped
    Salt to taste

Preheat grill. Place tomatoes on grill rack and grill until skin is charred. Peel and chop tomatoes. Meanwhile, cut the onions in half and grill until they soften. Also grill chiles until skin is charred or parched.

Chop onions. Peel and finely mince the chile.** Combine tomatoes, onions, and chile in a bowl with garlic, lemon juice, and cilantro. Add salt to taste.

Makes 4 cups.

*Habanero chile is the hottest, next hot is the serrano, and last usually is jalapeño as the mildest.
** If hot chiles burn your hands, wear rubber gloves. Lacking those, rub your fingers with cooking oil—any kind—before mincing the chiles.

Mexican Salsa

Originally from southern Mexico, this hot salsa is very differently flavored from, though with almost the same ingredients as, Chiltomate. It has proportionately more onion than American Southwest versions.

    1 1/4 cups chopped white onions
    1 cup chopped tomatoes
    1 1/2 teaspoons habanero chile, finely chopped or to taste
    1/2 cup fresh lime juice or lemon juice
    1/2 teaspoon or 1 clove garlic, minced

Combine onions, tomatoes, chile, juice, and garlic in a medium bowl. Allow to marinate, then serve at room temperature.

Makes 2 cups.

Chimichurri Salsa

In Argentina, this salsa is often served with melted mozzarella. Small "burros" are made by layering the melted cheese and salsa inside warm flour tortillas and rolling and eating them as an appetizer or snack. It's also often made prior to grilling a steak that has been marinated in teriyaki sauce and seasoned with lemon pepper. This salsa is then served as a topper on the steak.

1/2 cup olive oil
1/4 cup red wine vinegar
1/2 cup finely chopped onions
1 garlic clove, crushed
1 teaspoon ground Mexican oregano
1/4 teaspoon crushed pequin chile
1 1/2 teaspoons salt
1 teaspoon freshly ground black pepper
2 cups loosely packed fresh parsley, coarsely chopped

Place the oil, vinegar, onions, garlic, oregano, pequin chile, salt, and pepper in a blender or food processor; process until blended. Combine parsley and oil mixture in a small bowl. Let stand 30 minutes before serving.

Makes 1 1/2 to 2 cups.

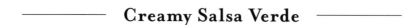

Creamy Salsa Verde

Cool and creamy, this is excellent when served with chicken and seafood dishes. It is a must to serve with the Crispy Chicken Tostados (recipe on page 105). Any leftovers can be used as a salad dressing, which is similar to ranch dressing.

> 1/2 cup sour cream
> 1/2 cup mayonnaise
> 1/3 cup Cold Salsa Verde (recipe on page 78)
> 1 Tablespoon fresh lime juice
> Crushed caribe chile or other crushed dried red chile (optional)

Combine sour cream, mayonnaise, salsa verde, and lime juice in a small bowl. Cover and refrigerate at least 1 hour. Sprinkle with crushed chile before serving.

Makes 1 1/4 cups.

Salsa Roja

This salsa is hot and typically New Mexican. It will keep for several days in the refrigerator and will freeze for at least six months. It's a common table salsa in northern New Mexico.

> 1 1/2 cups chopped fresh tomatoes or 1 (14 1/2-ounce) can petite diced tomatoes
> 1 Tablespoon finely crushed pequin chile or to taste
> 1 Tablespoon fresh lime juice
> 1 Tablespoon cider vinegar
> 1/2 teaspoon ground Mexican oregano
> 2 garlic cloves, minced
> 1 1/2 teaspoons ground cumin

Place tomatoes, pequin chile, lime juice, vinegar, oregano, garlic, and cumin in a blender jar and process briefly to completely blend the ingredients. If a coarser texture is desired, stir vigorously instead.

Makes 1 1/2 cups.

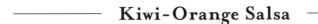

Kiwi-Orange Salsa

This flavorful salsa is especially nice over grilled fish.

    1 cup peeled, sliced, and quartered kiwifruit
    1 cup orange segments, separated with a knife so no membrane adheres
    2 jalapeño chiles, minced
    1 cup chopped Spanish onion
    1/3 cup freshly squeezed orange juice

Combine kiwi, oranges, jalapeño chiles, onion, and orange juice in a medium bowl. Serve over grilled fish. Allow to set 15 minutes before serving.

Makes 3 cups.

New Mexico Green Chile Sauce

This basic yet versatile sauce can be used as an enchilada sauce or over chimichangas or burritos. Or, when chicken or seafood is added, it becomes the sauce for enchiladas.

    1 Tablespoon butter or lard
    2/3 cup chopped onion
    2 Tablespoons all-purpose flour
    1 1/2 cups chicken broth
    4 to 6 New Mexico green chiles, parched and sliced in 3/4-inch crosswise
        slices or 1 cup chopped frozen or canned green chiles
    1 large garlic clove, finely minced
    3/4 teaspoon salt
    Dash of ground cumin
    2 cups poached chicken, coarsely chopped (optional) (recipe on page 94)

Melt butter in a saucepan over medium heat. Add onion and cook until softened. Stir in the flour, then gradually stir in the broth. Add green chiles, garlic, salt, and cumin.

Simmer, stirring, 10 minutes; serve as desired. To use in enchiladas, see Green Chile Chicken Enchiladas (recipe on page 176). Seafood enchiladas can be made the same using 2 cups seafood.

Makes 2 cups.

Hot Green Chile Sauce with Chicken

This is an alternative Green Chile Sauce, which has tomato instead of chicken stock for its basis. It can be used for saucing various tortilla-based dishes or to make enchiladas.

2 Tablespoons butter, lard, or bacon fat
2/3 cup chopped onion
1/4 cup all-purpose flour
1 (14 1/2-ounce) can stewed tomatoes
4 to 6 fresh green chiles, parched and sliced in 3/4-inch slices or
    1 cup chopped frozen or canned green chiles
2 large garlic cloves, finely minced
3/4 teaspoon salt
Dash of ground cumin
2 cups chopped cooked chicken (optional, used when making enchiladas, recipe on page 94)

Melt butter in a saucepan over medium heat. Add onion and cook until softened. Stir in the flour. Stir in tomatoes. Then add green chiles, garlic, salt, and cumin.

Simmer, stirring, 10 minutes. Add chicken and heat until hot. Serve as desired. To use in enchiladas, see Green Chile Chicken Enchiladas (recipe on page 176).

Makes 4 cups.

Red Chile Sauce

This is the basic red chile sauce used to create enchiladas and to serve over burritos, chile rellenos, tamales, and chimichangas.

2 Tablespoons butter, lard, or bacon drippings (omit if using ground beef in variation)
2 Tablespoons all-purpose flour
1/4 cup ground mild red chile
1/4 cup ground hot red chile
2 cups beef stock or water
1 garlic clove, minced
Pinch of ground Mexican oregano
Pinch of ground cumin
3/4 teaspoon salt (if not using stock)

Melt butter in a medium saucepan over low heat. Add flour and stir until smooth and slightly golden. Remove pan from heat and add ground chiles. Return to heat and gradually stir in stock. Add garlic, oregano, cumin, and salt, if using, and cook, stirring, about 10 minutes.

Makes about 2 1/2 cups.

VARIATION

Sauté 1 pound ground beef or beef cut in very small cubes. Omit the shortening, and continue as directed above. Use for enchiladas.

Magic Chile Sauce

The magic of this chile sauce is in its ingredients, which include chocolate and cinnamon. Slightly reminiscent of mole sauce, this is wonderful over any beef-filled tortilla dish such as burritos, enchiladas, and tamales. It can be frozen up to eight months.

2 cups Red Chile Sauce (recipe on page 84)
1/4 (1-ounce) square unsweetened chocolate
1 1/2 teaspoons light brown sugar
1/2 teaspoon red wine vinegar
1/8 teaspoon ground cinnamon
1 teaspoon ground almonds
1 teaspoon chopped raisins
Pinch of ground coriander
Pinch of ground cloves
Pinch of ground allspice

Combine chile sauce, chocolate, brown sugar, vinegar, cinnamon, almonds, raisins, coriander, cloves, and allspice in a medium saucepan. Simmer over low heat, stirring constantly, until chocolate is melted and flavors blend, about 20 minutes.

Makes 2 cups.

Mole Sauce

The traditional Mexican poblano-style mole is rich with chocolate, chiles, and spices. Poached chicken or turkey can be added and simmered in the sauce about five minutes to make Pollo Mole, which is generally served over rice. Or this sauce with the chicken or turkey chopped finely can be used in tamales, burritos, or chimichangas.

> 2-day-old air-dried corn tortillas, torn into pieces
> 2 Tablespoons seedless raisins
> 1 (1-ounce) square unsweetened chocolate
> 1/4 cup blanched almonds
> 1 small onion, chopped
> 3 green chiles, parched, peeled (see page 340), and chopped
>   or 1 green bell pepper, coarsely chopped
> 1 large tomato, quartered
> 1 garlic clove
> 3 Tablespoons all-purpose flour
> 1 Tablespoon ground hot chile
> 1/4 teaspoon ground cinnamon
> 1/4 teaspoon ground cloves
> 2 1/2 cups chicken broth (from poaching chicken if using
>   chicken in recipe, see recipe on page 94)

Process tortillas, raisins, chocolate, almonds, onion, green chiles, tomato, and garlic in a food processor or blender until ground. Place mixture in a medium saucepan.

Stir in flour, ground chile, cinnamon, and cloves. Add chicken broth and stir until well blended. Bring mixture to a boil, reduce heat, and simmer, uncovered, about 20 minutes, stirring occasionally. The sauce should be a little thicker than heavy cream. If necessary, thin with a bit more chicken broth.

Makes about 2 3/4 cups.

Ranchero Sauce

This is a standard tomato-based cooked sauce that is often served over eggs for a popular version of huevos rancheros. It is also served over chiles rellenos, burritos, omelets, and hamburgers.

1 Tablespoon corn oil
1 cup chopped Spanish onion
2 Tablespoons finely chopped serrano chile or jalapeño chile
2 (14 1/2-ounce) cans petite diced tomatoes
1 teaspoon salt
2 Tablespoons Italian flat parsley, finely minced

Heat oil in a skillet. Add onion and chile and cook until onion is softened. Add tomatoes, salt, and parsley. Bring to a boil. Reduce heat and simmer 10 minutes to blend flavors.
Makes 4 cups.

Sonoran Sauce

I developed this sauce after sampling a similar one in Juarez, Mexico. There it was served over eggs. This sauce has become my favorite for serving over poached or fried eggs for huevos rancheros.

1 Tablespoon butter
1 medium-size onion, thinly sliced and separated into rings
1 garlic clove, minced
1 Tablespoon all-purpose flour
6 green chiles, parched, peeled (see page 340), and cut into 3/4-inch-wide slices
1 1/2 cups chicken broth
1/2 teaspoon salt
2 medium-size tomatoes, cut into wedges

Heat butter in a skillet. Add onion and garlic, and cook until onion is softened. Stir in flour until well blended.

Add green chiles, broth, and salt. Cook, stirring, until the sauce is slightly thickened, then cook about 5 minutes to blend flavors. Add the tomato wedges, cooking slightly, about 3 minutes, and serve as a sauce with burritos, or use as a sauce over poached eggs atop tortillas for huevos rancheros.
Makes 2 cups.

Note: This sauce can be frozen for 3 months. Freeze without the tomatoes—adding them as above.

Sissy Sauce

Basically a creamy red sauce, this is somewhat reminiscent of cream of tomato soup with a lot more Mexican personality. It's very good over chicken and with chicken in it for enchiladas, or use it as a sauce for cheese enchiladas.

2 Tablespoons unsalted butter
3 Tablespoons all-purpose flour
1 Tablespoon ground mild chile
1 Tablespoon ground hot chile
2 cups chicken broth
1 (8-ounce) can tomato sauce
1/2 teaspoon minced fresh garlic (1 clove)
1/2 teaspoon salt
Pinch Mexican oregano

Melt butter in a medium saucepan. Stir in flour and cook until slightly browned over medium-low heat. Remove from heat and stir in ground chiles, then gradually stir in chicken broth. Add tomato sauce, garlic, salt, and oregano and simmer on low heat, stirring, until sauce is thickened.
Makes 3 cups.

West Texas Barbecue Sauce

A simple, robust sauce that is similar to the East Texas version but is thinner.

    1 cup tomato juice
    1/4 cup cider vinegar
    1/4 cup ketchup
    1/4 cup Worcestershire sauce
    2 Tablespoons brown sugar
    2 Tablespoons pure, mild red chile
    2 teaspoons dry mustard
    1 1/2 teaspoons onion salt
    1/2 teaspoon freshly ground black pepper
    Several dashes hot pepper sauce

Combine tomato juice, vinegar, ketchup, Worcestershire, brown sugar, red chile, mustard, onion salt, pepper, and hot pepper sauce in a 1-quart nonreactive saucepan and simmer, covered, 5 minutes.
Makes 2 cups.

East Texas Barbecue Sauce

This is wonderful over ribs, brisket, or most any meat.

    1 Tablespoon bacon drippings
    1/2 cup finely chopped Spanish onion
    1 garlic clove, minced
    1 (14-ounce) bottle ketchup
    6 Tablespoons Worcestershire sauce
    1/4 cup red wine vinegar
    1 teaspoon dry mustard
    2 Tablespoons molasses
    1/4 cup ground hot chile or to taste
    3/4 teaspoon ground cumin
    1 teaspoon liquid smoke

Heat bacon drippings in a 2-quart nonreactive saucepan over medium heat. Add onion and garlic and cook until the onion is softened. Add the ketchup, Worcestershire, vinegar, mustard, molasses, ground hot chile, cumin, and liquid smoke, reduce heat to low, and simmer, uncovered, 15 minutes, stirring occasionally.
Makes 3 cups.

Fiery California Barbecue Sauce

Packed with spices, brown sugar, and beer, this is wonderful on almost any meat or fish.

1 Tablespoon vegetable oil
2 cups finely chopped onions
3 large garlic cloves, minced
2 (8-ounce) cans tomato sauce
1 1/4 cups flat beer
6 Tablespoons packed brown sugar
1/4 cup vinegar
1/3 cup fresh lemon juice
1 Tablespoon Worcestershire sauce
1 1/2 Tablespoons soy sauce
1 teaspoon ground ginger
1 teaspoon ground allspice
1 teaspoon freshly grated nutmeg
1 teaspoon celery seeds
1 teaspoon crushed pequin chile
1 Tablespoon liquid smoke (optional)
Salt to taste

Heat oil in a skillet over medium heat. Add onions and garlic and cook until onions are softened but not browned. Transfer this mixture to a 2-quart nonreactive saucepan and add tomato sauce, beer, sugar, vinegar, lemon juice, Worcestershire, soy sauce, ginger, allspice, nutmeg, celery seed, and crushed chile.

Bring mixture to a boil over medium heat. Reduce heat and simmer, uncovered, 30 minutes. Remove from heat, add the liquid smoke, if using, and let the sauce cool. Taste, season with salt, and adjust seasonings.

Makes 3 1/2 cups.

POULTRY

Chicken in particular becomes a chameleon when combined with marinades and sauces with spicy, vibrant flavors. This is especially true in Southwestern dishes. Recipes featuring chicken, turkey, and duck present a range from traditional family favorites, such as the moles and drunken chicken, to very special creations with fresh citrus juices, garden produce, and Southwestern fresh and dried chiles and herbs.

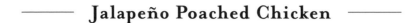

Jalapeño Poached Chicken

Use for pizzitas, chicken enchiladas, chicken tamales, chicken fettuccine, and quesadillas. Freeze in two-cup amounts in freezer-weight packaging for up to six months.

> 12 cups chicken broth
> 2 (2- to 3-pound) whole chickens
> 1/2 teaspoon salt
> 1 teaspoon pickled jalapeño chile juice

Place chicken broth in a large saucepan and simmer until reduced by half, to 6 cups. In a 5-quart saucepan, put chickens breast side up, then add broth, salt, and jalapeño chile juice and bring to a boil. Skim off the impurities that rise to the surface. Reduce heat and simmer, covered, about 45 minutes, or until chickens are tender. Remove from heat and slightly cool chickens in the broth. Drain, reserving the broth for another use.

Remove the meat from the bones. Discard skin and bones. Slice meat across the grain into julienne or pieces about 2 inches long for use in other recipes.

Makes 3 pounds.

Spicy Baked Chicken Thighs

These hot and spicy thighs are easy to make and possess excellent flavor.

> 1 lemon, zested, then halved and seeds removed
> 1 Tablespoon ground mild chile
> 2 teaspoons crushed caribe chile
> 2 teaspoons dried onion
> 2 teaspoons dried leaf Mexican oregano
> 4 garlic cloves, minced
> 1 teaspoon ground ginger
> 4 chicken thighs, trimmed

Preheat oven to 350°F (175°C). Zest the lemon and mix the zest with ground chile, crushed chile, onion, oregano, garlic, and ginger and sprinkle over all sides of the thighs. Place in a shallow baking dish and bake 30 minutes; turn and cook 10 to 15 minutes longer or until juices run clear when chicken is pierced. Juice the lemon and evenly sprinkle over the thighs, then serve.

Makes 4 servings.

— Duck Sauté with Chile-Nut Mole —

Ground seeds and tortillas are the thickeners for the sauce in this recipe. Subtly spiced, this entrée gets rave reviews from both adults and children every time. It can be frozen for up to six months.

 1 large (7- to 8-pound) duck
 8 cups chicken stock, reduced to 4 cups
 10 whole black peppercorns
 2 bay leaves

Mole Sauce
 2 Tablespoons unsalted butter
 1 medium-size onion, chopped
 1/2 cup sesame seeds
 3/4 cup hulled sunflower seeds or pumpkin seeds
 2 corn tortillas, torn into pieces
 Reserved broth
 1 to 2 Tablespoons ground mild chile
 2 green chiles or more, parched, peeled (see page 340), and chopped

Place duck in a large pot and cover with the chicken stock; add peppercorns and bay leaves. Bring to a boil; reduce heat and skim thoroughly. Cover and simmer until tender but still firm, 1 to 2 hours. Drain, reserving broth.

Prepare Mole Sauce: Melt butter in a skillet. Add onion and sauté over high heat until lightly browned. With heat still high, add seeds and corn tortilla pieces. Cook, stirring constantly, about 2 minutes. Stir in 1 1/2 cups of duck broth and green chiles. Add more broth if needed to thin sauce to a medium consistency. Taste and adjust seasonings. Add sauce to a blender jar and process until smooth.

Return sauce to skillet, then place duck pieces in sauce, turning to coat them evenly. Cover and simmer 15 minutes or until hot and duck is as tender as desired.

Makes 6 to 8 servings.

VARIATIONS:
If a spicier mole is desired, add more green or red chiles to taste.
Substitute 2 (3-pound) chickens for the duck.

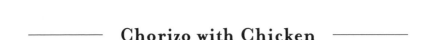

Chorizo with Chicken

A subtle, Spanish-inspired dish, this will freeze well for up to six months. It is best served with rice.

3 Tablespoons Spanish olive oil
1 (4-pound) chicken, cut up
2 or 3 chorizo links, sliced
2 medium-size onions, thinly sliced and separated into rings
2 garlic cloves, minced
2 large tomatoes, chopped
1 Tablespoon cilantro, coarsely chopped (optional)
1 teaspoon salt
1/4 teaspoon freshly ground black pepper
1 or 2 jalapeño chiles or to taste, finely chopped
Chicken broth, if needed

Heat oil in a large skillet over medium-high heat. Add chicken and cook until browned. Remove to a plate. In the same skillet cook the chorizo slices until browned; remove from skillet. Pour off all but 1 Tablespoon of the fat.

Add onion rings and garlic to the remaining fat, and sauté until onions are soft and lightly browned. Add the tomatoes, cilantro, salt, pepper, and jalapeño chiles. Cook, stirring, about 5 minutes. The sauce should be the consistency of gravy; if it is too thick, add a little chicken broth.

Return chicken and chorizo to the skillet, turning the pieces to coat with the sauce. Cover and simmer until tender, about 30 minutes.

Makes 4 to 6 servings.

Turkey Mole with Traditional Chocolate—Red Chile Sauce

The turkey is native to the Americas. Mole is a traditional Mexican dish dating back to early colonial times, reputedly having been created by a nun in a convent in Puebla, Mexico. This "national dish of Mexico" is delicious served with rice, frijoles, guacamole, or avocado and tomato vinaigrette, and fresh hot tortillas or bolillos. It can be frozen for up to six months.

- 1 turkey breast, cut into serving-size pieces
- 2 turkey thighs, about 3 pounds total, cut into serving-size pieces
- Water
- 1 carrot, cut into 1-inch pieces
- 1 small onion, halved
- 1 bay leaf
- 3/4 teaspoon salt
- 8 whole black peppercorns
- 1 recipe Mole Sauce (recipe on page 95)
- 1 Tablespoon sesame seeds

Place turkey breast and thigh pieces in a large pot and add enough water to just cover. Add the carrot, onion, bay leaf, salt, and peppercorns. Bring to a boil, skim off the foam, cover, and simmer until tender, about 1 1/4 hours. Drain and reserve the broth.

Prepare the mole sauce in a large, heavy skillet, using the turkey broth to prepare it. Place the cooked and drained turkey pieces in the sauce, turning to coat evenly. Cover and simmer 30 minutes, adding a bit more broth if sauce becomes too thick.

Meanwhile, toast the sesame seeds in a 300°F (150°C) oven 10 minutes or until browned, stirring frequently. Taste mole sauce and adjust seasonings. Remove to a deep serving platter, sprinkle with toasted sesame seeds, and serve.

Makes 6 servings.

Green Chile Chicken Bake

A south-of-the-border inspiration, this dish is somewhat lighter than the traditional mole. Serve with rice, tortillas, and your favorite salad. Leftovers, which can be frozen up to six months, are great in tacos and burritos.

1 (3- to 4-pound) chicken, cut for frying
2 cups water
1/2 teaspoon salt, plus more for seasoning
1 cup hulled pumpkin seeds
1 garlic clove, minced
1 recipe New Mexico Green Chile Sauce (recipe on page 83)
1 Tablespoon butter, lard, or bacon drippings
Freshly ground black pepper

Place chicken in a large, heavy skillet with the water and 1/2 teaspoon salt. Bring to a boil, reduce the heat, and skim off the foam. Cover and simmer until tender, about 45 minutes. Drain chicken, reserving the broth, and remove chicken from skillet.

Process pumpkin seeds in a blender until ground; add garlic and green chile sauce. Puree until smooth.

Melt butter in the skillet over medium-high heat, add puree, and cook, stirring constantly, 2 to 3 minutes. Thin to a medium consistency by adding small amounts of the reserved chicken broth. Taste and season with salt and pepper. Return chicken pieces to the skillet, turning to coat them evenly with sauce. Cover and simmer, without boiling, until hot, about 15 minutes.

Makes 3 to 4 servings.

Pecos Chicken

Select a very young fryer, not over 2 1/2 pounds, for this, and use the freshest, top-quality vegetables. The dish almost prepares itself once the chicken is browned and the vegetables are prepared. Use a large heavy skillet, a Dutch oven, or even a deep cast-iron pot, as long as it has a tight-fitting cover. You can cook this to the almost-done stage, then reheat it just before serving, a technique I prefer so that I don't have to watch the clock after my guests have arrived.

2 Tablespoons unsalted butter
1 (about 2 1/2 pound) chicken, cut into serving pieces
3 zucchini, cut diagonally into 3/4-inch slices
4 ears corn, kernels cut off, or 2 1/2 cups frozen whole-kernel corn
2 tomatoes (about 1 pound), peeled and cut into wedges
2 small white or yellow Spanish onions, sliced into rounds
3 garlic cloves, minced
1 jalapeño chile, chopped finely
1/2 teaspoon ground cumin
Pecos Pollo Salsa (recipe follows) (optional)

Melt butter over medium heat in a large 5- to 7-quart heavy pot. Add chicken, skin side down, and turn to brown evenly. When chicken is browned, add vegetables in layers, first zucchini, then corn, tomatoes, and onions.

Sprinkle garlic, jalapeño chile, and cumin over the top, cover, and steam, reducing heat to just maintain steaming. Check after 30 minutes that chicken is not sticking. Add water or chicken stock if mixture is too dry. (If cooking in advance, stop the cooking at this point before the vegetables are completely done.) Cook about 30 minutes or until vegetables are done.

Prepare salsa, if using. To serve, arrange everything on a platter with the chicken in the center and the vegetables around the sides. Serve with salsa.

Makes 4 servings.

Pecos Pollo Salsa
1 jalapeño chile or to taste, finely chopped
1 small tomato, chopped
2 (1/4-inch-thick) slices red onion, chopped

Combine all ingredients in a small bowl and serve alongside the chicken.

Christmas Chicken

In New Mexico, a favorite is to sauce dishes with half red chile sauce and half green chile sauce. This custom is called "Christmas" when you order this in a restaurant. So when I combined red and green chiles in one chicken dish, I decided Christmas was an appropriate name. Serve with tortillas for dipping into the flavorful sauce.

2 (3-pound) chickens, cut up
2 cups all-purpose flour
1 1/2 teaspoons salt
Freshly ground black pepper
4 Tablespoons unsalted butter, divided
4 Tablespoons olive oil, divided
4 garlic cloves, minced
1 large onion, chopped
2 tomatoes, peeled, seeded, and chopped
4 large New Mexico green chiles, parched, peeled (see page 340),
    and chopped or 1 (4-ounce) can chopped green chiles
2 cups chicken broth
1 cup pitted green olives, sliced
1/2 cup golden raisins
1/4 cup ground mild chile or to taste
8 medium-size new potatoes, cut in half

Preheat oven to 325°F (165°C). Rinse chicken pieces and pat dry with paper towels. In a shallow bowl combine flour, salt, and pepper and evenly coat chicken in the seasoned flour. In a large heavy pot with deep sides, heat 2 Tablespoons of the butter and 2 Tablespoons of the oil over medium heat. Add chicken, a few pieces at a time; fry until browned on all sides. Remove the pieces as they brown and set aside.

When all the chicken is fried, add garlic and onion; sauté until the onion is softened. Add tomatoes, green chiles, broth, olives, raisins, and ground chile and cook over medium-low heat until tomatoes are softened. Taste and adjust seasonings.

Heat remaining butter and oil in a large heavy skillet over medium-high heat. Add potatoes; cook, stirring occasionally, until browned. Add potatoes and chicken to the sauce, spooning it to cover the pieces. Cover and bake 45 to 60 minutes or until chicken is tender.

Makes 6 to 8 servings.

Citrus Turkey Breast in Champagne Vinegar Marinade

We first developed this marinade in our Woodstock, New York, kitchen. It was so terrific, especially when served with Golden Salsa napped over the center of each serving, that we put it on our restaurant menu.

 1/4 cup Champagne vinegar or white wine vinegar
 1/4 cup extra-virgin Spanish olive oil
 1/4 teaspoon finely grated orange peel
 1/4 teaspoon finely grated lemon peel
 1/4 teaspoon finely grated lime peel
 1 1/2 Tablespoons coarsely chopped cilantro
 1/4 teaspoon salt
 1 1/2 pounds boneless turkey breast, sliced 1/2-inch thick
 Golden Salsa (recipe on page 76)

Combine vinegar, oil, orange, lemon, and lime peel, cilantro, and salt in a large, shallow baking dish. Add the turkey, turning each piece to coat it, and marinate 30 minutes at room temperature or 2 hours in the refrigerator. (The turkey can even be frozen for up to 3 months in the marinade.)

Preheat grill. Grill turkey over medium-hot coals until no longer pink in center, 4 to 6 minutes on each side. Serve with the salsa drizzled over the center of each piece of turkey.

Makes 4 servings.

Pollo Borracho (Drunken Chicken)

This is a popular Sonoran chicken dish that is somewhat reminiscent of picadillo. You can use flat beer, or even frozen beer that's been left from a keg. It is one of my very favorite recipes for entertaining. I have only received rave reviews whenever I have served it—even in my New York City restaurant. The Pollo is wonderful served over the Peppered Rice (recipe on page 227).

1/4 cup vegetable oil
2 Tablespoons unsalted butter
2 (2 1/2-pound) chickens, cut into serving pieces, or 8 chicken legs with thighs
1/4 pound cooked ham, coarsely chopped
1 cup raisins
2 cups amber beer, such as Corona
1/8 teaspoon ground cloves
1/8 teaspoon ground cinnamon
1/8 teaspoon ground coriander
2 garlic cloves, minced
3/4 teaspoon salt
Freshly ground black pepper
1/2 cup piñon nuts (pine nuts)
1/2 cup pimiento-stuffed olives, halved
1 Tablespoon capers, drained (optional)

In a heavy, flameproof casserole dish with a lid, heat oil and butter. Add chicken pieces and sauté until golden. Add ham, raisins, beer, cloves, cinnamon, coriander, garlic, salt, and pepper. Cover and simmer until the chicken is tender when pierced with a fork, about 1 hour. Add the piñon nuts, olives, and capers and heat through, uncovered, about 5 minutes.

Makes 6 servings.

Sassy Southern Fried Chicken

Who doesn't like fried chicken? The chiles make this chicken even better than regular fried chicken.

1 cup all-purpose flour
1/2 cup cornflake crumbs
1 teaspoon crushed caribe chile or to taste
1/2 teaspoon ground pequin chile
1 teaspoon poultry seasoning
Freshly ground black pepper
1 (2 1/2-pound) whole chicken
About 1 cup buttermilk or milk
Vegetable oil
Southern Cream Gravy (recipe follows)

Process flour, crumbs, crushed chile, ground chile, poultry seasoning, and pepper in a food processor until fine; set aside.

Cut chicken into serving pieces. Soak in buttermilk 30 minutes at room temperature or in the refrigerator 2 hours, turning and rotating the pieces to coat uniformly.

Heat 2 inches of oil in a deep skillet over medium heat. To bread the chicken, lift the pieces out of the milk, shaking lightly. Then roll in the flour mixture and set on a waxed paper–covered baking sheet. Let stand about 5 minutes, then roll in the flour mixture again.

Place chicken pieces in the oil and partially cover the skillet. Cook 12 to 15 minutes or until golden (not too brown) on the first side. Turn, recover, and fry the other side. When chicken is uniformly golden and fork-tender, drain well on paper towels. Keep warm in a 200°F (95°C) oven. Do not cover tightly or it will become soggy. Prepare gravy. Serve chicken with mashed potatoes and cream gravy.

Makes 2 to 4 servings.

Southern Cream Gravy
1/4 cup all-purpose flour
1 cup half-and-half
1 cup milk
Salt and freshly ground black pepper to taste

Drain off all oil from the skillet except 1/4 cup, leaving any browned bits in the skillet. Add flour and cook, stirring, over medium heat until flour lightly tans. Gradually stir in half-and-half; cook, stirring constantly, until mixture is bubbly. Add milk; cook, stirring, until thickened and smooth. Taste and season with salt and pepper.

Chicken Avocado Fettuccine

I created this dish in my kitchen in Woodstock, New York, when I was searching for innovative Southwestern pasta dishes, and we all liked it very much.

4 Tablespoons unsalted butter, divided
2 cups sliced button mushrooms
1 1/2 cups cubed poached chicken breasts (recipe on page 94)
Salt and freshly ground black pepper
1 1/2 cups half-and-half, divided
4 ounces Monterey Jack cheese, cubed
2 New Mexico green chiles, parched, peeled (see page 340), and chopped
12 ounces green fettuccine noodles
4 ounces thin spaghetti
2 Haas avocados
1/2 cup freshly grated Parmesan cheese

Melt 2 Tablespoons of the butter in a large heavy skillet. Add mushrooms and sauté until lightly browned. Remove to a bowl. Melt the remaining 2 Tablespoons butter in same skillet and add the cubed chicken. Cook until lightly browned. Season with salt and pepper. Return mushrooms to the skillet and add 1 cup of the half-and-half, the cubed cheese, and green chiles. Cook over medium-low heat only until the mixture thickens, 3 to 5 minutes. Remove from heat. Cover and set the sauce aside.

Cook noodles and spaghetti in a large pot of boiling salted water until al dente. Reheat sauce, but do not boil, and add the remaining 1/2 cup of half-and-half. Meanwhile, peel the avocados, first scoring with a sharp knife, then removing the peel; cut into 1-inch cubes. When pasta is done, drain, rinse with hot water, and return to the cooking pot. Add sauce and avocados and toss. Serve on warm plates with Parmesan cheese.

Makes 4 servings.

Spicy Fried Chicken Strips

The crispy corn masa coating, with just a dash of chile and herbs, makes for a fabulous flavor. Freezing the coated chicken pieces before deep-frying assures greater breading retention and juiciness. The coated pieces can be frozen up to three months. This is a picture-perfect dish when the strips are crisscrossed on top of finely shredded lettuce in tostado cups dressed with Creamy Salsa Verde (recipe on page 82), dotted with tomato squares and sprinkles of caribe chile.

- 1/2 cup masa harina
- 1 teaspoon ground cumin
- 1 Tablespoon ground pure, mild red chile
- 1 Tablespoon ground pure, hot red chile
- 3/4 teaspoon salt, divided
- 1 Tablespoon minced fresh Italian flat-leaf parsley
- 1 teaspoon dried leaf Mexican oregano
- 2 garlic cloves, minced
- 1/2 cup all-purpose flour
- Freshly ground black pepper
- 3/4 cup milk
- 1 pound boneless, skinless chicken breasts
- 1 quart vegetable oil

Mix masa, cumin, ground chiles, 1/2 teaspoon of the salt, the parsley, oregano, and garlic in a flat, shallow bowl. Combine flour, the remaining 1/4 teaspoon salt, and pepper in another shallow bowl. Place the milk in a third shallow bowl.

Cut chicken into 3-inch-long strips about 3/4 inch wide and no more than 1/2 inch deep. Place waxed paper on a large baking sheet. Coat chicken pieces by first placing them in the milk, then the flour, then the milk, and finally into the masa mixture. Arrange the coated strips on waxed paper. Freeze until firm, at least 4 hours or preferably overnight.

To fry, heat oil to 350°F (175°C) in a deep fryer. Place several pieces of chicken in a frying basket and cook only until the bubbles begin to subside and the pieces are golden brown. If they are not done throughout, place in a 300°F oven to keep warm and finish cooking.

Makes enough for 12 tacos, 36 appetizers, or use on Chicken Fajita Salad.

Tostado Presentation

- 2 quarts vegetable oil
- 12 corn tortillas
- 6 leaves romaine lettuce
- 1/2 recipe Creamy Salsa Verde (recipe on page 82)
- 1/2 small tomato, cut in 3/8-inch squares
- 1 Tablespoon caribe chile

Heat oil to 375°F (190°C) in deep pan or electric deep fryer. Create a form to make shells by taking an 8-ounce tomato paste can and piercing 4 holes on the bottom of the can and 4 holes on the top side in between the top holes for the oil to circulate when frying. Using tongs, lower a tortilla on the top of the hot oil and plunge down the can centered on the tortilla and hold until crisp when the large bubbles of oil subside, about 22 seconds. Remove the crisp tostado carefully from the can and place a wad of paper towel in the center and invert to drain. Repeat until 12 shells are made. Place tostados on a platter in a 250°F (120°C) oven to crisp while preparing the rest of the ingredients.

Roll the rinsed leaves of lettuce tightly together and thinly slice. To serve, place lettuce in the bottom of each tostado. Place a crisscross of two crispy chicken pieces, then drizzle Creamy Salsa Verde over the chicken pieces. Dot with 3 tomato pieces and sprinkle with the caribe chile.

Chicken Fajitas with Pico de Gallo, Sour Cream & Tortillas

Chicken breast is perfect with the traditional fajita marinade. I have always preferred the fresh, pure flavors of lime and garlic to the "nontraditional flavors" such as soy sauce and pineapple juice. My favorite way to serve these chicken fajitas is with grilled rather than sautéed vegetables. Select large red onions and the biggest bell peppers you can find.

> 2 pounds lean boneless, skinless chicken breasts
> Juice of 2 limes
> 6 garlic cloves, minced
> 1 teaspoon salt
> Freshly ground black pepper
> 1/4 cup vegetable oil
> 2 large red onions, halved crosswise
> 1 each large red, green, and yellow bell pepper, cut into
>   quarters if grilling, strips if searing in a skillet
> Pico de Gallo (recipe on page 77)
> Sour cream
> 8 small (6-inch) flour tortillas, warmed

Cut each breast in half, following the natural division of the cartilage and removing any fat. Pound between sheets of plastic wrap to uniform thickness.

To prepare the marinade: Combine lime juice, garlic, salt, black pepper, and oil in a bowl. Dip each side of the chicken breast into the mixture and marinate 30 minutes at room temperature or up to 1 hour in the refrigerator.

Meanwhile, about 45 minutes before serving, preheat grill, using mesquite wood or chips to flavor the charcoal briquettes, if desired. To grill, start onion halves to cook 5 to 6 minutes before starting the bell peppers. Place the onion cut side down. Turn onion after 5 minutes, then add the chicken. Grill chicken about 3 inches from coals for 4 minutes on each side until charred on each side.

Cut the onion into thin wedges after they are cooked, removing the outer layers, and cut the peppers into 1/2-inch-wide strips. Toss all of the veggies together. Cut the chicken across the grain into strips about 1 inch wide.

To serve, on each plate divide onions and peppers and place chicken strips on top. Pass a napkin-lined basket of warm tortillas. Or, for a buffet, you can place the grilled veggies in the center of a platter and place the chicken pieces on top. Fold and tuck the tortillas in around the edges. Serve with bowls of pico de gallo and sour cream.

Makes 6 to 8 servings.

VARIATION

Serve Beef Fajitas (recipe on page 158) and Shrimp Fajitas (recipe on page 129) with Chicken Fajitas to have a sampling of each.

Duck Fajitas with Orange Raspberry Salsa

Duck adapts well to fajita-style preparation.

> 1 (4 1/2- to 5-pound) duck
> Juice of 2 limes
> 1/4 cup vegetable oil
> 6 garlic cloves, minced
> 1 teaspoon salt
> Freshly ground black pepper
> Orange Raspberry Salsa (recipe follows)
> Wild Rice Pilaf (recipe on page 228)
> 18 (6-inch) flour tortillas, warmed

Rinse and remove pin feathers from the duck, then slice the duck into 1/4- to 1/2-inch thick slices, trying to get as much meat as possible from the breast, thighs, and legs. Pound the thicker slices to uniform thickness.

To prepare the marinade: Combine lime juice, oil, garlic, salt, and pepper in a bowl. Dip each side of the duck slices into the mixture and marinate 30 minutes at room temperature or 2 hours in the refrigerator.

Prepare the salsa.

About 45 minutes before serving, preheat grill, using mesquite wood or chips to flavor the charcoal briquettes. Remove duck slices from marinade. Grill duck 3 inches from coals until charred on each side but still rare in the center (about 4 minutes a side). To serve, slice the larger pieces of duck into 1-inch-wide slices. Serve on rice with Orange-Raspberry Salsa. Pass a napkin-lined basket of hot tortillas.

Makes 6 servings.

Orange Raspberry Salsa

> 1 large navel orange, peel and pith removed, chopped
> 1 cup chopped red onion
> 1 cup red raspberries
> 2 teaspoons minced jalapeño chiles
> Juice of 1/2 lime

Mix oranges, onion, raspberries, jalapeño chiles, and lime juice together in a small bowl and refrigerate at least 1 hour.

VARIATIONS

If you prefer, the duck can be roasted in a 450°F (230°C) oven. Rub the outside skin with the lime juice and garlic and add the lime peels and 2 additional garlic cloves to the cavity before roasting. Or you can smoke the duck in a smoker.

FISH & SHELLFISH

The personalities that seafood takes on when combined with citrus, chiles, and other Southwestern ingredients are truly spectacular! Most of these dishes are quick and make a good contrast to the heavier meat-laden Southwestern dishes.

Many of the dishes use a simple marinade to add interesting flavor, and the fish is often quickly grilled. Try mixing and matching the various marinades and salsas for even more exciting entrées of your very own making.

Sandy's Margarita Snapper

Sandy, who adores New Mexico and all the specialties of the region, created this special marinade for guests. It has been a favorite ever since.

  6 red snapper fillets (about 1 1/2 pounds)
  6 Tablespoons fresh lime juice
  3 Tablespoons extra-virgin olive oil
  1 1/2 Tablespoons Triple Sec
  1/4 cup tequila
  1 teaspoon pickled jalapeño chile juice
  Crushed pequin chile

Rinse snapper fillets and pat dry. Combine lime juice, oil, Triple Sec, tequila, jalapeño chile juice, and crushed chile in a large shallow baking dish. Add the snapper fillets, turning to coat. Marinate at least 2 hours in the refrigerator.

Preheat oven to 350°F (175°C). Bake fish, covered, about 20 minutes or until fish just begins to flake when pierced with a fork. Serve with a favorite salsa.

Makes 6 servings.

Red Snapper Adobado

The robust adobado sauce, originally used on pork for carne adobado, is also wonderful on chicken breast or firm-fleshed fish, or even shrimp.

  1 pound fresh red snapper fillets
  1/2 cup Adobo Red Chile Sauce (recipe on page 84)
  1 medium-size onion, sliced and separated into rings

Preheat oven to 350°F (175°C). Rinse snapper fillets and pat dry. Lightly oil a 10-inch oval baking dish or a 9-inch-square baking dish. Pour 1/4 cup of the sauce into baking dish. Arrange the snapper on top of sauce. Pour remaining sauce over the snapper and turn fish to coat evenly. Cover with a layer of onion rings. Bake 15 minutes; then spoon sauce over fish and onion and bake another 15 minutes or until fish just begins to flake when pierced with a fork.

Makes 4 servings.

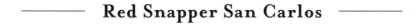

Red Snapper San Carlos

Red snapper is prevalent along Mexico's coast and is served in a special way in almost every seaside town.

1 (3- or 4-pound) red snapper, ready to cook
1 Tablespoon olive oil
1/4 cup finely chopped onion
1 cup thinly sliced mushrooms
8 ounces cooked and shelled baby shrimp
1/2 jalapeño chile, minced
1 teaspoon minced fresh tarragon or 1/2 teaspoon dried leaf tarragon
1 teaspoon minced fresh thyme or 1/2 teaspoon dried leaf thyme
1/2 teaspoon salt
Several grinds black pepper
About 1/2 cup dry sherry

Preheat oven to 375°F (190°C). Rinse red snapper and pat dry. Heat oil in a medium skillet over medium-high heat. Add onion and cook until softened. Add mushrooms, shrimp, jalapeño chile, tarragon, and thyme. Season with salt and pepper and cook until onion is clear, reducing heat if necessary. Stuff mixture into cavity of red snapper, then close opening with skewers.

Place fish in a large roaster with a lid. Just before placing into oven, drizzle with half of the sherry. Cover the pan. Baste fish frequently with wine in roaster as it bakes. Bake about 20 minutes or until done and fish just begins to flake when pierced with a fork. When fish is done, remove to a heated platter. Deglaze pan with remaining sherry and serve as a sauce.

Makes 4 to 6 servings.

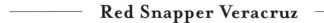

Red Snapper Veracruz

Veracruz, Mexico's oldest and largest port on the Caribbean, has played an important role in Mexican history. Veracruz-style sauce always contains tomatoes and usually olives.

    6 red snapper fillets
    1 Tablespoon olive oil
    1 small onion, finely chopped
    2 large garlic cloves, minced
    6 medium-size tomatoes, peeled, seeded, and chopped (about 2 cups)
    Juice of 1 lime
    1/2 teaspoon ground Mexican oregano
    1 jalapeño chile, seeded and minced
    1 teaspoon salt
    Steamed rice
    1/4 cup sliced pimiento-stuffed Spanish olives

Rinse snapper, pat dry, and set aside. Heat oil in a large skillet. Add onion and garlic and cook until onion is softened. Add the tomatoes, lime juice, oregano, jalapeño chile, and salt, and cook 10 minutes.

Reduce heat until sauce barely simmers and place the fillets on top of the sauce. Spoon some of the sauce over the top of each fillet. Cover skillet and simmer about 10 minutes or until fish just begins to flake when pierced with a fork. Taste the sauce and adjust the seasoning if desired. Serve fish on warm plates with a mound of rice alongside. Spoon some sauce over each portion. Garnish with the sliced olives.

Makes 6 servings.

Red Snapper in Tomatillo Sauce

The sauce is also delicious on grilled fish.

2 1/2 pounds red snapper fillets
Salt
3/4 cup all-purpose flour
1/4 cup olive oil
1 large onion, chopped
2 garlic cloves, minced
1 (10-ounce) can Mexican tomatillos, undrained*
2 large tomatoes, peeled and chopped
2 jalapeño chiles, seeded and chopped
1/4 cup minced fresh Italian flat-leaf parsley
2 Tablespoons coarsely chopped cilantro (optional)
1/4 teaspoon freshly ground black pepper
12 pitted ripe olives, sliced

Rinse snapper fillets and pat dry. Season with salt and lightly coat with flour. Heat oil in a large heavy skillet. Add fillets a few at a time and cook on both sides until golden. Remove to a platter and keep warm.

Add onion and garlic to skillet; cook until onion is softened. Add tomatillos and their liquid, the tomatoes, jalapeño chiles, parsley, cilantro, and pepper. Cook the sauce over medium heat until it is slightly thickened, 5 to 10 minutes. Pour sauce over snapper fillets, garnish with sliced olives, and serve.

Makes 6 servings.

*You may cook 3/4 pound fresh tomatillos about 5 minutes and add with about 1/2 cup of the cooking liquid.

Baked Cod with Lemon, Caribe Chile & Olive Oil

Simple yet flavorful.

6 (6-ounce) fillets of cod or any other firm, white fish such as snapper, sea bass, or halibut
1/2 cup all-purpose flour
1/4 cup olive oil
2 Tablespoons finely chopped green onions
1 Tablespoon chopped cilantro (optional)
2 teaspoons fresh lemon juice
3 Tablespoons minced Italian flat-leaf parsley
2 Tablespoons crushed caribe chile
1/2 teaspoon salt
1/4 teaspoon freshly ground black pepper
1 lemon, thinly sliced
Golden Salsa (recipe on page 76) or Seckel Pear & Tomatillo Salsa (recipe on page 76)

Rinse fish and pat dry. Preheat oven to 375°F (190°C). Butter a baking dish large enough to hold fish in a single layer.

Very lightly dust the fish fillets with flour and arrange them in buttered baking dish. Place oil, green onion, cilantro if using, lemon juice, parsley, crushed chile, salt, and pepper in a jar, cover, and shake well to combine. Pour evenly over fish. Bake 20 minutes. Arrange lemon slices over fillets and bake 5 minutes or until fish just begins to flake with pierced with a fork. Serve salsa on the side.

Makes 6 servings.

Catfish in Blue Corn Jalapeño Crumb Coating

The crunch of cornmeal is always a favorite for coating catfish. The added flavor of blue corn coupled with the finely minced jalapeño chile and garlic make a luscious combination.

1 1/4 to 1 1/2 pounds catfish fillets
3/4 cup blue cornmeal
1 jalapeño chile or to taste, finely minced
2 garlic cloves, finely minced
1/2 teaspoon salt
Vegetable oil for frying
Salsa
Lemon or lime wedges

Rinse and pat the fillets almost dry, leaving enough moisture on each for the meal mixture to stick. Combine cornmeal, jalapeño chile, garlic, and salt in a shallow bowl.

Heat about 1 inch of oil in a large skillet over medium-high heat. Dip each fillet into the meal mixture, then place in hot oil, turning when browned. Fry until other side is browned and fish just begins to flake when pierced with a fork. Serve with salsa and lemon wedges.

Makes 4 servings.

Grilled Catfish with Fresh Peach & Grilled Corn Salsa

Grilling the fish makes this dish quick and easy and of course contains less calories. It is yummy with this salsa.

1 1/4 pound catfish fillets
1/4 cup extra-virgin olive oil
1/4 cup fresh lime juice
1/4 cup tequila
1/4 cup chopped red onion
1 teaspoon crushed pequin chile
2 teaspoons fresh sage or 1 teaspoon dried
2 teaspoons Italian oregano or 1 teaspoon dried
2 teaspoons fresh tarragon or 1 teaspoon dried
Fresh Peach & Grilled Corn Salsa (recipe follows)

Rinse the fillets and pat dry. Combine oil, lime juice, tequila, onion, crushed chile, sage, oregano, and tarragon in a shallow baking dish. Add fillets, cover, and marinate 30 minutes at room temperature or 2 hours in the refrigerator, spooning the sauce over the top of the fillets and turning them periodically. Meanwhile, prepare the salsa.

Preheat grill to medium hot. Place catfish on grill rack and grill about 3 minutes. Turn and grill remaining side 3 minutes or until catfish just begins to flake when pierced with a fork. Serve on a bed of the salsa.

Makes 4 servings.

Fresh Peach & Grilled Corn Salsa

2 ears Grilled Mexican Corn (recipe on page 232), kernels cut off cob (about 1 cup)*
1 cup diced fresh peach
1 cup diced red onion
1/2 cup diced red or green bell pepper
1 (4-ounce) can chopped green chiles (1/2 cup)
2 garlic cloves, minced

Combine corn, peaches, onions, bell peppers, green chiles, and garlic in a small bowl. Cover and let stand at least 15 minutes for the flavors to blend.

*When preparing Grilled Mexican Corn, make extra to use for this recipe. If no leftover grilled corn or fresh corn is available, you can place 1 cup frozen corn kernels scattered over a cookie sheet under the broiler until the edges sear or become light brown.

Grapefruit Marinated Salmon with Kiwi-Orange Salsa

When you're in a hurry and would like to add an easy Southwestern flair to fish, try this. Buttered new potatoes with fresh dill and Caesar Salad Originale (recipe on page 56) will really make for a memorable meal.

    2 salmon steaks (1 pound)
    1/4 cup fresh grapefruit juice
    1/4 cup white wine
    2 garlic cloves, minced
    1 teaspoon fresh dill or dried dill weed
    Kiwi-Orange Salsa (recipe on page 83)

Rinse salmon and pat dry. Combine juice, wine, garlic, and dill in a small shallow baking dish. Add salmon, cover, and marinate 30 minutes at room temperature or 2 hours in the refrigerator, spooning the sauce over salmon steaks and turning them periodically. Preheat oven to 375°F (190°C). Cover dish and bake 20 minutes or until salmon just begins to flake when pierced with a fork and the very center is still translucent. Arrange salmon on plates. Serve with a ribbon of Kiwi-Orange Salsa over the top.
Makes 2 servings.

VARIATION
Marinate salmon in a microwave-safe dish. Cover with plastic wrap and cook in a microwave oven on high for 3 minutes.

Halibut with Triple Orange Marinade & Salsa

The tartness of the citrus really balances the flavor of this firm-fleshed fish. Accompany with Black Beans, Pintos, Garbanzos & Rice (recipe on page 221).

> 1 1/4 to 1 1/2 pounds halibut, orange roughy, or other firm-fleshed fish fillets
> 2 Tablespoons extra-virgin olive oil
> 1 1/2 Tablespoons fresh lemon juice
> 1/4 cup fresh orange juice
> 2 Tablespoons Triple Sec
> 1/4 cup coarsely chopped cilantro
> 2 garlic cloves, minced
> 1 fresh jalapeño chile or to taste, minced
> Salsa Tequila (recipe on page 77)

Rinse and pat the fish fillets dry. Combine oil, lemon juice, orange juice, Triple Sec, cilantro, garlic, and jalapeño chile in a shallow baking dish. Add fish fillets, cover, and marinate 30 minutes at room temperature, spooning sauce over fillets and turning them periodically.

Preheat oven to 350°F (175°C). Bake fish 10 minutes or just until fish begins to flake when pierced with a fork. Serve with salsa.

Makes 4 servings.

Grilled Swordfish

A juicy and flavorful way to serve swordfish. It's especially nice with Golden Salsa.

6 (4- to 6-ounce) swordfish steaks
6 Tablespoons fresh lemon juice
3 Tablespoons extra-virgin olive oil
3 Tablespoons tequila
Dash of crushed pequin chile
Golden Salsa (recipe on page 76)

Rinse swordfish and pat dry. Combine lemon juice, oil, tequila, and crushed chile in a shallow baking dish. Add swordfish, cover, and marinate 1 hour in the refrigerator, spooning sauce over swordfish and turning periodically.

Heat the grill to very hot, about 450°F (230°C). Oil rack and place fish on rack. Grill about 3 minutes per side or until fish just begins to flake when pierced with a fork. Serve with salsa.

Makes 6 servings.

Note: For a true Southwestern flavor, you can use mesquite chips, chunks of mesquite, or mesquite charcoal.

Patio Clams with Salsa Roja

We created these one day back East, when it rained and we couldn't do a real Down East Clambake. We just placed the grill on the patio under the overhang of the roof. If you serve these as a main course, you will want to have chunks of fresh crusty bread and a couple of hearty side dishes.

48 cherrystone or steamer clams
Cornmeal
1 recipe Salsa Roja (recipe on page 82) or favorite salsa

Prepare a moderate fire in the grill. In the meantime, for the clams, to remove the sand within the shell, sprinkle cornmeal over the top of the clams and add salted water to cover in a large pot. Prepare the salsa. When ready to grill, drain the water from the clams. Grill the clams directly on the grill. Place about 8 clams on the grill at a time and, as they pop open, serve them with the salsa.

Makes 4 servings.

— **Rocky Mountain Grilled Trout with Cilantro-Chile Pesto** —

The pesto adds a delicious zest to the trout and is easy to make.

4 (10- to 12-inch) boneless rainbow trout
Cilantro-Chile Pesto (recipe follows)

Rinse trout and pat dry inside and out. Make 3 (1- to 1 1/2-inch-long) slashes on each side, making cuts at a 45-degree angle.

Prepare pesto. Drizzle some pesto in trout cavities, then drizzle some pesto over both sides, dividing pesto over trout. Preheat grill to a moderate heat or 350°F (175°C). Place trout in an oiled fish holder or on individual pieces of foil. Grill 3 to 5 minutes per side, or until trout just begin to flake when pierced with a fork.

Makes 4 servings.

Cilantro-Chile Pesto
1 cup cilantro
1/4 chopped green chile
4 garlic cloves
6 Tablespoons olive oil
1/2 teaspoon salt

Combine cilantro, green chiles, garlic, oil, and salt in a blender or small food processor. Process until combined.

——— **Chipotle Sauced Scallops** ———

The pungency of the chipotles carries very well with the peppered rice.

2 dried chipotle chiles, soaked in 1 cup water with 1 teaspoon
 white wine vinegar, or 1 teaspoon chipotle powder
3 thick bacon slices, cut into thin strips
2 Tablespoons coarsely chopped onion
1 pound scallops, patted dry
Peppered Rice (recipe on page 227)

If using chipotle pods, prepare chipotle chiles by simmering in vinegar and water to cover until tender. Cook bacon in a skillet until almost crisp, then add onion and cook until softened. Drain off excess fat. Stir in the chipotle powder or minced chipotle. Over medium-high heat, add scallops and cook, turning after about 3 minutes or when lightly browned. Sauté just until opaque. Do not overcook. Serve with rice.

Makes 3 to 4 servings.

Barbara's Fruitwood Grilled Trout with Blueberry Salsa en Burrito

A few years back, one of my Santa Fe cooking school students shared this recipe with me. She had created this dish using what was at hand on a fishing trip to Lake Tahoe with great success.

4 (10- to 12-inch) whole trout, ready to cook
Juice of 2 limes, divided
Salt and freshly ground black pepper to taste
1 cup fresh blueberries
1 cup chopped onion
2 fresh jalapeño chiles, minced
2 garlic cloves, minced
8 (10-inch) flour tortillas

Rinse trout and pat dry. Then sprinkle with the juice of 1 lime and season with salt and pepper. Meanwhile, prepare salsa. Combine juice of remaining lime with the blueberries, onions, jalapeño chiles, and garlic.

Prepare a fruitwood fire or a charcoal fire topped with fruitwood chips. Place trout in an oiled fish holder or grill on individual pieces of foil. Grill 3 to 5 minutes per side or until trout just begin to flake when pierced with a fork.

When trout are almost done, place tortillas on the grill for just a few seconds per side. Fillet trout. Serve each person a trout, tortillas, and salsa, suggesting that each roll the burritos as desired.

Makes 4 servings.

Seafood Brochettes Campeche Style

Fruits of the sea from the gulf coast region of Campeche, Mexico, are delightful and pretty served this way. Serve with crusty bolillos (Mexican French bread–style rolls), your favorite green salad, and a Mexican rice.

1/2 pound cod fillets, cut in 1 1/2-inch pieces
1/2 pound sea scallops, cut in half if very large
1 pound large shrimp, shelled and deveined
2 green or red bell peppers, cut in 1 1/2-inch square pieces
1 bunch large green onions, white parts cut into 2 or 3 pieces, tops reserved for marinade
5 Tablespoons fresh lemon juice
2 Tablespoons fresh lime juice
1/4 cup dry white wine
1/2 cup very finely chopped green onion tops
1/2 cup olive oil
3 garlic cloves, very finely minced
1 small tomato, very finely chopped
1 Tablespoon ground pure, mild red chile
3/4 teaspoon salt
3/4 teaspoon ground Mexican oregano

Thread an alternating combination of cod, scallops, shrimp, bell peppers, and green onion pieces on each of 8 or 10 skewers. Place filled skewers on a large, shallow dish or baking pan.

To prepare marinade, combine lemon juice, lime juice, wine, green onion tops, oil, garlic, tomato, ground chile, salt, and oregano in a jar with a tight-fitting lid or in a bowl and whisk to combine. Shake well and pour over the brochettes. Marinate in the refrigerator at least 4 hours, turning occasionally.

Reserve marinade. Preheat broiler or grill and broil brochettes 5 inches from heat 5 to 7 minutes on each side, or until seafood is opaque and firm to the touch. Do not overcook. Place brochettes on a warmed serving platter. Bring reserved marinade to a boil and pour over brochettes.

Makes 8 to 10 servings.

Cozumel Crab with Shrimp

Superb, simple, and somewhat tropical.

2 Tablespoons olive oil
3 Tablespoons unsalted butter
2 Tablespoons finely minced shallots
1 large garlic clove, finely minced
1/2 pound shelled shrimp, deveined
1/2 pound lump crabmeat, picked over well
3 large tomatoes, peeled and chopped
3 or 4 green chiles, parched, peeled (see page 340), and chopped
1 1/2 teaspoons fresh lime juice
1/2 teaspoon minced fresh basil or 1/4 teaspoon dried leaf basil
Salt and freshly ground black pepper to taste
3 green onions, sliced in half lengthwise, then cut into 1-inch pieces
Avocado slices dipped in lime juice

Heat oil and butter in a large heavy skillet. Add shallots and garlic and sauté until they just barely begin to brown. Add the shrimp and crabmeat and sauté, stirring gently, about 2 minutes. Add the tomatoes, green chiles, lime juice, basil, salt, and pepper. Cover and simmer 5 minutes. Add green onions, cover, and simmer 3 minutes. Transfer to a warmed serving platter and garnish with avocado slices.

Makes 4 servings.

Southwest Seafood Pie

This unusual pie uses tortillas as the crust.

3 (8- to 10-inch) flour tortillas
1/4 cup vegetable oil
6 green chiles, parched, peeled (see page 340), and seeds removed, divided
1 1/2 cups shredded Monterey Jack cheese or Cheddar cheese, divided
1 (6 1/2-ounce) can flaked crabmeat or 3/4 cup fresh or frozen crabmeat, picked over well
3 chopped green onions, including some of the tops
1 Tablespoon chopped cilantro (optional)
4 large eggs
1 1/2 cups half-and-half
1/2 teaspoon salt
Freshly ground black pepper
3/4 teaspoon crushed caribe chile
1/2 cup sour cream (optional)

Select a round cake pan that is the same diameter as the tortillas so that they will just fit. Cut 2 of the tortillas in half. Heat oil in a heavy skillet and fry all tortillas until lightly browned on each side; drain on paper towels. Arrange the whole fried tortilla in the bottom of the pan, then stand tortilla halves around the rim of the baking pan, creating a crust.

Preheat the oven to 350°F (175°C). Using 4 of the chopped green chiles, place them in a smooth, uniform layer over the fried tortilla on the bottom of the cake pan. Top with 1 cup of the cheese, the crabmeat, green onions, and cilantro, if using. Meanwhile, beat eggs, half-and-half, salt, and pepper in a bowl. Pour mixture over crabmeat, then top with the remaining 1/2 cup of cheese and sprinkle with the crushed chile. Bake 30 to 40 minutes or until puffed and lightly browned. Serve garnished with the remaining 2 chopped green chiles and sour cream, if desired.

Makes 6 servings.

New Mexican Winter Bouillabaisse

Here, I modified Mediterranean Bouillabaisse to reflect the seafood ingredients readily available in the Southwest. The rouille is spiced up a bunch and thickened with corn tortillas instead of bread.

Rouille (recipe follows)
2 Tablespoons olive oil
1 cup chopped onion
3 medium-size garlic cloves, minced
1/2 pound shrimp, shelled, deveined, and butterflied
1/2 pound sea scallops
1/2 pound catfish fillets, cut into 1/2-inch chunks
1/4 cup sun-dried tomatoes packed in oil, slivered
1/8 teaspoon fennel seeds
1/2 teaspoon dried leaf thyme
Pinch of saffron
1 fresh bay leaf or 2 dried bay leaves
1 (2-inch) strip fresh lime peel
1 1/2 cups vermouth or dry white wine
Tortillas or crusty bread

Prepare rouille. Heat oil in a large saucepan. Add onion and garlic; sauté until onion is softened. Add seafood and cook, stirring, a few minutes. Add tomatoes, fennel seeds, thyme, saffron, bay leaf, lime peel, and vermouth. Simmer about 5 minutes or until seafood changes from translucent to opaque.

Discard lime peel and bay leaf. Ladle the bouillabaisse into 4 large soup bowls. Serve with rouille and tortillas.

Makes 4 servings.

Rouille

3 corn tortillas, ground in a blender or food processor
6 medium-size garlic cloves, finely chopped
2 Tablespoons ground hot chile
1 teaspoon ground Mexican oregano
1/2 teaspoon crushed caribe chile
1/2 teaspoon salt
1/4 cup olive oil

Combine ground tortillas, garlic, ground chile, oregano, crushed chile, and salt in a blender or food processor. Process until combined. Add oil and process until combined. If mixture is too dry, add a little hot water to make a paste.

Shrimp in Sunflower Seed Mole

Prepare this spicy, intriguing sauce in advance so that you can be a guest at your own party.

2 large tomatoes, peeled and chopped (about 1 1/4 cups)
2/3 cup sunflower kernels (raw or roasted)
2 garlic cloves, chopped
1 Tablespoon ground mild or hot chile or a combination
1/2 teaspoon coriander seeds
1 Tablespoon chopped fresh cilantro (optional)
3 Tablespoons olive oil
1 1/4 pounds shelled, deveined shrimp, lightly sprinkled with salt
1 medium-size onion, finely chopped
3/4 cup chicken broth
Juice of 1/2 lime
1/2 teaspoon salt
Freshly ground black pepper
3 cups hot cooked white rice

Place tomatoes, sunflower kernels, garlic, ground chile, coriander seeds, and cilantro in a blender. Process until smooth. Set the puree aside.

Heat oil in a large heavy skillet. Add the shrimp and stir-fry until shrimp are pink, 3 or 4 minutes. Remove from skillet and keep warm.

Add onion to skillet and cook until softened. With the skillet on medium-high heat, add puree to onion and cook, stirring constantly, 2 or 3 minutes. Add broth, lime juice, salt, and pepper. The sauce should be the consistency of heavy cream. If it is too thick, thin by adding a bit more chicken broth. Adjust seasonings, adding more ground chile if desired. Add cooked shrimp and cook together for about 3 to 5 minutes or until the shrimp are hot and the flavors are blended. Serve with rice.

Makes 4 servings.

Ensenada Shrimp

The wonderful blend of garlic, lime juice, and caribe chile makes any occasion a special one.

1 1/2 pounds large shrimp
6 Tablespoons unsalted butter
1/3 cup olive oil
1 large garlic clove, very finely minced
2 Tablespoons crushed caribe chile or 2 1/2 teaspoons ground mild red chile
2 Tablespoons freshly squeezed lime juice
2 Tablespoons finely chopped green onion
1/2 teaspoon salt
Freshly ground black pepper

Shell the shrimp, leaving on the tails. With a small, sharp knife, slit each shrimp down the back to butterfly and remove the vein. Rinse shrimp quickly under cold water and drain on paper towels.

Heat butter and oil over medium heat in a shallow flameproof baking dish or pan just large enough to hold the shrimp in a single layer. Add garlic and sauté until softened. Remove from heat and stir in the crushed chile, lime juice, green onion, salt, and a little pepper.

Preheat broiler to its highest heat. Arrange shrimp in the sauce and broil about 3 inches from the heat, 3 to 5 minutes; turn and broil 3 minutes. Serve hot.

Makes 4 to 6 servings.

Marinated Shrimp Achiote Style

The sauce for this Yucatán favorite is very similar in appearance to the adobado sauce; however, the flavor is much more subtle and less spicy.

    6 Tablespoons achiote paste
    Juice of 1 pound sour oranges or 2 cups orange juice concentrate plus the juice of 1 lemon
    2 teaspoons Worcestershire sauce
    1/2 cup chicken stock (could be made with chicken bouillon
        base such as "Better than Bouillon")
    1 pinch Mexican oregano
    3/4 teaspoon salt
    1 teaspoon freshly ground black pepper
    30 large shrimp

Dissolve achiote paste in the orange juice in a large glass or stainless steel bowl. Add Worcestershire, bouillon granules, oregano, salt, and pepper. Shell and devein shrimp. Stir shrimp into achiote mixture. Cover and marinate 2 hours in the refrigerator, turning occasionally.

Preheat grill. Drain shrimp, discarding marinade. Thread the marinated shrimp on skewers to make turning easier during grilling. Grill shrimp 3 inches from heat source about 3 minutes per side.

Makes 4 to 6 servings.

Shrimp Fajitas Galveston Style with Salsas & Guacamole

Shrimp are a popular favorite for fajitas. The same marinade is used for the Chicken Fajitas (recipe on page 107) and Beef Fajitas (recipe on page 158). The grilled veggies are great with the shrimp too.

2 pounds large to medium-large shrimp, shelled
Juice of 2 limes
1/4 cup vegetable oil, plus extra for brushing
6 garlic cloves, minced
1 teaspoon salt
Freshly ground black pepper
2 large red onions, halved crosswise, or 12 to 16 green onions, with the tops
1 each large red, green, and yellow bell peppers, quartered
18 (6-inch) flour tortillas, warmed on the grill

Butterfly shrimp, removing the large veins and leaving tails attached. Combine lime juice, 1/4 cup oil, garlic, salt, and pepper in a large shallow bowl. Carefully press each shrimp into the marinade. Cover and marinate at least 30 minutes at room temperature or several hours in the refrigerator before grilling.

About 45 minutes before serving, start the fire, using mesquite wood or chips to flavor the charcoal briquettes, if desired. Place onion halves on grill for 5 to 10 minutes, then add the bell peppers before adding shrimp. (Green onions only take about 10 minutes—5 minutes on each side.) Arrange shrimp on long skewers to facilitate turning. Grill shrimp over medium-hot fire until just done, about 5 minutes.

Cut the onion into thin wedges, removing the outer layers. Slice the cooked bell peppers into 1/2-inch thick slices and toss all together. Serve grilled veggies with the shrimp on the side. Pass a basket of warm tortillas. Or, for a buffet, you can place the grilled veggies in the center of a platter and place the shrimp on top. Fold and tuck the tortillas in around the edges.

Makes 6 to 8 servings.

VARIATION
Pan-sauté the onions and peppers using minimal oil, cooking only until slightly crisp.

PORK

Pork was introduced by the Spanish sometime after 1492, and the Native Americans and Mexicans found that either green or red chile and pork make a perfect combination. There are many wonderful dishes in Southwestern cooking, not the least of which is Carne Adobado, the signature dish of northern New Mexico.

Pork is the star attraction at many Southwestern barbecues, but it can also be served more formally when stuffed and rolled, as in Chorizo-Stuffed Loin of Pork with Jalapeño Glaze.

Carne Adobado (Pork with Red Chile Sauce)

This is one of the best, if not the very best-tasting, pork creations from northern New Mexico. Traceable back to conquistador days, this dish has somehow never gained favor outside of New Mexico. I think it is because crushed caribe chiles are hard to find outside of the area. I always make the full recipe because I like to have lots available for burritos, tacos, and enchiladas, or to serve over rice, beans, or eggs. Due to the great proportion of red chile, this dish can be frozen in meal-size quantities for up to a year.

 1/2 cup crushed caribe chile
 1/4 cup ground mild chile
 1/4 cup ground hot chile
 3 garlic cloves, minced
 2 Tablespoons ground cumin
 2 teaspoons ground Mexican oregano
 2 teaspoons salt
 4 cups water
 5 1/2 pounds pork shoulder chops, cut 1/2 inch thick (trimmed so
  as to keep a narrow layer of fat around the edges)

Place crushed chile, ground chile, garlic, cumin, oregano, salt, and water in a blender or food processor and process until smooth. (Many blenders and food processors do not have a large enough jar; if needed, process with 2 cups water and stir in the balance of 2 cups into the recipe after processing.) Pour into a large flat-bottomed glass or other nonreactive baking dish. Dip each pork chop into the marinade and lay to one side of the baking dish as you coat the rest. Let marinate 30 minutes at room temperature, periodically spooning chile mixture over the top and turning chops over. Then cover with plastic wrap and refrigerate overnight. (The pork can be frozen for up to 3 months at this point.)

In the morning, stir and coat each pork chop with chile sauce. Preheat oven to 350°F (175°C). Cover dish with lid or foil and bake chops, covered for the first 30 minutes. Remove cover and bake 1 to 1 1/2 hours longer, at 325°F (165°C), spooning the sauce over chops every 30 minutes. Let cool.

Using a sharp knife, remove bones and pull meat apart with your fingers to shred the pork. Place shredded meat back in the baking dish. Bake 30 minutes to allow the sauce to cook into meat. (If the sauce is thick, cover the pork on this last roasting. If the sauce is rather liquid, do not cover.) When done, the meat should be a bright rosy red color and very tender.

Makes 10 to 12 servings.

Picadillo (Spiced Pork)

A favorite dish in various Spanish-speaking countries—and what a treat! Serve as a main course in a crisp corn taco or a soft flour tortilla rolled into a taco. Accompany with rice, fresh fruit, and a vegetable. Picadillo can be frozen for up to two months.

1 1/2 pounds lean pork, cut into 1/2-inch cubes
2 garlic cloves, minced
1 large onion, chopped
1 1/2 teaspoons salt
1 1/2 teaspoons sugar
1 1/2 teaspoons ground cinnamon
1/2 teaspoon ground cumin
1/4 teaspoon ground cloves
3 Tablespoons vinegar
2/3 cup raisins
1/4 cup water
3 large tomatoes, peeled and chopped, or 1 1/2 cups canned tomatoes
3/4 cup slivered almonds, toasted

Place cubed pork in a large, heavy, well-seasoned skillet and brown well. Drain off excess fat. Add garlic and onion and cook until onion begins to soften. Add salt, sugar, cinnamon, cumin, cloves, vinegar, raisins, water, and tomatoes and simmer, covered, about 40 minutes or until pork is very tender.

Place the picadillo on a serving plate or in taco shells or warm flour tortillas. Garnish with the slivered almonds.

Makes 6 servings.

VARIATION
Beef chuck, coarsely chopped, can be substituted for pork.

Roast Loin of Pork in Green Chile Sauce

Great company fare—elegant, easy, and sumptuous. Leftovers may be frozen for up to three months.

1 (4-pound) boneless pork roast
1/2 teaspoon ground Mexican oregano
1/8 teaspoon dried leaf thyme
Salt and freshly ground black pepper
1 large tomato, peeled and cut into chunks
1 (10-ounce) can tomatillos, drained, or 1 cup coarsely chopped cooked tomatillos
4 green chiles, parched, peeled (see page 340), and coarsely chopped
1 onion, coarsely chopped
1 garlic clove, minced
1 Tablespoon minced parsley or fresh cilantro
1 Tablespoon olive oil
About 1 cup chicken broth or beef broth

Preheat oven to 350°F (175°C). Place roast in a baking pan and sprinkle with oregano, thyme, salt, and pepper. Bake uncovered about 2 1/2 hours or until a meat thermometer reads 145°F (70°C).

While the meat is roasting, prepare the sauce. Place tomato, tomatillos, green chiles, onion, garlic, and parsley in a blender or food processor. Process until pureed. Heat the oil in a heavy skillet. Add puree and fry it 3 to 4 minutes, stirring constantly. Add broth and salt and pepper to taste. The sauce should be the consistency of heavy cream; thin with a little broth, if necessary.

When roast is done, let it rest for about 20 minutes, then slice and arrange it on a warmed platter. Pour hot sauce over sliced roast and serve.

Makes 8 servings.

Note: For ease in dinner preparation, cook the roast and make the sauce earlier in the day. Slice roast, arrange on an ovenproof platter, pour sauce over the slices, and cover with a lid or foil. Warm, covered, in oven before serving—this incorporates the sauce flavor into the meat.

Pork Mole

Deliciously different—it contains no chocolate. Pork mole is wonderful served with rice, avocado vinaigrette salad or guacamole, flour tortillas, and icy cold beer. Leftovers may be frozen for up to three months and make terrific tacos.

2 pounds boneless pork
2 1/2 cups water
1 bay leaf
1/2 jalapeño chile or to taste
1 bread slice, half of 1 flour tortilla, or 1 corn tortilla
1 medium-size tomato, peeled
1 garlic clove, peeled
1/4 teaspoon ground cinnamon
1/8 teaspoon ground cloves
1/4 teaspoon freshly ground black pepper
1 Tablespoon vegetable oil
1/2 teaspoon salt or to taste

Trim fat from meat and cut meat into 1-inch cubes or thin strips. Place in a saucepan with the water and bay leaf. Bring to a boil and skim foam from the surface. Reduce heat, cover, and simmer about 30 minutes or until meat is tender. Drain, reserving broth.

Place jalapeño chile, bread, tomato, garlic, cinnamon, cloves, and pepper in a blender or food processor. Puree, adding reserved broth 1 Tablespoon at a time, if necessary, to achieve a medium-thick puree.

Heat oil in a large heavy skillet, add the mole puree, and cook, stirring constantly, 2 or 3 minutes. The mixture will be very pasty. Add meat, stir to coat it, then add 1 cup of the reserved broth. Cook, stirring, until sauce is smooth and thickened, at least 30 minutes. Add salt and adjust seasonings. If sauce is too thick, add a little more broth to thin it.

Makes 6 to 8 servings.

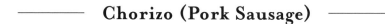

Chorizo (Pork Sausage)

Homemade chorizo is a treat. This recipe is leaner than most Mexican-style chorizo. You can experiment with the amount of fat to suit your taste.

> 3 pounds lean pork, chunked
> 8 ounces beef or pork fat
> 3 medium-size onions, quartered
> 12 garlic cloves, minced
> 1/2 cup cider vinegar
> 1/2 cup tequila
> 6 Tablespoons ground hot or mild chile
> 1 1/2 teaspoons ground cinnamon
> 2 teaspoons ground cumin
> 1 1/2 teaspoons ground Mexican oregano
> 2 1/2 teaspoons salt

Using a grinder or food processor, grind the meat, fat, and onions until finely ground. Add garlic, vinegar, tequila, ground chile, cinnamon, cumin, oregano, and salt. Refrigerate 2 hours. Form into a roll about 3 inches in diameter, rolling it in a piece of plastic wrap. Cover and refrigerate at least 8 hours before cooking. Freeze any sausage not used within 2 or 3 days. To cook, cut sausage into 1/2-inch rounds. Cook in a skillet over medium heat, turning, until cooked through.

Makes 3 1/4 pounds of bulk sausage.

Notes: To make grinding easier, place the pork in the freezer for a couple of hours or until slightly frozen for ease of use. If you have no food processor or grinder, buy triple-ground pork. The first time you prepare the recipe, fry a small patty, taste, and adjust the seasonings to suit your taste. To freeze, mold the sausage into 1/2-pound portions and freeze in plastic freezer bags up to 3 months.

Chorizo Stuffed Loin of Pork with Jalapeño Glaze

This beautiful and luscious roast is terrific for dinner parties and buffets. Serve with your favorite tangy dressed greens or fruit salad and Black Beans, Pintos, Garbanzos & Rice (recipe on page 221).

3 1/2- to 4-pound boneless, butterflied loin of pork*
1/4 teaspoon salt
1 pound chorizo (see Variation)
1/2 cup piñon nuts (pine nuts)
8 ounces jalapeño jelly

Lay pork roast out flat, with the inside (from which bone was removed) facing up. Sprinkle with salt. Remove casings from the chorizo and place meat in a bowl. Mix piñon nuts evenly into the sausage meat; then re-form the chorizo into a long roll and place it down the center of the roast. (If using Italian sausage or pork sausage, blend in the seasonings first before adding nuts.) Bring sides of roast together lengthwise. Tie every inch with white cotton twine. Place on a baking pan. Put in the oven and turn heat to 350°F (175°C).

Roast 1 hour. Spread the jelly on the outside of the roast. Roast an additional 1 1/2 to 2 hours, basting every 15 minutes, or until a meat thermometer reads 145°F (70°C). Let it rest 20 minutes before carving. Reserve the pan juices and serve on the side.

Makes 6 to 8 servings.

*To butterfly the roast, using a sharp knife, slice almost in half—allowing about 3/4 inch at the bottom—then slice each half almost in half, allowing about 3/4 inch at the bottom. Lay it out and stuff. When pulling it together and tying, it creates a very pretty star shape.

VARIATION

If chorizo is not available, use hot Italian sausage and add 1/2 teaspoon ground cumin and 1/2 teaspoon ground Mexican oregano. If hot Italian sausage is not available, use fresh pork sausage and add an additional 2 to 4 Tablespoons crushed, dried, hot red chile.

Southwest Barbecue

Barbecue is as hotly debated as chili as to its method of preparation and its origins—with one exception. Barbecue pitmasters or famous barbecue chefs simply do not exchange recipes. I'm always reminded of one famous Oklahoma barbecue chef who had a restaurant. When I requested his barbecue sauce recipe, he told me, "Madam, that recipe is just like my boots—it's going to die on me."

The origin of the word *barbecue* has three claims: French, English, and Spanish. The French theory comes from the old-fashioned roasting method of cooking game over an open fire, "barbe-a-queue," meaning beard to tail. The Spanish stake comes from the word *barbacoa*, derived from the Native American word for the framework of green wood on which meat or fish was cooked over a pit of coals. The English origins come via South Carolina, where over two hundred years ago a wealthy landowner by the name of Bernard Quayle became known for his lavish outdoor parties where assorted whole carcasses of meats were roasted over open pits. Supposedly he wasn't the only rancher who cooked this way, but his entertainment just had more flair and became the best known. Hence, the name of his ranch, the Bar-B-Q, became associated with open pit-cooked meats and outdoor eating.

The styles of barbecue vary widely and regionally. Almost all of them can be prepared in advance and kept either refrigerated or frozen for future enjoyment. There is nothing better than barbecue sauce to take the blahs out of most any dish! You don't need fancy equipment to enjoy barbecue. In fact, you can create the old-fashioned goodness of smoked meats, barbecued by grilling or broiling indoors, without even the benefit of a pit or grill. And, in good weather, most everyone really enjoys the gusto of outdoor grilled or smoked meats and vegetables.

Whenever you are grilling or smoking, take advantage of the heat in your grill for cooking whatever vegetables you plan to serve. For example, some truly fun dishes come from smoked potatoes, like smoky potato salad, smoky home fries, and smoky bakers with toppings.

Barbecue is often an area where men feel particularly comfortable. Perhaps it is because there are really no hard and fast rules. That is how so many variations got their start. With this spirit, I hope you enjoy the following barbecue recipes.

Texas Barbecued Ribs

In many parts of Texas, they like to use one of the rubs (recipes on page 329) on their ribs before they sear them in the oven or on the grill. True Texans will almost always build the fire out of mesquite or toss on some soaked mesquite chips just before placing meats directly on the grill.

For a true Texas taste, serve these ribs with coleslaw, baked beans, or corn on the cob, and sourdough biscuits or corn bread.

3 to 4 pounds pork spareribs
Pork Rub (recipe on page 329)
Favorite barbecue sauce (recipes on pages 90-91)

Preheat grill. Trim off any excess fat from ribs and work the rub into the ribs, keeping in mind that salt and chile are major flavors in the rub and you do not want to get the ribs too salty and spicy.

Place ribs on grill rack. The rack should be about 3 inches above the coals and the fire should be medium to medium-hot. Cover grill and allow ribs to smoke and/or cook about 30 minutes on the first side—depending on how thick and meaty the ribs are. When first side appears done, turn and spoon sauce over the ribs and cook until the ribs are tender and no longer pink in center.

Makes 6 to 8 servings.

VARIATION

Preheat oven to 450°F (230°F). Place ribs in a shallow baking pan. Cook in the oven and sauce as above.

—— Barbecued Ribs Socorro Style ——

The marinade coupled with the red chile creates a feisty flavor that is very memorable.

- **2 Tablespoons olive oil**
- **1/4 cup red wine vinegar**
- **1 1/2 teaspoons salt**
- **1/4 teaspoon crushed pequin chile or to taste**
- **2 teaspoons ground Mexican oregano**
- **3 garlic cloves, finely minced**
- **2 pounds country-style pork ribs or 3 pounds lean spareribs**
- **2 cups Red Chile Sauce (recipe on page 84), hot or mild**
- **1 medium-size onion, finely chopped**

Place oil, vinegar, salt, crushed chile, oregano, and garlic in a jar with a tight-fitting lid or in a small bowl. Cover and shake to combine. Arrange ribs in a single layer in a glass or nonreactive baking dish. Pour the marinade over the ribs and marinate 2 to 3 hours in the refrigerator.

Preheat oven to 350°F (175°C). Pour the Red Chile Sauce over the ribs, sprinkle with chopped onion, and bake, uncovered, 1 1/2 to 2 hours or until meat is very tender, basting occasionally.

Makes 4 servings.

Cazuela of Pork with Mussels & Clams Spanish Style

This flavorful casserole comes right from Spain but is adapted to the tastes of the American Southwest. It is a great dish for entertaining, as the meat can be marinated, then sautéed and refrigerated in its sauce for up to two days before finishing with mussels and clams.

12 mussels, rinsed and debearded
12 small hard-shelled clams, washed and thoroughly scrubbed
Cornmeal
1/2 cup double-strength low-sodium chicken broth*
1/2 cup dry white wine
2 Tablespoons ground hot chile
6 garlic cloves, minced, divided
1 small bay leaf
1 1/2 pounds lean boneless pork, cut into 1-inch cubes
1 Tablespoon olive oil
1/3 each large red, green, and yellow bell peppers, cut lengthwise
    into 1/4-inch strips, or 1 red or green bell pepper
2 medium-size onions, thinly sliced and separated into rings
2 medium-size tomatoes, finely chopped
1 teaspoon crushed caribe chile
1/4 cup cilantro, coarsely chopped
3 small green onions, finely chopped
1 lemon, cut into 6 or 8 wedges
Peppered Rice (recipe on page 227)

If serving as soon as dish is finished, place mussels and clams in a large bowl and cover with cold salted water. Sprinkle with a little cornmeal and set aside.

Combine broth, wine, and ground chile in a large bowl, and stir until thoroughly blended. Add 2 minced garlic cloves, bay leaf, and pork. Marinate 30 minutes at room temperature, turning the meat occasionally to keep it moist. With a slotted spoon, remove pork, discarding bay leaf. Reserve marinade. Pat pork dry with paper towels.

Heat a large heavy skillet over medium-high heat. Add pork; cook, turning frequently to brown pork quickly and evenly. When browned, add the reserved marinade, and bring to a boil over high heat, scraping bottom and sides of pan, until pork absorbs the marinade and mixture is thick.

Heat oil in another large, deep skillet, then add bell pepper strips. After turning peppers once, add onions and stir-fry about 5 minutes or until vegetables are soft, but not brown. Add remaining 4 minced garlic cloves, tomatoes, and crushed chile.

Drain and rinse mussels and clams. Spread mussels and clams, hinged-side down over the tomato sauce, cover the skillet tightly, and cook over high heat 10 minutes or until the mussels and clams open. Discard any mussels or clams that do not open. Stir in the pork with marinade and simmer 5 minutes or until pork is heated through. Mix the cilantro and green onions and sprinkle over the pork and clams. Garnish with lemon wedges. Serve over rice.

Makes 6 servings.

*To reduce chicken broth to double strength, heat 1 cup chicken broth until it is reduced to 1/2 cup or, if desired, using "Better Than Bouillon," prepare it double strength.

——— Rancher's Pork Chops ———

Cook this flavorful, quick entrée on top of the range or in a microwave oven. Use previously cooked or frozen ranchero sauce if you have some on hand instead of making the sauce as directed here.

    1 Tablespoon vegetable oil
    2 cups chopped Spanish onions
    1 (28-ounce) can whole peeled tomatoes with their juice
    4 large green chiles, parched, peeled (see page 340), and chopped,
        or 1 (4-ounce) can chopped green chiles
    2 garlic cloves, minced
    6 large, well-trimmed 2-inch-thick loin pork chops (2 to 2 1/2 pounds)
    Mushroom-Piñon Rice (recipe on page 226)

Place oil in a large, deep, nonreactive skillet with a tight-fitting cover. Add onions and cook until softened, about 5 minutes. Add tomatoes, green chiles, and garlic, and cook 10 minutes. Place pork chops on the sauce. Cover and cook over medium-low heat 40 to 60 minutes, spooning sauce over chops about every 5 minutes, until chops are tender when pierced with a knife and have an internal temperature of 145°F (65°C). Allow to rest at least 3 minutes, then serve hot on warmed plates with rice.

Makes 6 servings.

VARIATION
To cook in a microwave oven: Coat bottom of a 13 x 9-inch glass baking dish with oil. Add onions, cover with waxed paper, and microwave on High about 2 or 3 minutes or until the onion is softened. Add tomatoes, green chiles, and garlic. Cover with waxed paper and cook 3 minutes, stirring and rotating after 1 1/2 minutes. Place pork chops on the sauce, spooning about half of it over the tops of the chops. Cover with waxed paper and cook 15 minutes, turning every 4 minutes, spooning sauce over the top and rotating each time. Cook until juices run clear when chops are pierced with a knife and registers 145°F (65°C).

— California-Style Barbecued Ribs —

Californians often prefer fruitwood or grape cuttings to flavor their barbecue fires.

3 to 4 pounds pork spareribs
1 lemon, thinly sliced and seeds removed
2 medium-size onions, thinly sliced and separated into rings
Fiery California Barbecue Sauce (recipe on page 91)

Preheat grill. Trim off any excess fat from ribs. Place grill rack about 3 inches above the coals; the fire should be medium to medium-hot.

Place ribs on grill rack. Cover and allow to smoke and/or cook about 30 minutes on the first side, depending on how thick and meaty the ribs are. Then turn ribs; arrange lemon and onions on ribs. Spoon sauce over ribs and cook until ribs are tender and no longer pink in center.

Makes 6 to 8 servings.

VARIATION

Preheat the oven to 450°F (230°C). Place racks of ribs on a shallow baking sheet. Arrange lemon and onion rings on ribs. Cook in the oven 20 minutes; then turn, replacing lemon and onion rings on top. Reduce heat to 350°F (175°C) and spoon sauce over ribs.

BEEF

Beef has long been a popular meat on both sides of the Río Grande. With such vast ranges for grazing, the supply was assured. Its popularity probably grew because the flavor of beef is complemented by spicy chiles. Many of the dishes are from less tender cuts and benefit from long cooking with the chiles and other seasoning.

American burgers and steaks are not neglected in this chapter. They are just prepared with a Southwestern touch.

Gordon's West Texas–Style Brisket

Rubs have long been popular in Texas. They impart flavor and are easily applied. Brisket is very easy to cook this way and becomes quite juicy. Gordon McMeen, my deceased husband, a third-generation Texan partially raised in New Mexico, had been roasting these for family and friends for the last thirty years. He estimated that he has cooked "at least a million pounds for church and school groups." (Of course, this was probably a Texas exaggeration.)

1 (5- to 6-pound) beef brisket, trimmed
1/4 cup freshly ground black pepper
1/4 cup ground caribe chiles or ground medium-hot chiles
2 Tablespoons salt
1 1/2 Tablespoons garlic powder
1 large Spanish onion, sliced 1/4 inch thick
Minced parsley (optional)
Ground pequin chile (optional)

Preheat oven to 375°F (190°C). Trim excess fat layer off outside of brisket and bring meat to room temperature. Mix pepper, ground chile, salt, and garlic powder together. Then rub the seasoning mixture, or "rub," uniformly over all outside surfaces of the meat.

Place in a large roasting pan that has a tight-fitting lid. Top meat with onion. Close any steam vents. Roast 30 minutes. Reduce heat to 200°F (95°C) and roast 1 hour per pound or until beef is fork-tender. Do not peek for the first 3 hours. The brisket cooks in its own juice and will not need any added liquid.

When the meat is done, let it stand at room temperature about 20 minutes with the lid removed to allow roast to absorb some of the juice and to stabilize before carving. If desired, before carving, garnish the top with minced parsley and a sprinkle of pequin chile. Serve with the pan juices and your favorite barbecue sauce.

Makes 10 to 12 servings.

New Mexican Pot Roast

Pot roast with a twist, this is really somewhat German inspired. A bit of history here . . . After the Alamo, the remaining Texans decided to advertise free land in Germany and other countries in Europe. Many Germans came with their fine herds of cattle. The only hitch was, there was no way to get the beef to market until the railroads were built, so with beef so available in Texas, a great deal of recipes were developed. Here they called upon a favorite German way of cooking beef, called *sauerbraten*, and used chiles and other ingredients available.

To enjoy every last drop of the excellent sauce, serve with a big basket of warm flour tortillas. The uncooked pot roast can be frozen for up to eight months in the marinade. To cook, simply remove from the freezer, place in a 350°F (175°C) oven, and bake, covered, about 2 1/2 hours. Any leftover marinade can be frozen for later use.

1 (3-pound) beef chuck steak or round steak, about 2 inches thick
1 1/2 cups dry white wine
3 Tablespoons red wine vinegar
4 mild green chiles, parched, peeled (see page 340), and chopped,
    or 1 (4-ounce) can chopped green chiles
3 Tablespoons brown sugar
1 1/2 teaspoons salt
2 garlic cloves, finely minced
3 Tablespoons butter, lard, or bacon drippings
1 large onion, sliced crosswise, separated into rings
3/4 cup beef bouillon or broth
3 Tablespoons tomato paste

Place beef in a shallow flat-bottomed pan just large enough to hold the meat. Combine wine, vinegar, green chiles, brown sugar, salt, and garlic to make a marinade. Pour over beef and turn to coat evenly. Cover and marinate in the refrigerator overnight, turning at least two or three times and spooning sauce over the top. The next day, drain beef and reserve marinade.

Heat butter in a large heavy skillet or Dutch oven and brown beef thoroughly on both sides. Add 1 1/2 cups of the reserved marinade, the onion, bouillon, and tomato paste. Cover pan and simmer beef about 1 1/2 to 2 hours or until tender. Remove the cover and simmer a little longer, if necessary, to reduce and thicken the sauce to gravy consistency. Slice the beef and serve on a heated platter topped with some of the sauce. Pass the remaining sauce separately.

Makes 6 to 8 servings.

Rolled Flank Steak Stuffed with Vegetables

Called *matambre* in Spanish—literally translated this means "kill hunger"—this Argentinean specialty is quite attractive when sliced. You can serve it hot, cold, or at room temperature. We like it hot and enjoy dipping fresh crusty bread into the broth.

1 (2-pound) beef flank steak
1/4 cup red wine vinegar
2 garlic cloves, minced
1/2 teaspoon ground Mexican oregano
1/4 pound fresh spinach leaves, rinsed and stems removed
4 cooked whole carrots, about 6 to 8 inches long
2 hard-boiled large eggs, sliced
1/2 onion, thinly sliced and separated into rings
2 Tablespoons Italian flat leaf parsley, chopped
1/2 teaspoon crushed pequin chile
1 teaspoon salt
3 to 4 cups beef stock

Butterfly the flank steak (see note on page 137), trimming off all sinew and fat. Then lay it open and tenderize by pounding the meat as thin as possible without tearing. Sprinkle meat with vinegar, then with garlic and oregano. Arrange spinach over meat. Arrange carrots lengthwise across the spinach. Place a layer of eggs between the carrots and top with the onion rings. Sprinkle with parsley, chile, and salt.

Roll and tie roast. Place it in a deep heavy pot that is as long as the meat roll. Add enough broth to measure one-third of the way up on the beef. Cover and roast at 375°F (190°C) 1 to 1 1/2 hours or until meat is tender. Slice to serve.

Makes 4 to 6 servings.

Mexican-Style Shredded Beef (Carne Deshebrada)

Simple yet substantial, this flavorful meat dish has many uses. By merely altering the amount of liquid used in cooking, you can prepare an excellent main-dish topping for rice and beans, or a filling for enchiladas, tacos, burritos, taquitos, and empanadas. It will keep frozen for up to six months.

1 1/2 pounds beef chuck steak
4 cups water
1 teaspoon salt
2 Tablespoons butter, lard, or bacon drippings
1 onion, cut in half horizontally and sliced into thin half rings
2 garlic cloves, minced
1 Tablespoon all-purpose flour
3 medium-size tomatoes, finely chopped
1 jalapeño chile or to taste, minced
1 medium-size green bell peppers, cut into thin strips
Freshly ground black pepper

Place meat in a 3-quart saucepan and add the water and salt. Bring to a boil. Reduce heat, cover, and simmer until meat is very tender, about 1 1/2 hours.

Drain meat and reserve the broth. Using two forks, shred meat. Set aside.

Melt butter in a large heavy skillet. Add onion and garlic and sauté until softened. Stir in flour, add tomatoes, and simmer about 10 minutes or until tomatoes are soft. Add jalapeño chile, bell peppers, black pepper, shredded beef, and 3/4 cup of the reserved beef broth. Cover and simmer until bell peppers are soft. Taste and adjust seasonings.

Makes 6 servings.

VARIATION
For a one-dish meal, add 1 sliced fresh zucchini or 1 cup green peas when you add the bell pepper.

Tortilla Meat Loaf with Spicy Salsa

Here is a great way to use leftover or not-so-fresh tortillas. This recipe came about when I was given a case of corn tortillas by a manufacturer for me to judge the quality. As I remember, they were fine—but I had so many even after giving them to everyone I could think of so I developed this dish as a way to use them up. A few years later, my local CBS affiliate TV station staged a meat loaf contest among two local restaurants known for their meat loaf and me representing my cooking school. This recipe won first prize! I still think it has the greatest flavor and is less dense than most others.

1 1/2 pounds lean ground beef
1 cup finely chopped onion
2 garlic cloves, minced
1 large egg, slightly beaten
1/2 cup corn tortilla crumbs (about 6 tortillas)
1 Tablespoon Worcestershire sauce
1 teaspoon salt
1 teaspoon ground cumin
1 teaspoon ground sage
1 cup chopped fresh or canned tomatoes, divided
1/2 cup shredded Mexican cheese or Monterey Jack cheese
Salsa Roja (recipe on page 82) or Salsa Fresca (recipe on page 78)

Preheat oven to 350°F (175°C). Mix beef, onion, garlic, egg, tortilla crumbs, Worcestershire, salt, cumin, sage, and 1/2 cup of the chopped tomatoes in a bowl until combined. Press into a loaf shape and place in a baking dish. Top with remaining 1/2 cup tomatoes and the cheese, making a line of cheese down the lengthwise center of the loaf, centered with a line of tomatoes.

Bake 1 hour or until juices run clear. Allow juices to settle about 20 minutes before cutting. Serve on a bed of salsa or with a side dish.

Makes 6 servings.

Avocado-Stuffed Meat Loaf with Salsa

There's a surprise inside this spicy loaf.

2 pounds lean ground beef or 1 pound each ground beef and ground pork
2 bread slices, cubed, moistened with water, and squeezed
    dry, or 6 corn tortillas, ground in a blender
1 large onion, finely chopped
2 large eggs
3 garlic cloves, minced
1 Tablespoon ground hot chile
1 teaspoon salt
1 teaspoon ground cumin
2 or 3 mild green chiles, parched, peeled (see page 340), and chopped
1/3 cup tomato sauce
1 1/2 cups shredded Monterey Jack cheese, divided
1 large ripe avocado, sliced into wedges
Salsa of your choice

Preheat oven to 350°F (175°C). Combine beef, bread, onion, eggs, garlic, ground chile, salt, cumin, green chiles, and tomato sauce in a large bowl. Place half the mixture in a 9 x 5-inch loaf pan or 1 1/2-quart baking pan. Indent the center of meat mixture slightly, making a 1-inch margin all around, and arrange 1 cup of the cheese and the avocado slices on indented area. Top with remaining meat loaf mixture and press edges together to seal. Sprinkle the remaining 1/2 cup of cheese on top of meat loaf. Bake 1 1/4 to 1 1/2 hours or until juices run clear. Serve with salsa.
Makes 6 servings.

VARIATION
Prepare individual meat loaves and bake 30 to 45 minutes, or cook on an outdoor grill.

New Mexico Green Chile Cheese Burgers

These have become the focus of many a chef's contest, including on national television. A chain of fast-food restaurants in the sixties popularized these by calling them "Green Teen" burgers. Use mild or hot green chiles, according to taste.

1 1/2 pounds lean ground beef
1 garlic clove, crushed
Few grinds black pepper
1 teaspoon ground mild chile
1/2 teaspoon salt
4 1/4-inch-thick slices Monterey Jack cheese
4 sesame hamburger buns
4 green chiles, parched, peeled (see page 340), and chopped
4 red onion slices
1 medium-size tomato, sliced
Salsa Fresca (recipe on page 78) (optional)

Mix beef with garlic, pepper, ground chile, and salt in a large bowl. Shape into 4 flat patties. Preheat broiler or grill. Cook burgers to desired doneness. Just before serving, place the cheese on top of each burger bun. Toast the buns until they are lightly browned and the cheese is melted. Top each bun with a hamburger patty, green chiles, an onion slice, and a tomato slice. Serve immediately with fresh salsa on the side.

Makes 4 servings.

VARIATION
Chopped canned green chiles can be substituted.

Chili Burgers

There are chili burgers and then there are chili burgers made with the real stuff—the original cowboy chili without beans and tomatoes! These are very special.

1 1/2 pounds lean ground beef
1/2 teaspoon salt
Generous dash of freshly ground black pepper
2 cups Bowl o' Red (recipe on page 42)
4 hamburger buns (Kaiser or onion rolls, if possible)
1 Tablespoon butter (optional)
1/2 cup shredded mixed Monterey Jack and Cheddar cheeses
1/2 cup chopped Spanish onion
2 Tablespoons sliced, pickled jalapeño chiles (optional)

Mix beef with salt and pepper in a large bowl. Shape into 4 flat patties. Preheat broiler or grill. Cook burgers to desired doneness.

Meanwhile, heat the Bowl o' Red until it is warm enough to serve. Then split the buns, lightly butter them, if desired, and grill or toast them. To serve, place the burgers on the buns and top with chili, cheese, onion, and jalapeño chiles, if desired.

Makes 4 servings.

Salsa Burgers

Swiss cheese and freshly made Salsa Fresca make this burger superb. This cross-cultural burger is best when served on an English muffin.

        1 1/2 pounds lean ground beef
        1/2 teaspoon salt
        Generous dash of freshly ground black pepper
        1 Tablespoon butter
        4 English muffins
        1 teaspoon dried leaf basil
        1 teaspoon dried leaf tarragon
        4 Swiss cheese slices, about 4 inches square
        Salsa Fresca (recipe on page 78)

Mix beef with salt and pepper in a large bowl. Shape into 4 flat patties. Preheat broiler or grill. Cook burgers to desired doneness. Split and lightly butter muffins and sprinkle with the basil and tarragon, crushing the herbs as you sprinkle them on the top of the open muffins. Grill or toast muffins until lightly brown. To serve, place the burgers on muffins and top with the cheese. Broil to further melt the cheese, if needed. Serve topped with the salsa, and pass additional salsa.

Makes 4 servings.

Guacamole Burgers

Smooth guacamole, crunchy tostados, and refried black beans create a real taste sensation.

1 1/2 pounds lean ground beef
1/2 teaspoon salt
Generous dash of freshly ground black pepper
1 1/2 cups Frijoles Refritos (recipe on page 220 using black beans)
1/2 cup crushed corn chips
4 sesame hamburger buns, Kaiser rolls, or onion rolls
1 Tablespoon butter (optional)
1 1/2 cups Guacamole (recipe on page 13)
1/2 cup chopped Spanish onion
1/2 cup mixed shredded Monterey Jack cheese and Cheddar cheese
1/4 cup Salsa Roja (recipe on page 82) or purchased salsa
2 Tablespoons sliced pickled jalapeño chiles (optional)

Mix beef with the salt and pepper in a large bowl. Shape into 4 flat patties. Preheat broiler or grill. Cook burgers to desired doneness.

Meanwhile, prepare refried beans, substituting black beans for the pintos; or if time is short, use canned refried black beans. Top beans with the crushed corn chips.

Split buns, lightly butter them, if desired, and grill or toast them. To serve, place beans on the bottom half of a bun, then add a burger and layers of the following—guacamole, onion, cheese, salsa, and jalapeño chiles, if using. Top with the other bun half. Repeat.

Makes 4 servings.

Freddy's Favorite (Macaroni Beef Casserole)

This was always my brother's favorite family memory dish. Both my maternal grandmother's and my mother's versions were delicious. It is also known as Yamegetta, Glop, Kansas Chop Suey, and Goulash.

- 2 teaspoons salt, divided
- 2 cups elbow macaroni
- 1 pound extra-lean ground beef
- 1 cup chopped onion
- 1 garlic clove, chopped
- 1/4 teaspoon freshly ground black pepper
- 1 or 2 Tablespoons hot ground chile
- 1 (14 1/2-ounce) can petite diced tomatoes
- 1 (17-ounce) can whole-kernel corn, drained
- 1/2 cup tomato juice (optional)

Bring 3 quarts water and 1 teaspoon of the salt to a boil in a large pot, add macaroni, and boil 8 to 10 minutes or until tender to the bite.

Crumble meat into a 4-inch deep skillet with a lid. Cook, stirring to break up meat, until meat starts to brown, then add onion and garlic. Cook until onion softens. Push meat mixture to one side and drain off any fat. Drain macaroni. Season meat mixture with remaining 1 teaspoon salt, pepper, and ground chile. Then stir in the tomatoes and corn. Cover and simmer 5 to 10 minutes to blend flavors. Taste and adjust seasonings. Add the tomato juice if mixture is dry.

Makes 4 servings.

VARIATIONS
Add shredded Cheddar, Jack, or American cheese to taste. Other vegetables such as celery, green bell pepper, and mushrooms can be added and sautéed with the onion. It's a wonderful dish for using bits of leftovers.

Barbecued Beef Heart (Anticuchos)

This Peruvian meat kebab has a New Mexican accent. The recipe is a favorite of a dear friend of mine, Ann Moul, who lived in Bogotá, Colombia, before moving back to Santa Fe. Chunks of sirloin or other tender beef can be substituted.

 1 beef heart
 3 Tablespoons ground caribe chile
 6 Mexican garlic cloves, finely minced
 1 teaspoon freshly ground cumin
 1/2 teaspoon salt
 Few grinds, freshly ground black pepper
 1/4 cup oregano-flavored vinegar or red wine vinegar with 1
     teaspoon ground Mexican oregano stirred into it
 1/4 cup extra-virgin Spanish olive oil
 12 fresh mushrooms, wiped clean
 1 medium-size fresh green bell pepper, cut into 1-inch squares
 24 cherry tomatoes
 1 Spanish onion, cut into 1-inch squares

Clean and remove the membrane covering the heart with a sharp boning or paring knife. Remove the walls of major arteries, then cube the heart into 1 1/2-inch cubes and place in a glass or ceramic bowl. Combine the chile, garlic, cumin, salt, and pepper with the vinegar and oil. Pour over the meat, adding more vinegar as needed to cover it. Cover with plastic wrap and marinate 12 hours in the refrigerator, then drain.

Preheat grill or broiler. Alternate beef cubes with mushrooms, bell pepper, tomatoes, and 2 or 3 onion pieces on skewers. Grill to desired doneness, brushing marinade on vegetables and meat as it cooks.

Makes 4 to 6 servings.

Steak Tampico Style

This is inspired by workers from south of the border who are yearning for home. Serve as a London broil–type steak with salad and vegetables or as the filling for soft tacos. The cooked steak can be frozen up to eight months.

> 1 (3- or 4-pound) beef loin steak or beef tenderloin
> 1 Tablespoon olive oil
> 1 medium-size onion, finely chopped
> 3/4 cup red wine vinegar
> 1/2 teaspoon salt
> 1/2 teaspoon freshly ground black pepper
> 1/2 teaspoon ground chile
> 1/2 teaspoon ground Mexican oregano
> 1/2 teaspoon ground cumin
> 1/2 teaspoon ground cloves
> 1/2 teaspoon ground cinnamon
> 2 garlic cloves, minced
> 12 flour tortillas, warmed (optional)
> Salsa Roja (recipe on page 82) or Salsa Fresca (recipe on page 78) (optional)

Place the steak in a large shallow dish. In a small saucepan heat oil; add onion and sauté until it begins to soften. Add the vinegar, salt, pepper, ground chile, oregano, cumin, cloves, cinnamon, and garlic and simmer the marinade, covered, 10 minutes. Cool. Pour cooled marinade over steak, turn the steak over to coat evenly, and marinate 30 minutes at room temperature or 2 hours in the refrigerator.

Preheat grill. Grill steak, charring the outside and leaving the inside rare, basting with marinade as the steak cooks. Thinly slice and serve as is, or place a few strips in each tortilla; top with salsa, if using, and roll up.

Makes 10 servings.

VARIATION
Cut the beef into large chunks, marinate as above, and thread on skewers with fresh vegetables. Grill to desired doneness.

Chile Beef Taco Filling

This is a delicious and easy filling. Create tacos by warming or frying corn tortillas until crisp and bent into a U shape. (See page 162 for more information.) Place the beef filling in first, followed by shredded lettuce, chopped onion, grated cheese, dotted with fresh tomato, and salsa of your choice.

1 pound extra-lean ground beef
2 garlic cloves, minced
1 Tablespoon ground pure, mild red chile
1 Tablespoon ground, pure hot red chile
1 Tablespoon red wine vinegar or cider vinegar
1/4 teaspoon ground Mexican oregano
1/2 teaspoon ground cumin
1 teaspoon salt

Cook ground beef in a large skillet, stirring to break up meat, until browned. Drain off any fat, then add the garlic, ground chile, vinegar, oregano, cumin, and salt. Cook, stirring, to combine ingredients and blend the flavors. Serve hot.

Makes enough filling for 8 tacos.

Tacos al Carbon

I was first treated to these in Los Angeles by a Mexican-American woman. I loved them then and still do!

2 pounds beef sirloin steak
3 garlic cloves, minced
Coarsely ground fresh pepper
12 white or yellow corn tortillas, warmed
1/2 cup chopped Spanish onion
1 large tomato, chopped
1 cup shredded lettuce
Salsa Fresca (recipe on page 78)

Preheat charcoal grill. Season steak with garlic and pepper. Broil the steak about 3 inches from the coals to desired doneness. Meanwhile, wrap tortillas in foil and warm them, along with dinner plates, in a 350°F (175°C) oven. Thinly slice steak and arrange on a platter. Put the onion, tomato, lettuce, and salsa in bowls. Place the tortillas in a napkin-lined basket. Assemble the tacos by placing some steak in a tortilla, then adding layers of lettuce, onion, tomato, and salsa.

Makes 12 tacos.

Beef Fajitas

From their humble beginnings, fajitas have caught on like a prairie fire fanning out from South Texas. Originally this was the food that farm laborers along the border prepared for themselves from the trimmings their bosses gave them. Fajitas are made in the Southwest from relatively inexpensive skirt steak. In the North and East, one often has to settle for beef bottom round, which must be cut into very thin slices. The authentic smoky flavor comes from marinating the beef in lime juice and garlic and grilling it over mesquite, which for this recipe is optional but preferable. Fajitas are traditionally served on sizzling steak platters on top of sautéed slivered onions and tricolored bell peppers, accompanied by warm flour tortillas and sauced with peppery hot pico de gallo and sour cream.

> **2 pounds beef skirt steak or very lean scaloppini-cut bottom round steak**
> **Juice of 2 limes**
> **6 garlic cloves, minced**
> **1 teaspoon salt**
> **Freshly ground black pepper to taste**
> **2 large red Spanish onions, halved width-wise, then cut into slivers**
> **1 each green, red, and yellow bell pepper, cut in quarters, then cut into thin strips**
> **18 (6-inch) flour tortillas, warmed**
> **Pico de Gallo (recipe on page 77)**
> **Guacamole (recipe on page 13), if desired**

Trim the steaks, removing any fat and sinew. Pound as thin as possible between sheets of plastic wrap. Combine lime juice, garlic, salt, and a generous amount of pepper in a shallow bowl. Add steak pieces; roll and turn to get maximum amount of marinade absorbed into the meat. Marinate at room temperature 30 minutes or refrigerate 2 hours.

Meanwhile, about 45 minutes before serving, preheat grill, using mesquite wood or chips to flavor charcoal briquettes.

About 20 to 25 minutes before serving, place the onion halves on the grill, turning after about 5 minutes; place the bell pepper pieces on the grill for about 5 more minutes. Cut the onion into wedges and the peppers into 1/2-inch wide strips and mix together.

Grill beef strips about 3 inches from coals until charred on each side but still rare in the center. Cut into strips about 1 inch wide. To serve, divide onions and peppers on each plate and place steak strips on top. Pass a napkin-lined basket with hot tortillas and bowls of pico de gallo and guacamole, if using.

Makes 6 to 8 servings.

VARIATION

For a buffet or family-style service, place the mixed grilled vegetables in the center of a platter and cover with the beef slices. Tuck folded, warmed tortillas in around the edge of the platter.

Navajo Tacos with Beef & Beans

This uses a fried bread that is made by Native Americans in Arizona and New Mexico.

Navajo Fry Bread (recipe on page 257)
Chile Beef Taco Filling (recipe on page 157)
Vegetable oil for deep-frying
1 cup cooked pinto beans
1/2 cup finely chopped onion
2 tomatoes, coarsely chopped
2 cups very thinly shredded iceberg lettuce
2 cups salsa, your choice

Prepare fry bread dough and set aside. Then prepare filling. Preheat oil to 375°F (190°C) as directed in recipe. Fry bread disks, drain on paper towels, and keep warm.

Layer beef, beans, onion, tomatoes, and lettuce over bread, and serve warm with a side dish of the salsa.

Makes 6 to 8 servings.

VARIATIONS

Chicken & Jalapeño: Substitute 2 whole poached chicken breasts, cubed, for the beef. Add 2 or more finely chopped jalapeño chiles and sprinkle on top of the lettuce.

Chilied Vegetables & Sour Cream: Substitute 2 cups of Bean & Bulgur Chili (recipe on page 48) for the beef and add 1 cup sour cream, to be placed in dollops on top of the lettuce.

Chiles Rellenos with Picadillo Stuffing

Serve these stuffed chiles plain or dip in batter and fry until golden.

1 pound beef chuck, cut into 1/2-inch cubes or ground
1/4 cup chopped onion
2 garlic cloves, minced
1 cup water
1/2 teaspoon ground cloves
2 teaspoons ground coriander
3/4 teaspoon salt
1 cup raisins
12 large mild green chiles, prepared as for Chiles Rellenos de Queso (recipe on page 214)
California-Style Batter (recipe on page 215) (optional)
Vegetable oil (optional)
Salsa (optional)

Crumble beef and place in a heavy skillet. Cook and stir until browned. Add the onion and garlic and cook until onion is softened. Add the water, cover, and simmer until meat is tender, about 1 hour. Add cloves, coriander, salt, and raisins. Simmer, uncovered, and cook meat until meat mixture is thick but still moist.

Stuff the prepared green chiles with the meat mixture and serve. Or coat with batter and fry until golden in 2 or more inches of oil heated to 375°F (190°C). Drain and serve piping hot with salsa, if desired.

Makes 4 to 6 servings.

VARIATION

You can use 12 dried green chiles instead of fresh. Soak them in a little warm water to soften, coarsely chop them, and stir them into the meat mixture. Form the meat mixture into oval shapes. Dip the ovals in flour. Beat 3 egg whites until stiff and use this meringue for coating instead of batter. Deep-fry at 375°F (190°C) until golden. (This style is traditional Northern New Mexican.)

TORTILLA & TAMALE DISHES

Featured in this chapter are many of the traditional Southwestern favorites, such as tamales, burritos, chimichangas, and enchiladas, that have helped make this cuisine so popular, along with some innovative new twists such as Baja Seafood Tamales. Chiles figure in almost every dish in some way.

Many of the recipes that follow are for one-dish dinners, such as the tamale pies. These need only the addition of a crisp salad to have a complete meal. Several of the dishes can be made ahead and refrigerated or frozen.

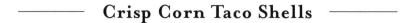

Crisp Corn Taco Shells

12 corn tortillas, preferably an assortment of yellow, white, and blue
2 quarts vegetable oil

Set up a cooking area, allowing ample space for draining the tacos. Place several layers of paper towels under a wire taco rack. If a rack is unavailable, make enough small wads of paper towels, about 1 1/2 inches in diameter, for each of the traditional U-shaped tacos you are creating. Meanwhile, heat the oil to 375°F (190°C) in a deep-fat fryer or in a 5-quart heavy pot, using a deep-fat thermometer to aid in maintaining the temperature, which is critical for good results.

To fry the traditional U shapes, place a tortilla in a taco fryer, making sure that the side of the tortilla with the least browned edges is on the outside (a tip to make bending easier and breaking less likely). Then immerse in the hot fat until the bubbles slow down, usually about 22 seconds. Fry each until it is crisp, dry, and not shiny looking, which indicates undercooking. Do not overcook, as the flavor and color will not be as good. As soon as each is fried, remove with tongs and drain, either on the rack or on its side with a wad of paper towels inside, which is important for draining the fat as well as keeping the taco shell from folding together.

If you are frying them with two tongs, form a U shape and grasp the two opposite sides of the tortilla with the tongs, making certain that the side of the tortilla with the least browned appearance is on the outside. Fry and drain as above. To create flat tacos or tostados, just hold one side of the tortilla with your tongs and fry until crisp. Drain as above, omitting the wads of paper, but topping each with additional paper towels. To create tostados compuestos, the little baskets, see Tips & Techniques (page 343).

Taco Bar

For a taco party, prepare an attractive assortment of ingredients for everyone to have the fun of stuffing his or her own.

2 or more taco fillings
24 to 36 Crisp Corn Taco Shells (opposite)
2 heads iceberg or romaine lettuce, finely shredded
3 large tomatoes, chopped
1 large Spanish onion, chopped
1 1/2 pounds mixed shredded Monterey Jack cheese and Cheddar cheese
2 salsas of your choice (pages 76–83)

Prepare fillings; keep warm, then place in bowls. Place lettuce, tomatoes, onion, cheese, and salsa in separate bowls.

Makes 12 servings.

Burritos

Burritos got their name quite by accident. They were named by the Spanish conquistadores for the little boys on burros tending the sheep that dotted the mountainous landscapes in Old Mexico. The boys would often be a long way from home and needed a portable food to take with them. The most popular snack was a portion of beans or other ingredients rolled into a tortilla. Conquistadores, being either greedy or hungry according to legend, would often snatch the tortilla snacks away from the boys, and thus was born the name burritos, "little boys on burros." As time wore on, the traditional burrito became a white flour tortilla wrapped around a portion of refried pinto beans topped with chopped onion and cheeses and other fillings.

I have developed infinite variations from this humble beginning. Burritos are one of the most popular Tex-Mex foods with people of all ages. They are delicious, satisfying, and can hold any range of ingredients, from seafood to New Mexico's carne adobado. Because burritos are filling as well as nutritious, a simple salad or even lettuce and a few wedges of tomato are often enough to make a complete meal. Garnishes of red or green chile–laced sauces, sour cream, guacamole, and cheese are especially good.

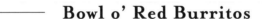

Bowl o' Red Burritos

These are always a favorite! Just like having Bowl o' Red, only better.

- 4 large flour tortillas
- 1 cup Frijoles Refritos (recipe on page 220)
- 2 cups Bowl o' Red (recipe on page 42)
- 2 Tablespoons pickled jalapeño chiles or to taste
- 1/4 cup chopped onion
- 1 cup mixed shredded Monterey Jack cheese and Cheddar cheese
- Sour cream (optional)
- Green onions (optional), finely minced

Preheat oven to 350°F (75°C). Wrap the tortillas in foil and warm them in the oven. Or warm them on a griddle or Mexican comal until soft. Spoon beans down center of each warm tortilla, allowing a 1 1/2-inch edge on one end, then top with the Bowl o' Red, jalapeño chiles, onion, and cheese. Roll, twisting the bottom edge closed. Return to oven to melt cheese, then garnish with a dollop of sour cream and green onion.

Makes 4 burritos.

VARIATION

For Carne Adobado Burritos, substitute 2 cups Carne, omit the pickled jalapeños, and serve with a dollop of sour cream on top and chopped fresh tomatoes sprinkled with caribe chile.

Green Chile & Chicken Burritos

These were a big favorite in my New York City restaurant. We were even judged the best burritos on the Upper East Side.

4 (12-inch) flour tortillas
New Mexico Green Chile Sauce (recipe on page 83)
1 1/2 cups Frijoles Refritos (recipe on page 220), warmed
2 cups bite-size pieces poached chicken (recipe on page 94)
1 avocado, sliced into thin wedges
2 green onions, chopped, tops included
2 cups shredded Cheddar cheese or Monterey Jack cheese, divided
1 medium-size tomato, chopped
1/2 cup sour cream

Preheat oven to 350°F (175°C). Wrap tortillas in foil and warm in oven 10 or 15 minutes. Or warm them on a griddle or Mexican comal until soft. Warm the sauce in a small saucepan. Spread beans down center of each tortilla; then add chicken, avocado wedges, green onions, 1 cup of the cheese, and chopped tomato. Roll burritos and place on plates. Top with remaining 1 cup cheese. Bake about 10 minutes or until cheese melts. Serve immediately with sauce spooned over the top of each, then add a dollop of sour cream.
Makes 4 servings.

VARIATION
Substitute Spicy Fried Chicken Strips (recipe on page 105) for the poached chicken.

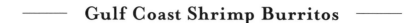

Gulf Coast Shrimp Burritos

Substituting rice for the beans in these burritos really makes them lower in calories. The Black Bean Salsa is a must to serve over them.

4 flour tortillas
2 cups Peppered Rice (recipe on page 227), warmed
16 medium-size shrimp, peeled, deveined, butterflied, and poached
1/4 cup chopped green onions
Black Bean Salsa (recipe on page 78)
Coarsely chopped romaine lettuce or red leaf lettuce (optional)

Preheat oven to 350°F (75°C). Wrap tortillas in foil and warm in oven. Or warm them on a griddle or Mexican comal until soft. Spread rice down the center of each warm tortilla, allowing a 1 1/2-inch edge on bottom end, then top with the shrimp and green onions. Roll each filled tortilla, twisting the bottom edge to close it. Spoon salsa over center of each burrito. Garnish with lettuce, if desired.

Makes 4 burritos.

Ham & Frijoles Slaw Burritos

These unusual burritos are made with ham and slaw that contains beans.

4 (12-inch) flour tortillas
3/4 pound thick-sliced cooked ham
1 1/2 cups shredded Monterey Jack cheese or Cheddar cheese, divided
1/2 cup Frijoles Slaw (recipe on page 65)
Cold Salsa Verde (recipe on page 78)

Preheat oven to 350°F (75°C). Wrap the tortillas in foil and heat in oven 15 minutes. Or warm them on a griddle or Mexican comal until soft. While tortillas are warming, fry ham slices in a skillet until hot and lightly browned.

Assemble burritos by placing ham, 3/4 cup of the cheese, the slaw, and a little salsa down the center of each tortilla. Roll filled tortillas and place in a baking dish. Top with salsa and remaining 3/4 cup cheese. Bake until cheese is melted. Serve with additional salsa on the side.

Makes 4 servings.

Santa Fe Burritos

These traditional burritos may be similar to the ones served to Cortez's armies over four hundred years ago. A must is to serve it with a warmed red or green chile sauce.

4 (12-inch) white flour tortillas
1 1/2 cups Frijoles Refritos (recipe on page 220)
About 2 cups Mexican-Style Shredded Beef (recipe on page 147)
1/3 cup sliced pitted ripe olives
Any warmed red or green chile sauce
1 1/2 cups shredded Monterey Jack cheese
Shredded lettuce
Guacamole (recipe on page 13)

Preheat oven to 350°F (175°C). Wrap the tortillas in foil and warm in oven 15 minutes. Or warm them on a griddle or Mexican comal until soft. Spread beans down center of each warm tortilla and top with beef and sliced olives. Roll and place in a baking dish. Spoon a little chile sauce over the top, then sprinkle with shredded cheese and bake until cheese is melted, about 10 minutes. Serve piping hot on plates garnished with shredded lettuce and guacamole. Pass additional warmed sauce in a separate bowl.
Makes 4 servings.

VARIATION
Substitute cooked pork or chicken, if desired.

Pastrami & Green Chile Burrito

A real favorite of mine, developed by a restaurant in Albuquerque. These were originally called the Sheep Herder Special.

4 (9-inch) flour tortillas
About 3/4 pound pastrami
4 or more green chiles, parched, peeled (see page 340), and cut into long, thin strips

Preheat oven to 350°F (175°C). Wrap the tortillas and pastrami separately in foil and warm in oven 15 minutes. Or warm them on a griddle or Mexican comal until soft. To assemble burritos, lay slices of hot pastrami along center of each warmed tortilla about two-thirds of the way down the length. Evenly divide green chile strips over meat. Fold the bottom one-third of the tortilla up, then fold the 2 sides over the pastrami and chiles. The sandwich will then be closed at one end to prevent dripping.
Makes 4 servings.

VARIATIONS
Substitute ham for pastrami. Try a combination of salami, spicy salsa, and shredded cheese—or use roast beef, chopped onion, and a tomato salsa. The combinations are endless!

Traditional Burritos

These burritos are vegetarian quite by accident. Hailing from Central Mexico, they were a simple and portable snack easily and inexpensively made. Originally the only tortilla was a corn one. We have altered the tortilla to the more predictable flour tortilla for this dish. The original burrito was made of just beans and a corn tortilla

    6 flour tortillas
    2 cups Frijoles Refritos (recipe on page 220)
    1/4 cup chopped onion
    2/3 cup mixed shredded Monterey Jack cheese and Cheddar cheese
    1/4 cup pickled jalapeños chiles (optional)
    Shredded lettuce (optional)
    Salsa of your choice, either cooked or a relish type (optional)
    1 tomato, cut in wedges (optional)
    Sour cream (optional)
    Crushed caribe chile (optional)

Preheat oven to 350°F (75°C). Wrap the tortillas in foil and warm them in oven. Or warm them on a griddle or Mexican comal until soft. Spoon beans down the center of each tortilla, allowing a 1 1/2-inch edge on bottom end, then top with onions, cheese, and a few rounds of pickled jalapeños, if desired. Roll each filled tortilla, twisting the bottom edge to close it. Bake until cheese is melted. Garnish, if desired, with the lettuce, salsa, tomato wedges, and sour cream, and sprinkle with caribe chile.

Makes 6 burritos.

CHIMICHANGAS

Chimichangas are a relative newcomer to the Tex-Mex or Southwestern entrées. In essence they originally were a fried burrito with the ends of the tortilla tucked in blintz style. Later, we have learned that baking them on a generously greased baking sheet yields almost the same result with lots less retained fat. The name *chimichanga* means "a bite for my loved one." Hence, they are fun to make for romantic occasions. The fillings can follow along the same ingredients as burritos, and you can mix and match to suit your own taste.

—— Bowl o' Red Chimichangas ——

As you can guess, our family really loves the Bowl o' Red chili. It is our favorite by far, so we use it in nearly everything! It does make a terrific chimichanga.

> 2 quarts vegetable oil (optional)
> 4 (10-inch) flour tortillas
> 1 Tablespoon lard, if baking
> 1 cup Frijoles Refritos (recipe on page 220)
> 2 cups Bowl o' Red (recipe on page 42)
> 1/2 cup chopped onion
> 1/2 cup mixed shredded Monterey Jack and Cheddar cheeses
> 12 to 16 pickled jalapeño chile slices
> Sour cream sprinkled with caribe chile
> Guacamole (recipe on page 13)
> Salsa of your choice (optional)

Heat oil in a deep-fat fryer or heavy pot to 375°F (190°C) if frying. Either warm the tortillas in a microwave oven or wrap them in foil and warm in a 350°F (175°C) oven until they are pliable. Or warm them on a griddle or Mexican comal until soft.

If baking, heat an oven to 425°F (220°C) and generously grease a baking sheet and build the chimichangas on the sheet. This will assist in greasing the top of the tortilla, enhancing browning.

Place a rectangle of beans on each tortilla, smoothing it out to about 1/4 inch thick and allowing a 2- or 3-inch margin all around beans. Top with chili, then onions, cheese, and jalapeño chile slices. Fold one side over the filling. Fold in the two ends, then roll to seal. Secure by stabbing with wooden picks.

Fry in the hot oil until lightly browned and crisp. Using the directions for baking and rolling them under the Tucson Chimichangas (recipe on page 172), bake for 12 to 15 minutes at 425°F on a generously greased baking sheet until lightly browned. Garnish as desired with sour cream, guacamole, and salsa.

Makes 4 chimichangas.

Pollo Verde Chimichangas

This light yet flavorful filling is a favorite of mine. You can temper the spiciness by the quantity of jalapeño chiles you use.

2 quarts vegetable oil
4 (10-inch) flour tortillas
1 Tablespoon lard, if baking
2 skinless, boneless chicken breasts, poached in chicken broth and cubed
1/4 cup minced fresh jalapeño chiles or to taste
1/2 cup cilantro, coarsely chopped
4 garlic cloves, minced
1/2 cup sour cream or chicken broth*
Sour cream sprinkled with caribe chile
Guacamole (recipe on page 13)
Salsa of your choice (optional)

Heat oil in a deep-fat fryer or heavy pot to 375°F (190°C) if frying. Warm the tortillas in a microwave oven or wrap them in foil and warm in a preheated 350°F (175°C) oven until they are pliable. Or warm them on a griddle or Mexican comal until soft.

If baking, heat an oven to 425°F (220°C) and generously grease a baking sheet and build the chimichangas on the sheet. This will assist in greasing the top of the tortilla, enhancing browning.

Combine the chicken with the jalapeño chiles, cilantro, garlic, and sour cream. Taste and adjust seasonings. Place a rectangle of filling on each tortilla, smoothing it out to about 1/2 inch thick and allowing a margin of 2 to 3 inches all around the filling. Fold one side up about one-third of the way. Fold in each of the remaining sides to create a rectangle. Secure with wooden picks by stabbing each in, not weaving it, as this may cause a tear.

Fry in the hot oil until lightly browned and crisp. Or bake for about 12 to 15 minutes in a preheated 425°F oven until lightly browned. (See directions for baking under the Tucson Chimichangas, page 172.) Serve garnished with sour cream, guacamole, or salsa, if desired.

Makes 4 chimichangas.

*Use the sour cream for a richer taste or the chicken stock for lower calories.

Tucson Chimichangas

These were all the rage a while ago. They are still popular, but their popularity has waned a bit, possibly because of the frying involved. However, I am offering a baking option that has the same great flavor and loads less calories. This recipe is for the original filling and is quite good.

2 pounds lean beef stew meat, coarsely chopped
2 medium-size potatoes, diced
6 medium-size hot green chiles, parched, peeled (see page 340), and chopped
1 cup chopped onion
2 garlic cloves, minced
2 teaspoons ground Mexican oregano
2 teaspoons salt
Water
Vegetable oil
12 to 18 (8-inch) tortillas
1 Tablespoon lard, if baking
1 head leafy lettuce, coarsely chopped
1 large tomato, chopped
Salsa of your choice
Sour cream
Guacamole (recipe on page 13) (optional)

Put beef, potatoes, green chiles, onions, garlic, oregano, and salt with water to barely cover into a saucepan. Simmer at least 1 hour, or until all ingredients are well done and very soft. Taste and adjust seasonings. Set the filling aside.

Preheat oven to 300°F (150°C). Heat about 4 inches of oil in a deep heavy saucepan or deep-fryer to 375°F (190°C) if frying. Wrap the tortillas in foil and warm them in the oven until they are pliable. Or warm them on a griddle or Mexican comal until soft. At the same time, warm 6 plates in the oven.

Or heat an oven to 425°F (220°C) for baking. If baking, generously grease a baking sheet and build the chimichangas on the sheet. This will assist in greasing the top of the tortilla, enhancing browning.

Divide the filling among warmed tortillas, placing about 2 heaping Tablespoons in center of each. Fold one side of the tortilla over the filling, then fold over each of the adjacent two sides, and finally fold the fourth side over the top. Secure by stabbing with wooden picks. Carefully fry the filled tortillas until golden, turning to assure even browning. Drain and place 2 on each warm plate in the oven until all are fried.

Or bake for 12 to 15 minutes until the tops are lightly browned.

Serve with lettuce and diced tomatoes. Serve with bowls of salsa, sour cream, and guacamole, if desired.

Makes 6 servings.

El Último Chimichanga

A potpourri of fillings in a giant-size tortilla with sauces and sour cream.

    1 Tablespoon lard, if baking
    1 (12- to 16-inch) flour tortilla, warmed
    2 cups Frijoles Refritos (recipe on page 220), warmed
    2 cups Carne Adobado (recipe on page 132)
    1/2 cup chopped onion
    1 cup mixed shredded Monterey Jack cheese and Cheddar cheese
    Vegetable oil
    2 to 3 leaves red leaf lettuce
    Sour cream sprinkled with crushed caribe chile
    Salsa Roja (recipe on page 82)
    Cold Salsa Verde (recipe on page 78)

Heat about 4 inches of oil in a deep heavy saucepan or deep-fat fryer to 375°F (190°C) if frying. Warm the tortillas in a microwave oven or wrap them in foil and warm in a preheated 350°F (175°C) oven until they are pliable. Or warm them on a griddle or Mexican comal until soft.

If baking, heat an oven to 425°F (220°C) and generously grease a baking sheet and build the chimichangas on the sheet. This will assist in greasing the top of the tortilla, enhancing browning.

Place warm beans in a strip down the center of tortilla, and top with Carne Adobado, chopped onion, and cheese. Fold one side of the tortilla up about one-third of the way. Fold in each of the remaining sides to create a rectangle, and secure by stabbing them with wooden picks.

Fry filled tortilla until it is golden brown on both sides, turning carefully with large spatulas. Drain on paper towels. Or bake 12 to 15 minutes until golden brown in a preheated oven to 425°F. (See rolling directions under the Tucson Chimichangas, page 172, if baking.) Serve on a bed of red leaf lettuce and garnish with sour cream, Salsa Roja, and Salsa Verde to replicate the Mexican flag. Dust with a sprinkle of caribe chile.

Makes 4 servings.

— Vegetarian Delight Chimichangas —

You can use any combination of vegetables you like, either quickly stir-fried or steamed. We've always liked the hearty, robust flavors of our vegetarian chili as a filling.

> **2 quarts vegetable oil**
> **1 Tablespoon lard, if baking**
> **4 (10-inch) flour tortillas**
> **2 cups Bean & Bulgur Chili (recipe on page 48)**
> **Sour cream sprinkled with caribe chile (optional)**
> **Guacamole (recipe on page 13) (optional)**
> **Salsa of your choice (optional)**

Heat about 4 inches of oil in a deep heavy saucepan or deep-fat fryer to 375°F (190°C) if frying. Warm tortillas in a microwave oven or warm them on a griddle or Mexican comal until soft or heat an oven to 425°F (220°C) and generously grease a cookie sheet and build the chimichangas on the greased cookie sheet. This will assist in greasing the top of the tortilla, enhancing browning.

Place chili in a rectangle on each tortilla, smoothing it out to about 1/2 inch thick and allowing a border of 2 to 3 inches all around the tortilla. Fold 1 side up about one-third of the way. Fold in each of the remaining sides to create a rectangle, and secure with wooden picks, just stabbing them in.

Fry filled tortillas until lightly browned and crisp on both sides, turning carefully with spatulas. Drain on paper towels. Or bake until golden for 12 to 15 minutes. (See rolling directions under the Tucson Chimichangas, page 172, if baking.) Serve garnished with sour cream, guacamole, or salsa.

Makes 4 chimichangas.

Enchiladas

Enchiladas have long been a favorite Southwestern and Mexican family meal. They are very popular with tourists as well. The meaning of *enchilada* is "in chile" or "in the chile sauce." I prefer the uniquely New Mexican flat enchiladas as they have more sauce and I think are more attractive. I like to encircle the flat enchiladas with coarsely chopped romaine, which is heat tolerant, then top with coarsely chopped red leaf or mesclun greens, which are not heat tolerant. Then I encircle the plates with tomato wedges placed equal distance, all facing the same direction.

Enchiladas Suizas

This dish originated in Old Mexico and was named Suizas, which is Spanish for Swiss, because Switzerland is known for its premium dairy products. It has been quite popular for some time.

Vegetable oil for frying
12 corn tortillas
New Mexico Green Chile Sauce (recipe on page 83)
2 cups shredded cooked chicken or pork
2 cups mixed shredded Monterey Jack and Cheddar cheeses
1 cup whipping cream
1/4 cup chopped green onions, tops included
Stuffed green olives, sliced
Cherry tomatoes

Preheat oven to 350°F (175°C). Heat 1/2 inch of oil in a heavy skillet. Add tortillas a few at a time and fry lightly, being careful not to make them too crisp to roll. Or heat them on a heavy griddle or comal until they are very soft. Dip each tortilla in green chile sauce. Place 2 heaping Tablespoons chicken or pork and 2 Tablespoons cheese down the center of each tortilla. Roll and place seam side down in a shallow baking dish.

After all the rolled tortillas are in the dish, spoon additional green chile sauce over them, then cover evenly with whipping cream. Sprinkle with remaining cheese and green onions. Bake, uncovered, 20 minutes. Serve immediately, garnished with olives and cherry tomatoes.

Makes 4 to 6 servings.

VARIATION
Some like this dish prepared with the tomatillo-based salsa on page 78 instead of the green chile sauce.

Green Chile Chicken Open-Face or Rolled Enchiladas

When you make these, make plenty of them. It's a delicious and festive meal that everyone is certain to love! This tends to be the favorite traditional entrée for visitors to our state. The enchiladas and/or the sauce can be frozen for up to three months.

Vegetable oil for frying, only for rolled enchiladas
8 to 12 white, yellow, or blue corn tortillas
Hot Green Chile Sauce (recipe on page 84), with 2 cups chopped cooked chicken added
1 1/4 cups mixed shredded Monterey Jack cheese and Cheddar cheese
1 medium-size onion, chopped
1/3 cup sour cream
Crushed caribe chile
Coarsely chopped lettuce
Tomato wedges

Preheat oven to 350°F (175°C). If rolling the enchiladas, heat 1/2 inch of oil in a heavy skillet. Add the tortillas and fry lightly in batches, being careful not to make them too crisp to roll. Or heat them on a heavy griddle or comal until they are very soft. Warm 4 plates in the preheated oven.

For Flat Enchiladas: For each enchilada, place a spoonful of chile sauce on a warmed ovenproof plate, then top with a tortilla (not necessary to fry) followed by cheese, onions, and more sauce. Repeat once or twice more, making a stack of 2 or 3 tortillas layered with cheese, onions, and sauce.* Top each enchilada with more sauce and cheese. Place in the preheated oven until the cheese melts. Top each enchilada with a dollop of sour cream and a few grains of caribe. Garnish with lettuce around the edge of the plate and a wedge of tomato spaced equally distant, all facing the same direction.

For Rolled Enchiladas: Dip the lightly fried tortillas into sauce, place a strip of shredded cheese and chopped onion down center of each, and roll up. Place 2 rolled enchiladas on each warmed plate and top with more sauce and cheese. Bake until cheese melts. Add lettuce and tomato wedges around edges before serving.

Makes 4 to 6 servings.

*Three tortillas make a very hearty serving. Most people prefer two.

VARIATION

To serve a crowd, double or triple the recipe. Place the rolled enchiladas in a large shallow baking dish but do not cover with sauce. They will keep 3 days in the refrigerator or can be kept for 3 months in the freezer. Just before serving, heat in a preheated oven. Warm the sauce separately and add just as you are ready to serve. Do not overcook or the enchiladas will be mushy.

— Red Chile Beef Open-Face Enchiladas or Rolled Enchiladas —

This is one of my very favorite dishes, especially when made with blue corn tortillas. It is a popular custom in New Mexico to place a soft-fried egg on top of each enchilada as soon as they come out of the oven. This enchilada is the favorite of natives and are served around the clock . . . great for after a party such as New Year's Eve.

> **Vegetable oil for frying, if rolling**
> **8 to12 white, yellow, or blue corn tortillas**
> **2 cups Red Chile Sauce, made with beef (recipe on page 84)**
> **1 cup shredded Monterey Jack or Cheddar cheese**
> **1 onion, chopped (may be cooked into the sauce)**
> **4 to 6 large eggs, soft fried (optional)**
> **6 to 8 lettuce leaves, coarsely chopped (optional)**
> **2 ripe tomatoes, cut in wedges (optional)**

Preheat oven to 350°F (175°C). If rolling the enchiladas, heat 1/2 inch of oil in a heavy skillet. Add tortillas and fry lightly in batches, being careful not to make them too crisp to roll. Or heat them on a heavy griddle or comal until they are very soft. Warm 4 plates in the preheated oven.

For Flat Enchiladas: Place a little chile sauce on a warmed ovenproof plate, then top with a tortilla (not necessary to fry) followed by cheese, onion, and more sauce. Repeat once or twice more, making a stack of 2 or 3 tortillas layered with cheese, onions, and sauce.* Top each enchilada with more sauce and cheese. Place in the preheated oven until the cheese melts. Top with an egg, if desired, and garnish with the chopped lettuce around the edge of each plate, then place the tomato wedges equidistant around the edges of each plate.

For Rolled Enchiladas: Dip a lightly fried tortilla into the sauce and place a strip each of shredded cheese and chopped onion down the center. Roll up, place 2 rolled enchiladas on each warmed plate, and top with more sauce and cheese. Place in oven until cheese melts. Arrange lettuce and tomato wedges, if desired, around the edges before serving.

Makes 4 to 6 servings.

*Three tortillas make a very hearty serving. Most people prefer two.

VARIATION
To serve a crowd, see variation (page 176) under Green Chile Chicken Enchiladas.

Seafood Enchiladas with Red Onion Salsa Cream

For those who like a somewhat lighter entrée, these have become quite popular.

> **Vegetable oil for frying, if rolling**
> **8 corn tortillas**
> **Red Onion Salsa Cream (recipe follows)**
> **2 cups New Mexico Green Chile Sauce, omitting chicken (recipe on page 83)**
> **2 cups cooked seafood—any combination of small shrimp, crabmeat, and scallops**
> **4 green onion brushes, made by shredding both ends of white**
>   **parts of green onions, chilled in water (optional)**
> **Red leaf, romaine, and curly green lettuces, coarsely chopped**

Preheat oven to 350°F (175°C). If rolling the enchiladas, heat 1/2 inch of oil in a heavy skillet. Add tortillas and fry lightly in batches, being careful not to make them too crisp to roll; or heat them on a heavy griddle or comal until they are very soft. Warm 4 ovenproof plates in the preheated oven. Prepare Red Onion Salsa Cream.

For Flat Enchiladas: Place a spoonful of sauce on a warmed plate, then top with a tortilla (not fried), then with some sauce, about 1/4 cup of seafood, and a generous spoonful of Red Onion Salsa Cream. Repeat once, making a stack of 2 tortillas layered with fillings, and warm in the oven until the cheese melts. To serve, garnish with a green onion brush angled across the top and with chopped lettuces encircling the plate.

For Rolled Enchiladas: Dip a lightly fried tortilla into the sauce. Place 1/4 cup seafood down the center of each tortilla and add a spoonful of Red Onion Salsa Cream. Roll up and place 2 rolled enchiladas seam side down on each plate. Place in a preheated oven 10 to 15 minutes. Warm the sauce separately and add just as you are ready to serve. Do not overcook or the enchiladas will be mushy. Garnish by angling a green onion brush on each and with chopped lettuces.

Makes 4 to 6 servings.

Red Onion Salsa Cream
> **1 cup finely diced red onion**
> **1 cup sour cream**
> **1 cup shredded Monterey Jack cheese**

Combine the red onion, sour cream, and cheese.

TAMALES

There are three basic steps to making these tamales: (1) the filling, (2) the masa, and (3) the stuffing and wrapping in softened corn husks. There are techniques that create fluffy, yummy, and memorable tamales that totally separate them from the usual greasy or dry ones. First, the masa should be coarsely ground and moistened repeatedly and carefully so as not to get lumps or be too dry. Very cold lard must be beaten very rapidly for a while so as to float on ice water. Then the two must be carefully folded together just before rolling the tamales. They should be steamed vertically after appropriately tying them with a loose bottom fold for the grease to escape. The boiling water in the steam should wick up about 1/2 inch into the bottom of the tamales.

You can package complete tamales in airtight plastic bags in serving-size quantities and freeze them for up to six months if not steamed. When steaming tamales from a frozen state, increase the cooking time by half. Any leftover masa mixture or filling can be stored in sealed containers, labeled, and frozen for later use.

Traditional Tamales with Red Chile Beef Filling

These were my mother's favorite tamales. They are delicious, especially when served with the Red Chile Sauce.

60 to 70 corn husks
Beef Filling (recipe follows)
Masa (recipe follows)
Red Chile Sauce (recipe on page 84)

Soak the corn husks in hot water until soft and pliable. Prepare filling and masa, carefully following the directions below. Spread about 2 Tablespoons of masa mixture on each softened corn husk, making a rectangle about 4 x 3 inches and leaving at least a 2-inch border of husk around the edges. Next spoon a strip of the meat filling down the center of each tamale, being careful not to place too much filling in each.

Fold one side of the husk toward the center, covering the meat filling with the masa, then roll the husk (still lengthwise) to form a long, round tamale. Fold the bottom of the husk up and tie loosely with a strip of corn husk, then twist top and tie. If you plan to freeze the tamales, do so at this point, before steaming them.

Stand the tamales upright on a rack in a large pot with water in the bottom to come 1/2 inch deep into the bottoms of the tamales. Steam the tamales in a conventional steamer 45 minutes. Frozen tamales need to steam for 1 1/2 hours. Serve with hot Red Chile Sauce.

Makes 60 to 70 tamales.

Beef Filling

1 1/2 pounds beef stew meat
1 1/2 Tablespoons bacon drippings or lard
1 garlic clove, minced
1/2 cup ground hot chile
3/4 teaspoon salt
1/4 teaspoon ground Mexican oregano

Simmer the meat in a large saucepan in just enough beef stock to cover and cook until tender, about 1 1/2 hours. Reserve stock. Cut the meat into very small cubes or chop in a food processor. Heat bacon drippings in a heavy skillet. Add meat, and cook until very lightly browned. Add the garlic and cook about 2 minutes. Remove pan from heat, cool slightly, and add the ground chile. Season with salt and oregano. Add a cup of meat stock and simmer the sauce, uncovered, stirring frequently, for about 15 minutes or until sauce is thick. Taste and adjust flavor.

Masa

3 1/2 cups warm water, plus more cold water to gain proper texture
6 cups tamale grind masa (yellow, white, or blue)
2 cups very cold lard, cubed into 1 inch cubes
1 1/4 teaspoons salt

Using your hands or a long steel spoon, combine 3 1/2 cups warm water into the masa to make a very thick mixture that holds together; then immediately add about 1/2 cup cold water to yield a softer masa, being sure to squeeze out any lumps. Let it stand.

For the lard, using first a low speed on a heavy-duty electric mixer to break up any lumps, beat until lard is smooth. Switch to highest speed, then whip the lard and salt until very fluffy and will float on water. Combine lard with the masa in the mixer bowl and use the lowest speed to just combine the lard and masa into a smooth mixture.

Baja Seafood Tamales

A medley of spicy seafood tucked into a creamy white masa crust makes for a different, milder flavor.

60 to 70 corn husks
Seafood Filling (recipe follows)
Masa (recipe on page 180), using white masa
New Mexico Green Chile Sauce (recipe on page 83)

Soak the corn husks in hot water until soft and pliable. Prepare filling and masa. Spread about 2 Tablespoons of masa mixture on each softened corn husk, making a rectangle about 4 x 3 inches and leaving at least a 2-inch border of husk around the edges. Next, spoon a strip of the filling down the center of each tamale, being careful not to place too much filling in each.

Fold one side of the husk toward the center, covering the filling with the masa, then roll the husk (still lengthwise) to form a long, round tamale. Fold the bottom of the husk up and tie loosely with a strip of corn husk, then twist top and tie. If you plan to freeze the tamales, do so at this point, before steaming them.

Stand the tamales upright on a rack in a large pot with water in the bottom to come 1/2 inch deep into the bottoms of the tamales. Steam the tamales in a conventional steamer 45 minutes. Frozen tamales need to steam for 1 1/2 hours. Serve with hot green chile sauce.

Makes 60 to 70 tamales.

Seafood Filling
1/2 pound red snapper, cut into small pieces
1/2 pound small shrimp
1/2 pound crabmeat or baby scallops
1 Tablespoon dried shrimp or mixed seafood seasoning
2 Tablespoons crushed caribe chile or to taste
2 Tablespoons jalapeño chiles, minced
1/4 cup cilantro leaves, coarsely chopped
About 1/4 cup white wine

Simmer the snapper, fresh shrimp, scallops, and dried shrimp in a saucepan in just enough water to cover just until shrimp is pink and fish is opaque. Reserve stock for another use. Add crushed chile, jalapeño chiles, and cilantro. Add enough wine to moisten.

Cheesy Chicken Tamales in Blue Corn Masa

Blue corn is one of the most cherished delicacies of northern New Mexico. Part of the heritage of the Pueblo Indians, who are still its chief cultivators, blue corn has a nutlike flavor due to its deeper pigmentation, piñon (pine) roasting, and lava-wheel grinding. If you can't obtain it, substitute white or yellow corn masa.

60 to 70 corn husks
Chicken Filling (recipe follows)
Masa (recipe on page 180), using blue corn masa
12 New Mexico hot green chiles, parched, peeled (see page 340), and sliced into strips

Soak the corn husks in hot water until soft and pliable. Prepare filling and masa. Spread about 2 Tablespoons of masa mixture on each softened corn husk, making a rectangle about 4 by 3 inches and leaving at least a 2-inch border of husk around the edges. Place 1 or 2 green chile strips down the center of each tamale. Next, spoon a strip of filling over the green chiles, being careful not to place too much filling in each.

Fold one side of the husk toward the center, covering the filling with the masa, then roll the husk (still lengthwise) to form a long, round tamale. Fold the bottom of the husk up and tie loosely with a strip of corn husk, then twist top and tie. If you plan to freeze the tamales, do so at this point, before steaming them.

Stand the tamales upright on a rack in a large pot with water in the bottom to come 1/2 inch deep into the bottoms of the tamales. Steam the tamales in a conventional steamer 45 minutes. Frozen tamales need to steam for 1 1/2 hours.

These are very juicy and flavorful and do not need a sauce.

Makes 60 to 70 tamales.

Chicken Filling

2 cups boned, shredded, cooked chicken
1 cup sour cream
2 cups shredded Monterey Jack cheese
Salt (optional)

Combine the chicken with the sour cream and cheese. Season with salt, if desired.

Green Chile Pork-Filled Tamales

In New Mexico, pork and green chile are a favorite combination and are wonderful in tamales!

> 60 to 70 corn husks
> Pork Filling (recipe follows)
> Masa (recipe on page 180), using blue corn masa
> New Mexico Green Chile Sauce (recipe on page 83)

Soak the corn husks in hot water until soft and pliable. Prepare filling and masa. Spread about 2 Tablespoons of masa mixture on each softened corn husk, making a rectangle about 4 x 3 inches and leaving at least a 2-inch border of husk around the edges. Next, spoon a strip of filling down the center of each tamale, being careful not to place too much filling in each.

Fold one side of the husk toward the center, covering the filling with the masa, then roll the husk (still lengthwise) to form a long, round tamale. Fold the bottom of the husk up and tie loosely with a strip of corn husk, then twist top and tie. If you plan to freeze the tamales, do so at this point, before steaming them.

Stand the tamales upright on a rack in a large pot with water in the bottom to come 1/2 inch deep into the bottoms of the tamales. Steam the tamales in a conventional steamer 45 minutes. Frozen tamales need to steam for 1 1/2 hours

Serve with green chile sauce.

Makes 60 to 70 tamales.

Pork Filling

> 1 1/2 pounds lean, stewed, shredded pork
> 1 garlic clove, minced
> 3/4 teaspoon salt
> 1/4 teaspoon ground cumin
> 8 to 12 hot green chiles, parched, peeled (see page 340), and chopped (about 1 cup)

Combine shredded pork, garlic, salt, cumin, and green chiles in a large bowl. Taste and adjust seasoning.

Southern Arizona Green Corn Tamales

Rarely seen, these are wonderful as a side dish or even as a light main dish with a salad. You must steam these horizontally! These are a seasonal specialty as the corn must still be in all layers of the husk with the dark green tendrils still intact.

> **6 ears yellow or white corn in untrimmed husks**
> **1/2 pound Monterey Jack cheese, shredded**
> **1/2 teaspoon salt or as desired**
> **2 Tablespoons sugar (optional)**
> **1/2 pound butter, softened**
> **About 2 Tablespoons half-and-half (optional)**
> **6 green chiles, parched, peeled (see page 340), and cut in matchstick strips**
> **1/4 pound sharp Cheddar cheese, cut in matchstick strips**

Cut stalk end of each ear of corn flush with the base of the ear. Carefully shuck corn, removing each layer of the husk at a time to keep husks intact for wrapping tamales. Rinse and drain the husks and place in a large pot to briefly boil to soften. Cut the corn off the cobs. In a food processor or with a meat grinder, grind corn with the Monterey Jack cheese. Add salt to taste. Taste corn and determine the need for the sugar.

Using an electric mixer, whip butter until fluffy and combine with the corn-cheese mixture. Continue beating until the mixture is very fluffy, like whipped cream. If mixture seems dry, add half-and-half to make a pudding-like texture.

Cut the roasted green chiles into long strips. Spread about 2 Tablespoons of the corn mixture on each husk, leaving about a 2-inch border of husk on all sides. Top with 1 or 2 strips of chile, then add a strip of Cheddar cheese. Roll and tie tamales, using a strip of the dark green outer husks. Stack them horizontally in a basket over 1 inch of water. Steam 20 minutes or until an inserted knife comes out clean. Do not oversteam as they will fall apart.

Makes about 48 tamales.

— Chilied Beef Tostados with Cheeses, Onion, Lettuce & Tomato —

The original! These were served decades before the popularization of the taco salad. You might say this was the original taco salad. The sauce can be frozen up to three months.

Chilied Beef Sauce (recipe follows)
Salad Mixture (recipe follows)
3 cups Frijoles Refritos (recipe on page 220)
1 jalapeño chile, chopped, or to taste
1 medium-size Spanish onion, thinly sliced
8 corn tortillas, fried crisp and left flat or formed into cups (see page 343)
9 ounces sharp Cheddar cheese, cut into thin strips or shredded
1 avocado
1 cup shredded Monterey Jack cheese
8 thin slices of red onion, separated into rings
Salsa of your choice

Prepare the Chilied Beef Sauce and keep it warm. Prepare Salad Mixture and refrigerate. Preheat oven to 325°F (165°C). Heat beans with the jalapeño chile and onions in a small saucepan. Place 2 crisp-fried tortillas on each of 4 ovenproof plates. Spread each with one-eighth of the bean mixture and top with strips of Cheddar cheese. Next, top each with one-eighth of the beef sauce, and bake 25 to 30 minutes.

Peel avocado and cut into thin slices. To serve, top each tostado with Salad Mixture, and garnish with the avocado strips and shredded Monterey Jack cheese. Top with onion rings. Serve salsa on the side.

Makes 4 servings.

Chilied Beef Sauce
1 Tablespoon bacon drippings or butter
1 1/4 pounds beef stew meat, cut into 1/2-inch cubes or 85% lean hamburger
1 medium-size onion, chopped
2 garlic cloves, minced
1/4 cup ground pure, hot red chile
1 cup beef stock
Salt (optional)

Heat bacon drippings in a heavy skillet over medium heat if using stew meat. (Omit the bacon drippings if using hamburger.) Add beef and cook until browned, stirring occasionally. Add onions and garlic, and cook until onion is soft. Drain off excess fat. Remove skillet from heat. Stir in ground chile, add beef stock, and stir. Simmer 1 to 2 hours until meat is very tender and flavors blend. Add salt, if desired.

Salad Mixture

 3 green onions, thinly sliced
 1/2 cup sliced pitted ripe olives
 1 tomato, cut into thin wedges
 2 1/2 cups finely shredded lettuce (iceberg or romaine)

Combine green onions, olives, tomato, and lettuce in a small bowl.

Black Bean Tostados with All the Trimmings

Old San Diego (Old Town), the site of California's first mission (established in 1769 by Father Junipero Serra), boasts many fascinating historic sites and some wonderful restaurants serving such delights as this.

3 cups Frijoles Refritos (recipe on page 220 using black beans)
6 crisp-fried tortillas, corn or white flour
2 avocados
1 green onion, thinly sliced
1 garlic clove, mashed
1 teaspoon finely chopped jalapeño chile
1 1/2 Tablespoons fresh lime juice or to taste
4 to 5 cups finely shredded lettuce (iceberg or romaine)
1 1/2 cups shredded Longhorn cheese* or mild Cheddar cheese
1 to 1 1/4 pounds cooked crabmeat, chicken, or assorted vegetables
3/4 cup pitted ripe olives, halved
12 cherry tomatoes
Creamy Salsa Verde (recipe on page 82), or salsa of your choice

Heat beans in a saucepan and keep warm. Warm the tortillas in a 225°F (105°C) oven. Peel and pit avocados and cut into 1/2-inch cubes. Place avocado cubes in a medium bowl, then gently mix in green onion, garlic, jalapeño chile, and lime juice to taste.

Divide lettuce evenly among 6 plates and top with a warm tortilla. Place some hot beans on top and sprinkle with cheese and crabmeat. Top with avocado mixture, sprinkle with a bit more cheese, and garnish with olive halves and cherry tomatoes. Serve immediately, while beans are still hot, with salsa verde.

Makes 6 servings.

*Longhorn cheese has a softer texture and a milder texture than Cheddar and was so named as it originally was sold in round, cylindrical shapes. Longhorn cheese is also called Colby, but then it is sold in flat disks, often cut in half.

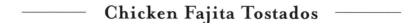

Chicken Fajita Tostados

A delightful salad for luncheon or a light supper.

   Chicken Fajitas (recipe on page 107)
   3 cups shredded lettuce, preferably at least 3 types, or could be mesclun greens
   4 (12-inch) flour tortillas, fried into tostado shells (see page 343)
   Guacamole (recipe on page 13)
   Salsa Fresca (recipe on page 78), Salsa Vinaigrette (recipe on page 73), or salsa of your choice

Prepare fajitas and grill, then cut into 1/2-inch strips. Place shredded lettuce in tostado shells, then top with grilled and sliced chicken pieces. Spoon guacamole over chicken and top with salsa.
   Makes 4 servings.

Flautas

Flautas got their name from their flutelike shape. These crisp rolled tortillas can be filled with your choice of shredded meat, seafood, or refried beans. These can be frozen for three months for later reheating.

   1 quart vegetable oil
   12 corn tortillas
   1 1/2 cups shredded cooked meat, cooked seafood, or Frijoles Refritos (recipe on page 220)
   2 cups shredded lettuce
   1 cup Guacamole (recipe on page 13)
   Sour cream
   Salsas of your choice

Heat about 1 inch of oil to 375°F (190°C) in a deep heavy skillet. Quickly fry the tortillas in the hot oil and drain.
   Place about 2 Tablespoons of the meat, seafood, or beans in a narrow strip down the center of each tortilla. Roll tightly and secure with wooden picks.
   Fry rolled tortillas in the hot oil; turn to brown evenly. Drain well on paper towels. Place on a bed of shredded lettuce with guacamole and sour cream and serve with your favorite salsas.
   Makes 4 to 6 servings.

Shrimp Tostados with Creamy Salsa Verde

A delightful salad for luncheon or a light supper.

2 cups chicken broth
1/4 teaspoon salt
1 Tablespoon pickled jalapeño chile juice
1 1/2 teaspoons fresh lime juice
1/2 pound fresh shrimp, shelled and deveined
1/2 pound bay scallops (or quartered sea scallops)
1/2 pound cod, flounder, or other firm-fleshed white fish, cut in 1 1/2-inch pieces
3 cups shredded lettuce
12 flour tortillas, shaped into tostado shells (see page 343)
Creamy Salsa Verde (recipe on page 82) or salsa of your choice
Crushed caribe chile

Bring chicken broth, salt, pickled jalapeño chile juice, and lime juice to a boil in a saucepan. Add shrimp and poach over low heat 2 minutes or until they turn pink, then remove with a slotted spoon. Add the scallops and fish to the hot broth and cook until opaque, about 7 minutes. Do not overcook. Drain and set aside broth for another use.

Place shredded lettuce in tostado shells, then add seafood. Spoon salsa over salads and sprinkle with crushed chile.

Makes 6 to 8 servings.

Old-Fashioned West Texas Tamale Pie

This simple, straightforward tamale pie can be varied by using chicken instead of beef and by adding more vegetables, even chiles, to the filling.

6 cups water, divided
1 cup yellow cornmeal
2 teaspoons salt, divided
1 pound ground beef
1 medium-size onion, chopped
1 (14 1/2-ounce) can petite diced tomatoes
2 pimientos, chopped
2 garlic cloves, minced
1/2 teaspoon red (cayenne) pepper or to taste

Grease a 3-quart casserole dish. Heat 3 cups of the water to boiling in a large heavy saucepan. Mix cornmeal, teaspoon salt, and remaining 3 cups of water together in a bowl and pour into boiling water, stirring constantly. Cook until thickened into a mush, about 30 minutes. Before it cools, line the bottom and sides of the prepared casserole with three-fourths of the mush, reserving remainder for top. Preheat oven to 325°F (165°C).

Put the meat in a large skillet and cook until red color disappears, stirring to break up meat. Add onion and cook until softened. Add tomatoes, pimientos, garlic, cayenne, and remaining 1 teaspoon salt. Spoon meat mixture into lined casserole dish. Cover with reserved mush and bake, uncovered, 2 hours or until filling is bubbly and the topping is browned.

Makes 4 to 6 servings.

Black Bean, Chipotle & Turkey Tamale Pie

Serve this dish with a tangy green salad or fruit salad for rave reviews.

6 cups water, divided
1 1/2 cups white, yellow, or blue cornmeal
1 teaspoon salt
2 cups cooked black beans with broth
1 (4-ounce) can chopped green chiles
1/2 cup finely chopped onion
2 garlic cloves, minced
2 Tablespoons ground hot chile or to taste
1 chipotle chile (reconstitute if dried, page 341), finely minced, or 1/2 teaspoon powdered
1 teaspoon ground cumin
2 pounds coarsely chopped cooked turkey, could be leftover, poached, or fried ground turkey
1 cup mixed shredded Monterey Jack cheese and Cheddar cheese

Grease a 3-quart casserole dish. Heat 3 cups of the water to boiling in a large heavy saucepan. Mix cornmeal, salt, and remaining 3 cups of water together in a bowl and pour into boiling water, stirring constantly. Cook until thickened into a mush, about 30 minutes. Before mush cools, line bottom and sides of prepared casserole with three-fourths of the mush, reserving remaining mush for the top. Preheat oven to 325°F (165°C).

Combine black beans, green chiles, onion, garlic, ground chile, chipotle chile, and cumin in a large saucepan. Cook, stirring, over low heat to blend flavors. Add turkey and cook until hot. Spoon turkey mixture into the lined casserole and cover with reserved mush. Bake, uncovered, 2 hours or until filling is bubbly and topping is browned. Top with cheese and bake until cheese melts and begins to brown.

Makes 4 to 6 servings.

Pueblo Pies

These are individual tamale pies that are perfect for a supper gathering, or bake in a large casserole dish for a buffet.

    8 cups water, divided
    3 cups yellow, white, or blue cornmeal
    1 Tablespoon salt
    3 pounds ground beef
    1 pound chorizo, chopped
    1 small onion, finely chopped
    1/2 cup chopped celery
    1/2 cup chopped green pepper
    1 cup canned or frozen whole-kernel corn
    1 cup shredded sharp Cheddar cheese
    1 cup pitted ripe olives
    1 cup chicken broth
    1 (28-ounce) can petite diced tomatoes
    2 to 4 Tablespoons ground pure, hot red chile
    1 teaspoon ground cumin
    1 cup shredded Monterey Jack cheese
    12 stuffed green olives, sliced (optional)

Grease 10 to 12 small casserole dishes or one very large casserole dish. Heat 5 cups of the water to boiling in a large heavy saucepan. Mix cornmeal, salt, and remaining 3 cups of water together in a bowl and pour into boiling water, stirring constantly. Cook until thickened into a mush, about 30 minutes. Before the mixture cools, use it to line the bottom and sides of individual casserole dishes or a large casserole dish. Reserve one-quarter of the mush for the topping. Preheat oven to 325°F (165°C).

Cook ground beef, chorizo, and onion in a very large skillet until the red color disappears, stirring to break up the meat. Add the celery, green pepper, corn, Cheddar cheese, ripe olives, chicken broth, tomatoes, ground chile, and cumin. Simmer, stirring to break up the tomatoes, until mixture is somewhat thickened. Taste and adjust seasoning. Spoon the mixture into the mush-lined casserole dishes or dish and top with reserved cornmeal mixture. Bake small casseroles 45 minutes to 1 hour or large casserole about 2 hours or until filling is bubbly and topping is browned. Sprinkle with Monterey Jack cheese and sliced olives, if using. Bake until cheese melts and begins to brown.

Makes 10 to 12 servings.

Blue Corn–Crusted Chicken Pie

This is somewhat lighter, both in flavor as well as calories, than the usual tamale pie. You can make it ahead of time and even freeze it for up to three months.

5 cups water
1 teaspoon salt
2 cups blue cornmeal (white or yellow cornmeal can be substituted)
2 pounds chopped, poached chicken (see page 94) or leftover roasted chicken
2 cups green chiles, parched, peeled (see page 340), and chopped
    or 1 pint frozen or 2 (8-ounce) cans green chiles
2 garlic cloves, minced
1/2 cup chopped Spanish onion
1 (12-ounce) can reduced-fat evaporated milk or 3/4 cup reduced-fat sour cream
Salt to taste
3/4 cup shredded Monterey Jack cheese
1/4 red bell pepper, cut into slivers, or 2 Tablespoons chopped, canned pimiento

Bring the water and salt to a boil in a large heavy saucepan. Gradually stir in the cornmeal and cook until it is thick, about 30 minutes. Set aside to cool slightly.

Preheat oven to 375°F (190°C). Butter a 3-quart casserole dish. When the cornmeal mush is cooled enough to work with, carefully smooth it around the sides and bottom of prepared casserole dish to form a crust about 3/4 inch thick.

Mix together the chicken, green chiles, garlic, onion, milk, and salt in a bowl. Spoon chicken mixture into the mush-lined casserole dish. Sprinkle with cheese and arrange the bell pepper slivers over cheese. Bake 45 minutes or until browned on top and hot throughout.

Makes 4 to 6 servings.

Note: To make ahead, cool quickly, wrap in heavy foil, and freeze for up to 3 months.

Green Chile Beef & Cheese Casserole

While not terribly authentic, this dish is both easy and delicious. It has long been popular for buffet fund-raisers.

1 pound processed cheese, chopped
1 (12-ounce) can evaporated milk
1 pound ground beef
3/4 teaspoon salt
2 garlic cloves, minced
12 corn tortillas
Vegetable oil for frying (optional)
1 (4-ounce) can chopped green chiles
1/2 cup chopped onion

Preheat oven to 350°F (175°C). Grease a 2-quart casserole dish. Melt cheese in evaporated milk in a medium saucepan over low heat, stirring frequently. Reserve. Cook ground beef in a large skillet until browned, stirring to break up meat. Stir in salt and garlic and set aside.

If desired, fry the tortillas: Heat 1/2 inch of oil in a skillet over medium-high heat. Add tortillas, one at a time, and fry on each side only until soft. Drain on paper towels. (Omit frying to decrease calories.)

Place ingredients in greased casserole dish in layers starting with tortillas, then ground beef, green chiles, and onion; repeat layers. Pour reserved cheese sauce over the entire dish and cover. Bake 25 to 30 minutes or until hot.

Makes 4 servings.

VARIATIONS
Add a layer of 1 1/2 cups cooked pinto beans. Substitute ground chicken or turkey for beef.

Spicy Pork Sausage with Red Chile Cream Sauce Bake

The subtle, creamy flavors that combine to create this dish are a definite blend of two cultures . . . Spanish and Pueblo Indians of New Mexico.

12 corn tortillas
1/2 cup vegetable oil (optional)
2 cups shredded Cheddar cheese
2 cups shredded Monterey Jack cheese
1 cup chopped Spanish onion
1 pound spicy fresh pork sausage, crumbled, cooked, and drained
1 (15-ounce) carton ricotta cheese
1 cup half-and-half
1 cup Red Chile Sauce (half the recipe on page 84)

Preheat oven to 350°F (175°C). Grease a 13 x 9-inch baking dish. If desired, fry the tortillas: Heat 1/2 inch of oil in a skillet over medium-high heat. Add the tortillas, one at a time, and fry on each side only until soft. Drain on paper towels. (Omit frying to decrease calories.)

Arrange 3 tortillas in bottom of greased baking dish. Add a layer of one-fourth of the Cheddar cheese, Monterey Jack cheese, onions, sausage, and ricotta. Repeat to make 4 layers. Combine half-and-half and Red Chile Sauce, and pour evenly over the casserole. Bake, uncovered, 30 minutes or until bubbly.

Makes 6 servings.

Southwestern Seafood Lasagne

Seafood combines amazingly well with tomatillos, cream, and green chiles.

    12 corn tortillas
    1/2 cup vegetable oil (optional)
    4 green chiles, parched, peeled (see page 340), and chopped,
        or 1 (4-ounce) can chopped green chiles
    1 (13-ounce) can tomatillos, drained, or 1 cup chopped cooked fresh tomatillos (about 1 pound)
    1/2 cup sour cream
    1 large garlic clove, minced
    1/2 teaspoon salt
    1 1/2 cups shredded Monterey Jack cheese
    6 green onions, thinly sliced
    1/2 pound small shrimp, cooked, shelled, and deveined
    1/2 pound bay scallops, cooked and drained
    2 cups half-and-half or evaporated skim milk

Preheat oven to 350°F (175°C). Grease a 10-inch round baking dish. If desired, fry the tortillas: Heat 1/2 inch of oil in a skillet over medium-high heat. Add tortillas, one at a time, and fry on each side only until soft. Drain on paper towels. (Omit frying to decrease calories.)

Process green chiles, tomatillos, sour cream, garlic, and salt in a food processor or blender until pureed to make a sauce. Place 1 or 2 spoonfuls of sauce in prepared dish and overlap 3 tortillas over sauce. Add a layer of one-fourth each of the cheese, green onions, shrimp, scallops, and sauce. Repeat to make 4 layers. Pour the half-and-half evenly over the dish. Bake, uncovered, 30 minutes or until bubbly.

Makes 6 servings.

Chorizo Lasagne a la Tortilla Flats

Similar to a traditional lasagna, but made with all the flavors and ingredients of the Southwest substituted for the Italian ones.

   1/2 cup vegetable oil (optional)
   12 corn tortillas
   2 cups shredded Cheddar cheese
   2 cups shredded Monterey Jack cheese
   6 green onions, thinly sliced
   1 pound chorizo,* removed from its casings, and chopped, cooked, and drained
   1 (15-ounce) container ricotta cheese
   3 cups half-and-half or 2 (12-ounce) cans evaporated skim milk

Preheat oven to 350°F (175°C). Heat oil in a heavy skillet over medium-high heat, if using. Arrange paper towels over paper plates for draining the tortillas. Lightly fry the tortillas, one at a time, only until soft. Drain well. (Omit frying to reduce calories.)

Using some of the oil, lightly oil a 13 x 9-inch baking dish. Arrange 3 tortillas in bottom of prepared dish. Add a layer of one-fourth each of the Cheddar and Monterey Jack cheese, green onions, chorizo, and ricotta cheese. Repeat to make 4 layers. Pour half-and-half evenly over the dish. (The lasagne can be refrigerated at this point up to 8 hours, or frozen.) Bake, uncovered, 30 minutes, or until bubbly.

Makes 6 servings.

* If chorizo is difficult to find in your local markets, you can make it at home (page 136), or use hot Italian sausage according to the directions on page 137.

Corn Chip Pie

This recipe is based on the one for Individual Frito Pies (see Variation below), but its size makes it perfect for a buffet dinner or fund-raiser.

5 cups broken corn chips
2 cups coarsely chopped Spanish onion
1 recipe Bowl o' Red (recipe on page 42) or 4 cups other favorite chili
1 1/2 cups shredded Monterey Jack cheese
1 1/2 cups shredded Cheddar cheese

Preheat the oven to 350°F (175°C). Butter a 14 x 10-inch baking dish or 2 9-inch-square baking dishes. Spread half of the broken chips in the baking dish. Top with the onion, then add the chili in an even layer. Top with the rest of the corn chips. Mix cheeses together, and sprinkle uniformly over the top of the corn chips. Bake 15 minutes or until bubbly.

Makes 8 servings.

VARIATION

Individual Frito Pie: You can make this tasty little treat right in the small snack-size bag of Fritos corn chips. To do so, crunch the bag with your hand, then cut a lengthwise slash down the bag and cut a crosswise dash at right angles. Top with any favorite heated chili, onions, and cheese, and cook in a microwave oven on High about 1 1/2 minutes or until cheese melts.

Eggs & Cheese

Chiles and chile-laden sauces take eggs out of the realm of the ordinary into the sublime. Huevos rancheros, or ranch-style eggs, are quite possibly one of the world's most special egg dishes. Often only one version is offered in restaurants, but the variations are endless.

Eggs are even popular as a topper for stacked enchiladas and are an excellent foil for a very hot dish. Chorizo, the Mexican pork sausage, offers many more variations with eggs, chiles, and potatoes.

Cheese is an important garnish for many Southwestern specialties, but in some cases, such as chiles rellenos, the cheese is an important part of the dish.

Huevos a la Sonora

Sonora is the Mexican state just south of Arizona. It has had a major influence on the Mexican cooking in Arizona.

Sonoran Sauce (recipe on page 88)
8 corn tortillas
8 large eggs
1 cup shredded Monterey Jack cheese or sharp Cheddar cheese
2 cups coarsely shredded romaine lettuce

Prepare sauce. Preheat oven to 350°F (175°C). Wrap tortillas in foil and set in preheated oven. (At the same time, you can also warm any extra tortillas to be served as bread.)

Poach the eggs. To serve, unwrap the warm tortillas and place 2 in the center of each of 4 ovenproof plates. Top each tortilla with a poached egg. Spoon sauce over eggs, dividing it equally among the 4 servings. Top each serving with 1/4 cup of the shredded cheese.

Place in the oven until the cheese melts, 2 to 5 minutes. Garnish each plate with a tuck of shredded lettuce between the tortillas and serve.

Makes 4 servings.

Huevos Rancheros con Pollo (Ranch-Style Eggs with Chicken)

Here the traditional green chile and tomato sauce is enhanced by the addition of chicken.

4 large flour tortillas
6 green chiles, parched, peeled (see page 340), and cut into 1-inch slices
1 onion, chopped
1 tomato, peeled and chopped
2 cups chicken broth
1 garlic clove, minced
1 pinch of ground Mexican oregano
1/2 teaspoon salt
2 cups chopped poached chicken (recipe on page 94)
8 large eggs
1 cup coarsely chopped lettuce (optional)
1 tomato, cut into wedges (optional)

Preheat oven to 350°F (175°C). Wrap tortillas in foil and set in preheated oven. (At the same time, you can also warm any extra tortillas to be served as bread.) Or heat on a hot griddle or comal. Put 4 ovenproof plates in the oven to warm.

Simmer green chiles, onion, tomato, broth, garlic, oregano, and salt in a skillet. When onion is tender, add chicken and cook together 10 minutes.

Break 1 egg into a cup. Stir a small portion of the sauce in a circular motion, then slip the egg into the stirred sauce. Repeat with the rest of the eggs. Cover the skillet and cook until the eggs are set. Place 1 tortilla on each warmed plate. Place 2 eggs on each tortilla and cover with the sauce. Garnish with lettuce and tomato, if desired.

Makes 4 servings.

VARIATION
Brown 1/2 pound lean ground beef, drain, then add onions and chiles to cooked beef. Continue as above, using beef stock for chicken broth. If a thinner sauce is preferred, use more beef stock.

Huevos Rancheros (Traditional Ranch-Style Eggs)

Often found on Mexican restaurants' menus, this is easy to prepare at home. However, to cut corners, many Southwestern/American Mexican restaurants just use the Green Chile Sauce and the Red Chile Sauce they use for enchiladas, etc., instead of making this, which is the original huevos rancheros. This sauce can be made in advance, so breakfast or brunch is simply a matter of poaching or frying the eggs.

    1 recipe Ranchero Sauce (recipe on page 87)
    8 corn tortillas, plus extra for serving
    8 large eggs
    1 cup shredded mixed Monterey Jack cheese and sharp Cheddar cheese
    3 Tablespoons thinly sliced green onions, tops included
    1 avocado, sliced into thin wedges
    1 large tomato, cut into wedges

Prepare sauce and keep it warm. Wrap tortillas in foil and heat in a 325°F (165°C) oven 15 minutes. Or heat on a hot griddle or comal. Heat 4 ovenproof plates in the oven.

Fry eggs or poach them. Assemble the dish by placing 2 tortillas on each plate and topping with an egg; then pour about 1/4 cup of sauce over each.

Sprinkle 1/4 cup cheese and a few green onion slices over each serving. Place plates back in the oven only long enough to melt the cheese, about 5 minutes. Garnish each plate with avocado and tomato wedges. Pass remaining warm sauce and tortillas separately.

Makes 4 servings.

Huevos Río Grande (Eggs with Cheese Sauce)

These eggs with cheese sauce are a special dish for any occasion.

8 corn tortillas, plus extra for serving
Chile con Queso (recipe follows)
8 large eggs
1 large ripe tomato, thinly sliced
Cooked broccoli or asparagus

Wrap tortillas in foil and heat in a 325°F (165°C) oven 15 minutes to soften. Or heat on a hot griddle or comal. Heat 4 serving plates in same oven. Prepare sauce and keep warm.

Fry or poach eggs. Place 2 tortillas on each of the warm plates, then top with tomato slices and an egg on each tortilla. Pour sauce over eggs. Serve immediately with broccoli or asparagus and the remaining warmed tortillas.

Makes 4 servings.

Chile con Queso

3 Tablespoons butter
1 small onion, chopped
6 green chiles, parched, peeled (see page 340), and cut into 1-inch slices
3 Tablespoons all-purpose flour
1/2 teaspoon salt
Freshly ground black pepper
2 cups milk
1 cup shredded mixed Monterey Jack and sharp Cheddar cheeses

Melt butter in a saucepan over low heat. Add onion and green chiles and sauté until onion is tender, raising the heat to medium. Stir in flour, salt, and pepper. Gradually stir in milk and cook, stirring, until smooth and thickened. Add the cheese and cook, stirring, until melted. Keep the sauce warm over the lowest heat.

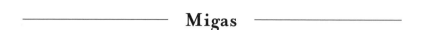

Migas

Sometimes called megas, these eggs are a good way to use up not-so-fresh corn chips and leftover chopped onion, tomato, and chiles. In fact, you could substitute leftover salsa for the separate ingredients.

2 Tablespoons butter
1/2 cup chopped onion, plus extra for garnish
1/2 cup diced tomato, plus extra for garnish
8 large eggs, beaten
2 Tablespoons milk
1 cup coarsely crushed corn chips
2 Tablespoons pickled jalapeño chile slices, plus extra for garnish
1/2 cup mixed shredded Monterey Jack cheese and Cheddar cheese, plus extra for garnish

Melt butter in a large heavy skillet. Add onion and tomato and cook until onion is transparent. Beat eggs in a medium bowl and add milk and crushed corn chips. Mince half the jalapeño chile slices.

Add the egg mixture to the skillet and cook, stirring, just until eggs begin to set. Add cheese. Mince remaining 1 Tablespoon chile slices and add to egg mixture. Continue cooking eggs until set. Serve on warmed plates, topping each serving with a sprinkling of cheese, chopped onion, tomato, and a slice or two of pickled jalapeño chiles.

Makes 4 servings.

Mini Quiches with Green Chile Crusts

The green chiles form the crust for this delicious combination of eggs and cheese.

8 whole green chiles, parched and peeled (see page 340), or 1 (8-ounce) can whole green chiles
1 cup mixed shredded Monterey Jack cheese and Cheddar cheese
6 large eggs
1/2 cup milk
1/2 teaspoon salt
Freshly ground black pepper

Preheat oven to 350°F (175°C). Butter 8 large muffin cups. Cut green chiles open and use one to line each muffin cup, allowing the tops of the chiles to extend up about 1/2 inch around cup tops. Spread cheese evenly over chiles.

Beat eggs in a medium bowl until frothy; add milk, salt, and pepper and beat together. Pour into the chile-lined cups. Bake 20 minutes or until eggs are set and top is lightly browned.

Makes 8 servings.

Chorizo con Papas y Huevos

Mexican hash and eggs, this recipe makes a hearty and rib-sticking brunch.

1 recipe Papas con Chorizo (recipe on page 235)
4 to 8 large eggs
1/2 cup shredded sharp Cheddar cheese (optional)

Prepare Papas con Chorizo according to the recipe. While the hot potato mixture is still in the skillet, make 4 to 8 indentations in it and break an egg into each indentation. Cover skillet and cook about 5 minutes or until eggs are cooked to your preference. Sprinkle with shredded cheese, if desired.

Makes 4 servings.

Ham & Egg Pinwheel with Salsa

Gorgeous is the only word to describe this whirl of brilliant color. A pinwheel omelet is fun to make, and once you've mastered its techniques, there is no limit to the variety of fillings. The major trick is buttering the waxed paper generously enough; otherwise, what should be a puffy baked omelet immediately becomes very thin and wrinkled looking. Plan carefully so that the omelet, once done, can be served immediately. Have the eggs separated, the pan ready, and the fillings laid out in advance. Then allow twenty to twenty-five minutes to prepare the omelet and bake, roll, and serve it.

12 (about 4-inch-square) thin slices of cooked ham
12 extra-large fresh eggs, separated
3/4 teaspoon salt
Freshly ground black pepper
6 large green chiles, parched, peeled (see page 340), and coarsely chopped
6 large red lettuce leaves, rinsed and drained (optional)
1 cup fresh salsa of your choice

Preheat oven to 350°F (175°C). Cut a piece of waxed paper to exactly fit the bottom of a 14 x 10-inch jellyroll pan. Generously butter pan, place paper in the bottom, and generously butter paper. Place ham in the oven to heat while beating eggs.

Beat egg whites in a large bowl until very stiff but not dry using an electric mixer. In another bowl beat egg yolks, salt, and pepper with a whisk until thick and lemon-colored. Then fold together, carefully blending the two and retaining as much air as possible; the mixture should stand in definite peaks. Spoon one-fourth of the mixture in each corner of prepared pan. Working gently with a spatula, smooth to uniform thickness, making certain that the mixture is smoothed to all sides of the pan. Air pockets will make a ragged-appearing edge.

Place the pan in the center of oven. (Ovenproof plates can also be placed in the oven to warm.) Bake 15 to 20 minutes or until dry when pierced with a sharp knife or wooden pick. Set the pan on a wire rack and cut around the outside edge to free the omelet from the pan. Add a layer of the ham, spreading to cover the top of the omelet. Sprinkle the green chiles uniformly over the top.

Begin to roll by lifting up the long side next to the edge and rolling it like a jellyroll, gently pressing the omelet down and removing the paper as you roll. (The first time, you may want a helper for this.) Continue to roll until you have completely rolled the omelet into one large, long roll. Do be very careful not to rip or tear the omelet as this will destroy the overall appearance. Serve slices of the omelet immediately on warmed plates, garnishing each with a lettuce leaf if using and some salsa. Serve extra salsa alongside.

Makes 6 servings.

Breakfast Burritos

Scrambled eggs are truly versatile. Here's just one more way to serve them. You can add almost any ingredients and use virtually any of the fresh or cooked salsas over them.

4 corn tortillas or flour tortillas
4 teaspoons butter
1/2 cup chopped onion
2 medium-size potatoes, cooked and sliced
1/2 cup chopped green chile
1/2 cup mixed shredded Monterey Jack cheese and Cheddar cheese
8 large eggs, beaten
1 cup salsa of your choice
1/4 cup sour cream (optional)
Cilantro or parsley (optional)

Wrap tortillas in foil and warm in a 350°F (175°C) oven while preparing the filling (or heat in the microwave oven without foil for 10 to 15 seconds just before adding filling). Melt butter in a large skillet over medium heat, then add the onion and potatoes and cook until lightly browned.

Push potato mixture to the side, reduce heat to medium-low, and add eggs. Cook, stirring gently to mix with potatoes, until eggs begin to set. Add green chiles and cheese and cook, stirring, until hot. Spoon one-fourth of mixture down the center of each warm tortilla and roll. Then place on plates and top with salsa and sour cream and cilantro, if using.

Makes 4 servings.

New Mexico Potato Omelet

A Spanish potato omelet spiced Southwestern style. In Spain, the word *tortilla* refers to baked omelet-style eggs with a potato crust.

6 Tablespoons butter or Spanish olive oil, divided
1 large Spanish onion, chopped
1 garlic clove, minced
2 medium-size potatoes, thinly sliced
1/2 teaspoon salt, plus more to taste
Freshly ground black pepper
8 large eggs
1/4 cup water or beer
2 Tablespoons ground hot or mild chile or 4 to 6 parched, peeled (see page 340), and chopped
1 (4-ounce) can chopped green chiles
1/4 cup shredded Monterey Jack cheese
1 cup Salsa Fresca (recipe on page 78)

Melt 3 Tablespoons of the butter in a large heavy skillet over low heat. Add onion and garlic, and sauté until onion is clear, raising the heat to medium.

Add potatoes and cook, turning occasionally, until tender and slightly browned. Season with a little salt and pepper, remove from heat, and let cool 5 to 10 minutes.

In a large bowl beat together eggs, water, 1/2 teaspoon of salt, pepper to taste, and ground chile. Stir in the green chiles and cooled potato mixture. Heat 3 Tablespoons more butter in the skillet, pour in the egg mixture, and, as it sets on the bottom, gently shake the skillet and slide a spatula under egg mixture to keep omelet from sticking.

When omelet is almost firm, cook the top in one of the following two ways: Place a plate on top of the skillet and invert both so that the omelet is on the plate, bottom side up, and then slide back into the skillet to briefly cook the other side. Or place skillet under a preheated broiler about 4 inches from heat and broil until just set but not dry, 2 or 3 minutes. Sprinkle with cheese and cut into wedges. Serve Salsa Fresca separately.

Makes 4 servings.

Vegetable Omelet

The cooked vegetables add flavor and act almost like a sauce for the omelet.

2 Tablespoons extra-virgin Spanish olive oil
3 cups chopped tomatoes
1 onion, chopped
2 celery stalks, thinly sliced
1 garlic clove, minced
1/2 teaspoon salt
1/4 cup cooked green peas
4 green chiles, parched, peeled (see page 340), and sliced into 1-inch rings
6 large eggs
1/4 cup water
1/2 teaspoon salt
Freshly ground black pepper
Coarsely shredded lettuce (optional)

Heat oil in a large skillet. Add tomatoes, onion, celery, garlic, and salt, and cook just until onion is softened. Add peas and green chiles and cook until hot. Remove vegetables from skillet and keep warm.

Beat eggs, water, salt, and pepper until combined. Pour all at once into the skillet and cook until eggs set, lifting with a spatula to let uncooked eggs flow to bottom of pan. Slide the omelet onto a platter and spoon most of the vegetables over one side of the omelet, then fold the omelet over and top with remaining vegetables. Garnish with lettuce and serve.

Makes 2 to 3 servings.

Chilaquiles con Huevos

A hearty, flavorful way to use dry corn tortillas or not-so-crisp corn chips.

2 Tablespoons butter
1 medium-size onion, finely chopped
1 garlic clove, minced
3 Tablespoons ground pure, mild red chile
1/2 teaspoon salt
1/4 teaspoon ground cumin
1 large tomato, cut into thin wedges
1/4 cup tomato juice
1/4 cup chopped canned green chiles or to taste
3 cups corn chips or corn tortilla pieces torn into approximately sixths
8 large eggs
3/4 cup shredded Monterey Jack cheese
1/4 cup ripe olive slices

Preheat oven to 350°F (175°C). Heat butter in a saucepan over low heat. Add onion and garlic and sauté until onion is softened, using medium heat. Remove from heat and stir in ground chile, salt, cumin, tomato, tomato juice, and green chiles. Return to heat and simmer about 5 minutes. Stir corn chips into the hot sauce, simmer 2 minutes, and pour into a large, shallow ovenproof serving dish.

Poach or fry the eggs and arrange them on top of the chilaquiles. Sprinkle with cheese. Bake about 10 minutes or until cheese is melted. Garnish with olives and serve immediately.

Makes 4 servings.

Chorizo Custard Pie

A real taste treat. The fluted crust is attractive, crisp, and delicious.

Vegetable oil or lard for frying
1 (12-inch) flour tortilla (if making your own, use pieces of
    dough the size of a tennis ball) (see page 242)
2 or 3 Tablespoons tomato sauce mixed with 1/2 teaspoon jalapeño pickle juice, Red Chile
    Sauce (recipe on page 84), or New Mexico Green Chile Sauce (recipe on page 83)
1/2 pound chorizo
4 large eggs
1 cup half-and-half
1 Tablespoon coarsely chopped fresh cilantro
1/2 teaspoon salt
Freshly ground black pepper
1 cup shredded Monterey Jack cheese
1/2 cup sliced green onions, tops included
1 small tomato, seeds removed, chopped
Salsa of your choice

Preheat oven to 375°F (190°C) (350°F, 175°C if using a glass pie plate). Butter a 9-inch pie plate and set aside. Heat 1/4 inch of oil in a large skillet over medium-high heat. Add tortilla and fry very briefly, being careful not to make it too crisp to fit into the pie plate. Fit the tortilla into the pie plate and brush it with tomato sauce mixture.

Remove chorizo from its casing, crumble it into a skillet, and fry, using medium heat until well browned. Drain chorizo well and scatter it over the tortilla shell. In a medium bowl beat eggs with the half-and-half, cilantro, salt, and pepper. Stir in cheese, green onions, and tomato. Pour the egg mixture into the tortilla shell and bake for about 30 minutes or until the eggs are set. Serve with sauce on the side.

Makes 6 servings.

VARIATION
Substitute crabmeat or chopped cooked chicken for the chorizo, add green chiles, and garnish with sour cream.

Chile-Cheese Omelet

Serve this special easy-to-prepare dish for brunch, lunch, or supper. Serve fresh fruits and your favorite hot rolls.

2 cups Chile con Queso (recipe on page 17)
8 large eggs
1/4 cup milk
1/2 teaspoon salt
Freshly ground black pepper
1 Tablespoon butter
4 to 6 green chiles, parched and peeled (see page 340), or 1 (4-ounce) can whole green chiles
1 medium-size tomato, diced
1 fresh jalapeño chile, cut in thin slices

Prepare Chile con Queso and set aside. In a medium bowl beat eggs with a whisk or fork until foamy. Add milk, salt, and pepper. Mix well. Melt butter in a heavy 10-inch skillet using medium-low heat. Pour egg mixture into the skillet and cook until eggs are just set, lifting with a spatula to let uncooked eggs flow to bottom.

To serve, remove to a large oval or rectangular platter and place green chiles evenly over one side of the omelet. Fold the other half over chiles and drizzle top with the Chile con Queso. Place a few squares of tomato on top of sauce, then arrange 2 or 3 jalapeño chile slices on tomatoes.

Makes 4 servings.

Huevos Argentinean (Eggs with Chimichurri Salsa)

The crisp, fresh Chimichurri Salsa has yet another use!

4 thick ham slices
Vegetable oil, if needed
4 medium-size potatoes, peeled and sliced
1/2 cup coarsely chopped red onion
2 Tablespoons unsalted butter
8 large eggs
1 cup Chimichurri Salsa (recipe on page 81)
Crushed caribe chile
1 medium-size tomato, cut into 8 wedges

Cook the ham in a large heavy skillet over medium heat until browned on both sides. Transfer to 4 plates and place the plates in a 250°F (120°C) oven. Add enough oil to the ham fat in the skillet to measure about 2 Tablespoons. Add the potatoes and cook, turning occasionally, until lightly browned. Add the onion to the potatoes and stir to mix well. Cook until potatoes are tender.

When potatoes are almost done, melt butter in another large heavy skillet over medium-low heat. Break eggs, one at a time, into a cup, then slip each egg into the skillet. Spoon Chimichurri Salsa evenly around the whites of the eggs. Cover and steam until eggs are set.

Spoon potatoes onto the warmed plates with the ham. Place 2 eggs on each plate, spooning the salsa remaining in the skillet around the eggs. Sprinkle a little crushed chile over egg yolks. Garnish each plate with tomato wedges.

Makes 4 servings.

Chiles Rellenos de Queso

Relleno means "stuffed" in Spanish. Stuffed chiles have become known as chile rellenos and have long been popular in the states along the Mexican border. The New Mexico batter is more versatile as the chiles can be held in a warm 250°F (120°C) oven for up to two hours before serving. Also, any leftovers can be served warmed and cut into one-inch pieces as appetizers or served whole and warmed. The California batter doesn't hold up well if held.

> 1/2 pound Monterey Jack cheese, cut into 12 long, narrow strips
> 12 large green chiles, parched and peeled (see page 340), with
>   stems on, or 3 (4-ounce) cans whole green chiles
> New Mexico–Style Batter (recipe follows) or California-Style Batter (recipe follows)
> Vegetable oil for frying
> Red Chile Sauce (recipe on page 84) or New Mexico Green Chile Sauce (recipe on page 83)

Insert cheese strips into green chiles, using the small slit that was cut for steaming (or cut a small slit just below the stem). Make sure that the cheese strips do not burst the chiles or overfill them. Drain chiles thoroughly on paper towels on both the bottom and top to ensure that the batter will coat them well. Prepare your choice of batters.

Preheat 3 to 4 inches of oil to 375°F (190°C) in a deep heavy skillet, large saucepan, or deep-fat fryer, using a deep-fat thermometer for accurate temperature. Dip the stuffed chiles in the batter. Place in hot oil and fry until golden. Tongs work best to hold and turn them. Drain well on paper towels. Serve piping hot with chile sauce.

Makes 4 to 6 servings.

New Mexico–Style Batter

> 1 cup blue, white, or yellow cornmeal
> 3/4 cup all-purpose flour
> 1 teaspoon baking powder
> 1/2 teaspoon salt
> About 1 cup milk
> 2 large eggs or 3 large egg whites

Combine cornmeal, flour, baking powder, and salt in a shallow bowl. Beat milk and eggs together in a small bowl, then add to the cornmeal mixture. Mix until smooth. If necessary, add a little more milk to make a smooth batter that will coat the chiles.

California-Style Batter

4 1/2 Tablespoons all-purpose flour
3/4 teaspoon baking powder
1/4 teaspoon salt
4 large eggs, separated

Combine flour, baking powder, and salt in a small bowl. Beat egg whites in a medium bowl until soft peaks. Beat the yolks in another medium bowl until thick, adding a couple of spoons of the beaten whites. Add the flour mixture slowly to the yolks, and stir to blend well. Beat whites until stiff, but not dry. Gently fold in the egg whites.

—— Corn-Stuffed Chile Relleno Bake ——

A simplified way to prepare chiles rellenos. The flavor remains and the chiles are softer in texture.

2 Tablespoons butter, lard, or bacon fat
1 medium-size onion, chopped
1 garlic clove, minced
3 cups fresh or frozen whole-kernel corn, thawed
1 large tomato, peeled and chopped
1/4 to 1/2 teaspoon salt
Freshly ground black pepper
Pinch of ground Mexican oregano
2 1/2 cups shredded Monterey Jack cheese or mild Cheddar cheese or a mixture, divided
12 green chiles, prepared as for Chiles Rellenos de Queso (recipe on page 214)
1 cup half-and-half
Ranchero Sauce (recipe on page 87)

Preheat oven to 350°F (175°C). Melt butter in a large heavy skillet using a low heat. Add onion and garlic, turning the heat to medium, and cook until onion is soft. Add corn, tomato, salt, pepper, and oregano, and simmer, uncovered, 15 to 20 minutes, to reduce the liquid. Remove from heat. Stir 2 cups of the cheese into the corn mixture and let cool.

Stuff green chiles with corn mixture and place them in a large shallow baking dish. Pour half-and-half evenly over the chiles and sprinkle with the reserved 1/2 cup cheese. Bake, uncovered, 25 minutes or until sauce is bubbly and cheese is lightly browned. Spoon Ranchero Sauce down the center of the chiles and serve any remaining sauce on the side.

Makes 4 to 6 servings.

SIDE DISHES

The two typical side dishes for many Southwestern restaurants are refried beans and Mexican rice. Delicious, more versatile versions of each are included here. In this chapter, rice is combined with mushrooms, piñon nuts, bell peppers, and spicy chiles. Beans and rice are also combined in new ways in such recipes as Black Beans, Pintos, Garbanzos & Rice. Some of the Southwest's traditional foods are featured, particularly corn, beans, and squash, often creatively flavored with chiles. Eating your vegetables is definitely not boring in this cuisine!

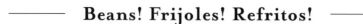

Beans! Frijoles! Refritos!

Pinto beans are the king of Southwestern cooking, much the same as the black bean is the king of Latin cooking. Increasingly, however, there are more and more varieties of beans being combined. And you might be amazed to learn that the pinto is the healthiest of all beans. With pinto beans, freshly harvested, the beans are white or light tan with brown flecks. The older the beans, the more browned they become and the longer it takes to cook them to the desired doneness.

The lowly bean is praised and appreciated more than it used to be as people have come to recognize beans as a very positive source of nutrients and fiber. They fit perfectly into today's desire for less fat and smaller amounts of meat, and are no longer thought of as the poor man's meat substitute.

In fact, my railroader grandfather, who hobnobbed with the cowboys running the cattle drives, learned that the cowboys used beans to stretch the meat as the chili (usually made from meat with no beans) ran thin on the drives. And further, they added tomatoes to the thin chili to keep it red. That is how Kansas chili (with beans and tomatoes) came into being, because Kansas was the end of the trail.

When there was no meat in sight, beans were the meal, often served with corn bread. Beans are a popular filling, and in fact are the traditional filling for burritos. They are served under stews and chili, used as a stuffing for both corn and flour tortillas and even sopaipillas, and as a topping for Navajo fry bread.

Beans were often the "potatoes" served on West Texas ranches, where to feed large numbers of cowboys, the steaks were deep fried and served with stewed pinto beans. Sometimes on Saturdays we would fix three different kinds of beans at a time. Each type and preparation has its unique personality, both in appearance and flavor, making a delicious feast with our favorite toppers of chopped fresh onions, jalapeño chiles—fresh or pickled—hot pepper sauces, and the ubiquitous corn bread, spoonbread, or hoe cakes. I must admit that just the thought of one of those bean dinners makes me hungry!

Beans take well to the addition of different flavors. However, when you're cooking them, always wait to add salt until the beans soften. Water is best for starting the cooking process; then, once they have started to soften, chicken stock, beef stock, chiles, herbs, and any member of the onion family can be added. Pork, especially smoked pork, is traditional for flavoring most all types of beans.

Once cooked, beans can be cooled quickly, packed into freezer containers, and frozen for up to six months without any measurable loss of flavor or nutrition. Beans can also be used for numerous dishes—from salsas to salads, soups, sandwiches, casseroles, and tortilla dishes.

Black Beans with Ham Hocks

When served with fresh lime juice, chopped green onions, and a topping of sour cream, this can be either a side dish or a light main dish.

    1 pound dried black beans
    2 ham hocks
    1 cup coarsely chopped Spanish onion
    4 garlic cloves, minced
    2 Tablespoons ground hot chile
    2 teaspoons cumin
    1 teaspoon salt or to taste
    3 or 4 cups rich chicken stock as needed

Rinse and sort beans, picking out any foreign objects. Place beans and ham hocks in a heavy 5-quart pot. Add enough water to come about 3 inches above the level of the beans and meat. Boil 10 minutes,using high heat; reduce heat and simmer 30 minutes, uncovered. Add the onion, garlic, ground chile, and cumin; simmer 1 hour or until a bean will mash easily against the side of the pot, cooking uncovered for the entire period. Add chicken stock as needed to keep the liquid level to about 1 inch above the level of the bean mixture. When beans are done, cook to reduce the liquid to the desired consistency. Taste and adjust seasonings.

Makes 2 quarts or 4 to 6 servings.

Gordon's Famous Frijoles

More highly flavored than ordinary beans, these can be served as a side dish or as a main course with sliced ham on the side. In any case, top them with chopped onions and pickled jalapeño chiles. Corn bread is a must.

    1 pound dried pinto beans
    1 ham hock, ham bone, or 1/2 pound salt pork
    Water
    1/2 teaspoon freshly ground black pepper
    2 garlic cloves, minced
    2 cups Spanish onion, coarsely chopped
    3 to 4 cups rich chicken stock, as needed
    1 teaspoon salt or to taste

Rinse and sort beans, picking out any foreign objects. Place beans and ham hock in a heavy 5-quart pot. Add enough water to come about 3 inches above the level of the beans and meat. Boil 10 minutes on high heat, reduce heat, and simmer 30 minutes, uncovered. Add the pepper, garlic, and onion and simmer 2 hours or until a bean will mash easily against the side of the pot. Add chicken stock as needed to keep the liquid level about 1 inch above the level of the bean mixture. Taste and determine the need for salt and salt accordingly. When beans are done, cook to reduce the liquid to the desired consistency.

Makes 2 quarts or 4 to 6 servings.

Frijoles Refritos (Refried Beans)

When made this way, refried beans are very flavorful and excellent as a side dish and in nachos and many Southwestern specialties. They are the basis for burritos.

    2 Tablespoons butter, bacon drippings, or lard
    1 garlic clove, minced
    2 Tablespoons finely chopped Spanish onion
    4 cups cooked pinto beans or 2 (16-ounce) cans pinto beans
    Salt and freshly ground black pepper
    1 cup mixed shredded Monterey Jack cheese and Cheddar cheese (optional)

Melt butter in a large heavy skillet over medium heat. Add the garlic, and as soon as it starts to turn golden, add the onion. When the onion begins to soften, add the pinto beans with a little liquid and mash them as they fry, leaving some beans whole for contrast, using a potato masher or a heavy wooden spoon adding additional liquid as needed. (The liquid could be water or chicken stock.)

Fry over medium heat about 5 minutes, turning to prevent burning, until the beans reach a thick, paste-like consistency. Top with cheese, if desired, and serve piping hot.

Makes 6 to 8 servings.

Black Beans, Pintos, Garbanzos & Rice

This three-bean, two-rice dish is excellent alone or with most any entrée.

1 1/2 teaspoons unsalted butter
1 1/2 Tablespoons chopped onion
1 garlic clove, minced
2 cups cooked white rice*
2 cups cooked brown rice*
1/2 cup cooked or canned pinto beans, drained
1/2 cup cooked or canned black beans, drained
1/2 cup cooked or canned garbanzo beans, drained
Salt to taste
1/4 teaspoon cumin

Melt butter in a large saucepan. Add onion and garlic and cook until softened. Add the white and brown rice, beans, salt, and cumin. Cook over medium-low heat, stirring occasionally, until hot. If mixture is too dry, add a little water or chicken stock.

Makes 4 servings.

*To cook white rice, add 3/4 cup rice to 2 cups boiling chicken broth. Stir and cover. Simmer over low heat 15 minutes. For brown rice, use 1 cup rice and 2 1/2 cups chicken broth. Simmer 45 minutes.

Mexican Fried Rice

This is a very popular side dish in Mexican-American restaurants. This rice can be frozen for up to three months.

   2 cups chicken broth
   3/4 cup long-grain white rice
   1 teaspoon salt (optional)
   3 Tablespoons vegetable oil
   1 (8-ounce) can Spanish-style tomato sauce or 1 cup Bloody Mary mix
   2 Tablespoons chopped fresh green bell pepper
   1 Tablespoon minced onion

Bring the broth to a boil, using high heat, in a medium heavy saucepan. Add rice and salt, cover, and cook over medium heat 15 minutes or until tender but not mushy. Heat oil in a heavy 10-inch skillet using medium heat, reducing to low. Add the rice and stir-fry 10 minutes. Add the tomato sauce, bell pepper, and onion and stir until well mixed. Cover and cook over low heat, stirring occasionally, 5 minutes.

Makes 4 to 6 servings.

Dulce (Sweet Rice)

This sweet rice is a refreshing complement to many spicy Southwestern specialties like moles and picadillo. It can be frozen for up to three months.

   2 cups water
   1 Tablespoon light brown sugar or honey
   3/4 cup long-grain white rice
   1/2 teaspoon salt
   2 Tablespoons butter
   1/2 cup raisins, coarsely chopped
   1/2 cup piñon nuts (pine nuts) or slivered almonds, toasted

Place water, sugar, rice, and salt in a medium heavy saucepan. Bring to a boil, using high heat; immediately reduce heat to low, stir in butter, raisins, and toasted nuts, and cover tightly. Simmer without peeking 15 minutes or until rice is tender and liquid is absorbed. Spoon into a warmed serving dish and serve hot.

Makes 4 servings.

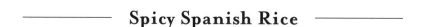

Spicy Spanish Rice

Spicier than most rice dishes, this one contains three kinds of chiles and beans.

2 Tablespoons butter or bacon drippings
1 cup long-grain white rice
1 cup chopped Spanish onion
1 cup chopped canned tomatoes
1 1/2 cups chicken stock
1 Tablespoon ground hot chile
1 1/2 Tablespoons crushed caribe chile
1 teaspoon drained chopped canned jalapeño chile
1 garlic clove, minced
1/8 teaspoon ground cumin
1/8 teaspoon ground Mexican oregano
1/2 teaspoon salt
1 cup cooked or canned red kidney beans

Melt butter in a saucepan over low heat. Add rice and onion and cook, using medium heat, stirring, until onion is translucent. Stir in tomatoes, chicken stock, ground chile, crushed chile, chopped jalapeño chile, garlic, cumin, oregano, and salt and bring to a boil. Reduce heat to low, cover, and simmer 15 minutes or until the rice is done, but not mushy. Add the beans and simmer 5 minutes, or until the rice is tender.

Makes 4 to 6 servings.

Black Beans with Rice

When made with black-eyed peas, this dish is called "Hoppin' John." It's an excellent side dish for grilled meats.

    2 Tablespoons butter
    3/4 cup each red and green bell pepper, diced
    1/2 cup yellow bell pepper, diced
    1 cup Spanish onion, diced
    1/2 teaspoon minced garlic (1 clove)
    1 1/2 cups long-grain white rice
    2 1/2 cups chicken broth
    1 teaspoon ground cumin
    1/2 teaspoon salt
    1 cup cooked or canned black beans

Melt butter in a large saucepan over low heat. Turn up the heat to medium and add the bell peppers, onion, and garlic and cook until onion is translucent. Stir in rice, then add broth, cumin, and salt and stir well. Cover and simmer 15 minutes or until rice is tender and liquid is absorbed. Stir in beans and heat over low heat until thoroughly heated.

Makes 4 to 6 servings.

VARIATION
Use cooked pinto beans instead of black beans.

Rice with Vegetables

The vegetables add bright bits of color and flavor to this savory rice. The dish can be frozen for up to three months.

3 tablespoons butter, lard, or bacon fat
1 cup long-grain white rice
1 cup chopped onion
2 garlic cloves, minced
1 medium-size carrot, shredded
1/2 cup uncooked green peas
1 medium-size tomato, peeled and chopped
1/2 teaspoon salt
2 green chiles, parched, peeled (see page 340), and chopped
1 3/4 cups chicken broth

Melt butter in a heavy skillet over low heat. Add rice and cook, raising the heat to medium, stirring until golden. Add onion and garlic and cook until onion begins to soften. Stir in carrots, peas, tomato, salt, green chiles, and broth. Bring to a boil, using high heat, then immediately reduce heat to very low, and cover. Simmer 20 minutes. Taste and adjust seasonings and serve hot.
Makes 6 servings.

Mushroom-Piñon Rice

Piñon nuts, or pine nuts, are a traditional food in the Southwest and are gathered in the fall by the Native Americans. This highly flavored rice is a good accompaniment to pork or poultry dishes.

2 Tablespoons butter
1 cup chopped onion
1 1/2 cups chopped fresh mushrooms
1 1/2 cups long-grain white rice
5 garlic cloves, minced
3/4 teaspoon dried leaf Mexican oregano
2 cups chicken broth
1/4 cup piñon nuts (pine nuts)
1 teaspoon salt
2 Tablespoons raisins (optional)

Melt butter in a large saucepan with a tight-fitting cover over low heat. Add onion and mushrooms, raising the heat to medium, and cook until onion is softened. Add rice, garlic, and oregano and stir until well mixed. Stir in broth, piñon nuts, salt, and raisins, if using. Cover and simmer 15 minutes without peeking, then stir. If the rice is not as tender as desired, cook to the desired doneness, adding more stock if needed.

Makes 4 servings.

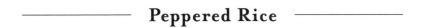

Peppered Rice

An excellent rice side dish with peppers and cumin. It's one of my favorites with fajitas and most any Southwestern entrée.

2 Tablespoons butter
1 cup diced green, red, and/or yellow bell pepper
1 cup chopped onion
2 garlic cloves, minced
2 teaspoons ground cumin, divided
1 1/2 cups long-grain white rice
About 2 1/2 cups chicken broth

Melt butter in a large saucepan over low heat. Add bell pepper and onion, raising the temperature to medium, and cook until onion is softened. Add garlic, 1 teaspoon cumin, and rice and stir until well mixed. Add broth. Cover and steam 15 minutes without peeking, then stir. If not as tender as desired, cook to the desired doneness, adding more stock if needed. Stir in remaining 1 teaspoon cumin and taste and adjust seasonings.

Makes 6 to 8 servings.

Wild Rice Pilaf

This pilaf is excellent with poultry and game dishes, and it is a luxury with fajitas.

1/4 cup butter or margarine
1/2 pound fresh mushrooms, sliced
1 garlic clove, minced
1 Tablespoon minced green bell pepper
1 cup wild rice, rinsed and drained
1/2 cup slivered almonds
1 teaspoon salt
Freshly ground black pepper
3 cups chicken broth

Preheat oven to 350°F (175°C). Melt butter in a large skillet using low heat and add mushrooms, garlic, bell pepper, wild rice, almonds, salt, and pepper, raising the temperature to medium. Stir-fry 2 minutes. Spoon into a large shallow baking dish. Add broth. Stir until mixed. Cover tightly. Bake about 1 hour or until rice is tender and liquid is absorbed.

Makes 4 to 6 servings.

Calabacitas Picantes (Zucchini with Chiles)

This recipe is also very good with yellow summer squash, chayote, and green or wax beans. It can be frozen up to six months without the sour cream.

2 Tablespoons butter
1 onion, chopped
1 garlic clove, minced
3 or 4 zucchini (each about 8 inches long), sliced
2 large tomatoes, peeled and chopped or 1 (14 1/2-ounce) can petite diced tomatoes
1 teaspoon chopped cilantro or parsley
2 green chiles, parched and peeled (see page 340), sliced into thin strips
Salt and freshly ground black pepper to taste
1 cup shredded Monterey Jack cheese
1/2 cup sour cream (optional)

Melt the butter in a large skillet over low heat. Add onion and garlic and cook over medium heat until onion is softened. Add the zucchini, tomatoes, cilantro, green chiles, salt, and pepper. Cover and simmer, reducing the heat to low until squash is tender, 10 to 15 minutes.

Preheat broiler. Place vegetables in a flameproof serving dish, sprinkle with cheese, and broil just long enough to melt the cheese. Serve immediately with dollops of sour cream, if desired.

Makes 4 servings.

Grilled Marinated Veggie Kabobs with Salsa

For greatest flavor, color, and control over cooking time, I recommend grilling each vegetable individually in kabobs, rather than alternating them on a skewer with meat, as is so often done. You can make substitutions for some of the vegetables if necessary.

    4 small yellow summer squash
    4 small zucchini
    2 small eggplant
    12 cherry tomatoes
    1 teaspoon salt
    12 small white onions
    24 large mushrooms
    1/2 cup virgin olive oil
    1/2 teaspoon ground Mexican oregano
    1 Tablespoon crushed caribe chile

Rinse the yellow squash, zucchini, eggplant, and tomatoes. Cut the yellow squash and zucchini into 1-inch-long pieces; have at least 12 equal pieces of each. Cut eggplant into at least 12 cubes, leaving the peel on. Salt the eggplant cubes generously and place between 2 double layers of paper towels. Peel the onions and parboil about 5 minutes, if large. Clean the mushrooms with a moist cloth, removing the stems.

Combine oil, oregano, and chile in a small bowl. Alternate vegetables or cook each individually on 6 12-inch skewers, putting tomatoes in the very center and a mushroom on each end.

Preheat grill. Brush kabobs with oil mixture, then grill over a medium fire, turning frequently and brushing with the rest of the oil mixture, about 20 minutes, or to the desired degree of doneness.

Makes 6 servings.

Chile Corn Custard

The combination of flavors and the proportions are the very best! You can keep this warm in a low oven or on a warmer up to one and a half hours, making it a great buffet or party dish.

2 large eggs, beaten
4 cups yellow or white cream-style corn
3/4 cup yellow or white cornmeal
1/2 teaspoon salt
1 garlic clove, minced
1/2 teaspoon baking powder
1/4 cup melted butter
4 ounces canned chopped green chiles
3/4 cup shredded sharp Cheddar cheese

Preheat oven to 375°F (190°C). Place eggs, corn, cornmeal, salt, garlic, baking powder, butter, green chiles, and cheese in a blender or food processor and puree until uniformly smooth. Pour into a buttered 1 1/2-quart casserole. Bake 30 minutes, then check for doneness. An inserted knife near center should come out clean.
Makes 4 to 6 servings.

Chile, Corn & Greens

Substitute any of your favorite greens for the spinach.

1 1/2 pounds fresh spinach
1 Tablespoon butter or bacon drippings
3 Tablespoons chopped onion
2 ears corn, cooked and kernels cut off, or 1 cup canned whole-kernel corn
1 (4-ounce) can chopped green chiles or 2 to 4 fresh chiles,
    parched, peeled (see page 340), and chopped
3/4 teaspoon salt

Wash spinach and remove large stems. Steam, covered in a medium saucepan, 10 minutes, using medium heat and stirring occasionally. Drain and chop spinach. Melt butter in a large skillet on medium heat. Add onion and cook until softened. Add corn, spinach, green chiles, and salt. Cook a few minutes just to blend flavors.
Makes 4 to 6 servings.

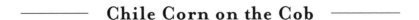

Chile Corn on the Cob

Fresh corn on the cob takes very well to spicy cooking water. The vinegar supplies just the right flavor balance.

    2 quarts water
    1/4 cup crushed caribe chile
    2 Tablespoons cider vinegar
    1 teaspoon salt
    4 ears corn, shucked

Combine water, crushed chile, vinegar, and salt in a large pan, and bring to a boil. Add corn and cover. Cook about 5 minutes or just until milk in corn is set. Drain immediately and serve hot. *Makes 4 servings.*

Grilled Mexican Corn

This is one of our family's favorites. Whenever you have the grill hot and corn handy, do try this version of corn on the cob. The Mexicans like this with mayonnaise sprinkled with red chile flakes, such as caribe!

    6 ears fresh corn, shucked
    About 2 Tablespoons olive oil
    1 fresh lime (optional)
    1 Tablespoon crushed caribe chile (optional)
    1/2 cup mayonnaise or to taste (optional)

Lightly brush each ear of corn with oil. Then place on a grill rack over hot coals and cook, turning each side as the kernels get light touches of browning. The ears should cook until all the kernels are somewhat dried out and milk is set when pierced with a fork, about 15 minutes. When done, either squeeze lime juice over each ear and sprinkle with crushed chile to taste, or serve with bowls of mayonnaise and caribe chile for guests to spread on the corn. Serve hot.

Note: Any leftovers can be used in salads or other vegetable dishes.

Texas-Style Green Beans & Potatoes with Bacon

Texans really prefer their green beans literally boiled until soft. They eat them with hot pepper sauce.

1/4 pound thick-sliced bacon, cut into 1/2-inch pieces
1/2 cup chopped onion
1 pound small red new potatoes, quartered
1 1/2 pounds fresh green beans
Water
1 cup chicken stock
Hot pepper sauce

Sauté bacon in a large heavy skillet over medium heat until crisp. Drain off all but 1 Tablespoon of fat and then add onion and cook until softened. Add potatoes and cook, turning occasionally, until potatoes are slightly brown, then add green beans and enough water to cover. Cook, covered, about 30 minutes. As the water level goes down, add chicken stock. Serve with hot pepper sauce.

Makes 6 to 8 servings.

Fried Tomatoes with Cream

This dish was intended to be prepared with red ripe tomatoes, but green tomatoes are okay.

> 1/4 cup all-purpose flour
> 1 teaspoon salt
> 1/8 teaspoon pepper
> 2 teaspoons fresh basil, minced
> 4 tomatoes, sliced 1 inch thick
> 1/4 cup butter
> 1 1/2 cups half-and-half or sour cream

Combine flour, salt, pepper, and basil in a shallow bowl. Coat tomato slices with the flour mixture.

Melt butter in a large skillet over low heat. Add tomato slices, turning the heat to medium, and fry 10 minutes, turning once. Remove tomatoes. Stir in half-and-half or sour cream and mix well with the juices in the skillet. Simmer 5 minutes. Pour over the tomatoes.

Makes 4 servings.

Fried Green Tomatoes with Green Chiles

The blue corn coating adds a distinctive touch, as do the green chiles.

> 3/4 cup finely ground blue cornmeal
> 1/2 teaspoon salt
> 1 1/4 pounds green tomatoes
> 2 Tablespoons or more of butter or bacon drippings
> 4 green chiles, parched, peeled (see page 340), and chopped

Combine blue cornmeal and salt in a shallow bowl. Slice tomatoes and dip each slice into the cornmeal, pushing down to make sure that the cornmeal sticks. Meanwhile, melt the butter in a heavy skillet over low heat. Add tomato slices, turning heat to medium high, and brown on both sides. Spread green chiles evenly over the tops of the tomato slices, cover the skillet, and steam about 5 minutes or until the chile juices are hot and blended in with the tomatoes.

Makes 4 to 6 servings.

Papas Fritas (Spicy French Fries)

This spicy version of french-fried potatoes has drawn many a rave at both restaurants where I've chefed, as well as from friends. In fact, when I had a restaurant in New York City, several customers stated that my fries were the best in the Big Apple!

2 quarts vegetable oil for deep-frying
1 pound russet potatoes
1/4 cup ground mild or hot chile
1/4 cup sea salt or kosher salt
1/4 cup sugar

Heat oil in a deep-fat fryer to 375°F (190°C). Scrub potatoes (do not peel) and slice into strips for french fries. Fry a handful of strips at a time until golden. Meanwhile, mix ground chile, salt, and sugar together and place in a shaker or a large shallow bowl. As the fries are done, shake or toss in the seasoning mix. Serve hot.

Makes 4 servings.

Papas con Chorizo (Potatoes with Sausage)

This is terrific with scrambled eggs for brunch.

3/4 pound chorizo
1 large onion, chopped
2 large potatoes, cut into 1/4-inch-thick slices
2 to 4 green chiles, parched, peeled (see page 340), and chopped (optional)

Remove chorizo from its casing, crumble, and cook in a large skillet over medium-low heat until lightly browned, stirring to break up meat. Stir in the onion and potatoes, and cook over high heat to crisp the outside edges of the potatoes. Cover and cook until potatoes are very tender, stirring occasionally. The potatoes will take on a wonderful reddish color from the sausage. If using, add green chiles just as the potatoes are almost done. Serve piping hot.

Makes 4 servings.

Sopa Seca de Fideo

The Mexican version of pasta, this is somewhat similar to Mexican or Spanish rice in flavor.

3 Tablespoons vegetable oil
1 (7-ounce) package fideo or very fine noodles, broken up*
1 cup finely chopped onion
2 garlic cloves, minced
1/4 cup chopped green bell pepper
1/2 cup chopped red bell pepper
1 jalapeño chile, minced
1/2 cup chopped tomato
1 1/2 cups hot chicken broth
1/4 cup Italian flat leaf parsley, chopped

Heat oil in a large skillet over medium-high heat. Add fideo and brown. It is more delicate than rice so be careful not to burn. Drain off excess oil. Push the fideo aside, add onion, garlic, bell peppers, and jalapeño chile, and cook until onion is soft. Add tomato and mix together with the fideo. Add hot chicken broth, cover, and cook over low heat until the liquid is almost completely absorbed. Sprinkle with parsley and serve.
Makes 4 to 6 servings.

VARIATION
Add 1 cup cooked chicken for a main-dish meal.
 *Angel hair pasta broken into about 1 inch pieces may be substituted.

Steamed Kale

This colorful vegetable dish will do double duty—substituting for both the salad and a side dish.

    2 Tablespoons butter
    1/4 medium red onion, thinly sliced
    1 garlic clove, minced
    1 small head purple flowering kale or other type kale, thinly sliced
    1/2 teaspoon salt
    Freshly ground black pepper

    Melt butter in a large skillet on low heat. Add onion, raising the temperature to medium, and cook until softened. Add garlic and cook 1 minute. Add kale, salt, and pepper and stir. Cover and cook over low heat 5 minutes, or until the kale is tender, stirring occasionally.

Makes 4 servings.

Seared Carrots & Onions, Mexican Style

In Mexico, the carrots always seem to have more flavor; it's because they do not boil them.

    2 Tablespoons vegetable oil
    4 large carrots, sliced diagonally
    2 large onions, cut in half vertically and sliced into sections
    1 teaspoon ground Mexican oregano
    3/4 teaspoon salt
    Freshly ground black pepper
    1 teaspoon fresh mint, minced

    Heat oil in a large skillet on medium-high heat. Add carrots and stir-fry about 3 minutes. Then add the onions and stir-fry until onions are caramelized on the edges and lightly browned. Add oregano, salt, pepper, and mint, and stir to blend.

Makes 6 servings.

BREADS

In Southwestern cooking, quick breads such as tortillas, corn bread, and biscuits are more traditional than yeast rolls. Cornmeal is a very popular ingredient in breads and muffins; however, cornmeal is not used to make corn tortillas, which require masa (ground corn treated with lime). Sopaipillas are a puffy fried bread that is very popular in New Mexico.

Breads, particularly when spread with butter, are a terrific way to soothe the taste buds after one too many hot chile dishes. Beware though—sometimes chiles are even added to the breads!

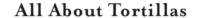

All About Tortillas

Tortillas are a traditional food in Mexico that date back to ancient times. They are the main ingredient in many dishes, such as enchiladas, tacos, and burritos, as well as the bread that is most often eaten with meals. They often serve as a spoon or eating utensil, either in the soft, just-baked form or as crispy chips.

Corn tortillas are very simply made, just requiring masa harina, which can be purchased in the instant form ready for preparation. Or the masa can be purchased already moistened, just needing to be pressed in a tortilla press or shaped with the palms of the hands.

Corn tortillas were the first and are still the most popular tortillas throughout Mexico. The earliest were most probably made from white corn, as it was the first cultivated corn. In recent times, with the development of more varieties, yellow corn has become popular, especially in the United States.

More recently, blue corn has become popular. In New Mexico, blue corn was always the ritual grain, and it has found increasing favor, although it is still not commonly found throughout the United States, Canada, or Mexico.

Tortillas are never discarded. If slightly stale, they are used as an ingredient in casseroles such as chilaquiles, tamale pies, or soups or as a thickener for sauces, such as moles. Or they can be crisply fried whole, when they are known as a tostado, or in pieces, when they are called a tostadita or chip.

The masas on the market today are all instant, not requiring the thirty minutes or so of rest—often called for in older recipes—before rolling. To form tortillas, locals pat balls of moistened masa with their hands until they get a thin round disk, which they bake on top of a hot well-seasoned griddle or comal. In Old Mexico, a popular cooking surface has been the large round lid from an oil drum.

Contemporary cooks usually favor a hot seasoned griddle, or comal, which can be a cast-iron stove lid or a cast-iron griddle. It must be heated to at least 450°F (230°C). Tortilla presses are used to shape the dough, as it requires lots and lots of practice to make uniformly shaped tortillas by hand.

Flour tortillas were introduced by the Spanish when they brought wheat into Mexico and the Southwest. They are popular in New Mexico, the entire Southwest, and northern Mexico. Flour tortillas are made differently from corn ones. The dough, once made, must be kneaded until gluten develops and the appearance is smooth. Then the dough must rest until it relaxes enough to be rolled into a thin, round tortilla. For this, a short, uniformly round rolling pin, known as a bolillo, is used. Once rolled, it is also baked on a hot, seasoned cast-iron griddle or comal.

Corn Tortillas

The Mayans of ancient Mexico worshiped the god of corn and believed that man was created from corn dough, or masa, meaning that eating food made from corn was a special or even sacred experience.

These tortillas are to be served warm as bread, or fried to become the basis for tacos, tostados, or other dishes. They can be frozen for up to six months.

2 1/2 cups masa from white, yellow, or blue corn
1 teaspoon salt
About 1 1/4 cups hot water

In a medium bowl combine the masa and salt, and make a well in the center of the mixture. Mix in 1/2 cup of the water. Continue adding water a little at a time, mixing well, until a firm dough is formed. Finish mixing with your hands; this will give the best dough. It should be firm and springy to the touch, not dry, crumbly, or sticky.

To test, roll a small ball of dough and flatten it between your hands. If cracks form, add more warm water; if it is too moist and sticks to your palms, add more masa. For the best-quality tortillas, the dough should be easily handled.

Preheat a comal or well-seasoned griddle until it is very hot. Pull off one ball of dough at a time about the size of a Ping-Pong ball. Keep remaining dough covered with plastic wrap. Roll each ball until round, then place it between sheets of waxed paper. Flatten in a tortilla press or with a rolling pin or the bottom of a cast-iron pan. Trim the edges, if you wish, to get a round shape.

Place the tortillas, one at a time, on the hot ungreased surface and cook 1 or 2 minutes on each side, or until they bubble up a bit and have brown specks and become "dry" on the surface. Stack them as they cook, and wrap in a warm towel or napkin.

Makes 12 (6-inch) tortillas.

VARIATION
The dough can also be used to make 16 (5-inch), 24 (4-inch), or 40 (3-inch) tortillas.

Blue Corn Tortillas
The dough for blue corn tortillas normally must be more moist. However, if you still have trouble rolling and baking them, add 1/2 to 1 cup white or yellow masa and more warm water to make the dough easier to shape into tortillas.

White Flour Tortillas

These taste best when they're fresh, but they freeze well for up to three months (only half as long as the corn tortillas).

>   4 cups unbleached flour
>   2 teaspoons baking powder
>   1 teaspoon salt
>   1/2 teaspoon sugar
>   1/4 cup lard or butter
>   1 1/2 cups warm water

Stir together the flour, baking powder, salt, and sugar in a large bowl. Cut in the lard or butter with a pastry blender, food processor, or mix with your fingers.

Add all of the water to form a rather soft dough. Turn dough out onto a board or other hard surface and very carefully knead in extra flour a little bit at a time, until a smooth, soft dough results. Cover with the mixing bowl and allow to sit until the dough has relaxed and your finger will easily push to the bottom when poking it. Cut the dough into 12 equal portions and work each to form a round ball of dough, about 2 inches. Cover the balls of dough with plastic wrap. Roll out each ball with a rolling pin into circles about 6 inches in diameter and 1/8 inch thick.

Meanwhile, set a cast-iron comal or griddle over medium-high heat. Rub it with oil and then wipe it dry with a paper towel. When it is hot, bake the tortillas about 45 seconds on the first side, or until small brownish spots appear on the cooked surface. Turn with a spatula and cook for just a few seconds on the other side until it is done and has no shiny spots. Keep warm and serve immediately.

Makes 12 (6-inch) tortillas.

VARIATION
Whole-Wheat Flour Tortillas: To make whole-wheat tortillas, substitute whole-wheat flour for one-half of the unbleached flour. Follow directions above.

Blue Corn & Jalapeño Skillet Bread

The best blue cornmeal is smoked in adobe ovens and then lava-wheel ground to a fine flour consistency. With the popularity of blue corn, a lot of blue corn on the market is "filled," or blended with white or yellow corn. For the best flavor, buy pure blue cornmeal. The moist quality of this bread has long made it a favorite with campers and picnickers.

    2/3 cup butter, melted
    1 cup sour cream
    2 large eggs, beaten
    2 cups cooked or canned whole-kernel corn, drained
    1 cup blue cornmeal
    1 1/2 teaspoons baking powder
    3/4 teaspoon salt
    1/4 pound Monterey Jack cheese or Cheddar cheese, or a
        combination of the two, sliced 1/4 inch thick
    1/4 cup sliced jalapeño chiles, either pickled or fresh

Preheat oven to 375°F (190°C). While oven is preheating, place the butter in a 9-inch cast-iron skillet or a 9-inch round or square cake pan. Watch carefully and when butter is melted, pour it into a bowl (leave enough butter in the pan to coat) and combine it with the sour cream, eggs, and corn. In a separate bowl mix the cornmeal, baking powder, and salt together and make a well in the center. Add butter mixture and mix until just combined.

Pour almost half the batter into the prepared pan. Cover with the sliced cheese and jalapeño chiles. Pour the remaining batter over cheese and chiles and smooth to cover the filling. Bake 30 to 40 minutes or until golden and a wooden pick inserted in the center comes out clean. Serve warm.

Makes 9 to 12 servings.

Blue Corn Sticks

Blue cornmeal, used by the Pueblo Indians living along the northern Río Grande in New Mexico, makes these corn sticks special. I have always thought that blue cornmeal improves the taste of any recipe in which it is used. If you can't find blue cornmeal, it can be ordered by mail. These bread sticks can be frozen, tightly wrapped, for up to three months.

2 large eggs, beaten
3/4 cup milk
1/2 cup butter or bacon drippings, melted
1 1/2 cups blue cornmeal or cornflour
2 Tablespoons sugar
1 1/2 teaspoons baking powder
1/2 teaspoon salt

Preheat oven to 350°F (175°C). Thoroughly grease and flour a cast-iron corn stick pan. In a small bowl combine eggs, milk, and butter. In a medium bowl combine cornmeal, sugar, baking powder, and salt. Add the egg mixture all at once to the cornmeal mixture; stir only until thoroughly moistened.

Pour batter into prepared pan, filling two-thirds full. Bake 15 to 20 minutes or until bread pulls away slightly from the sides of pan and is lightly browned. Allow to cool 10 minutes on a cooling rack, then carefully remove.

Makes 18 to 24 corn sticks.

VARIATION
Add 3 or 4 seeded and chopped mild green chiles to the batter.

Blue Corn Piñon Pancakes

I created these very special pancakes for my New York City restaurant when I was longing for New Mexico's blue corn and piñon nuts. I like to serve these with butter and honey or fruited yogurt.

1 cup buttermilk
1 large egg, beaten
2 Tablespoons vegetable oil
1/2 cup all-purpose flour
1/2 cup blue cornmeal
1 Tablespoon sugar
1 teaspoon baking soda
1/2 teaspoon salt
1 Tablespoon piñon nuts (pine nuts) toasted*

Combine buttermilk, egg, and oil in a small bowl. Combine flour, cornmeal, sugar, baking soda, and salt in a medium bowl. Add the buttermilk mixture all at once to the flour mixture and stir until just combined. Fold in nuts.

Preheat a griddle over medium heat. Drop batter from a large spoon to make 4- to 6-inch-diameter pancakes. Cook until bubbles form over the top; turn and cook the other side until brown.

Makes 2 to 3 servings.

*Toast the piñon nuts on the griddle on which you will be baking the pancakes. Toast only until they darken somewhat. Watch carefully since they burn easily.

Piki Bread

Piki is a paper-thin, crisp bread that is baked for feast days and ceremonies by Native Americans. Lard is the traditional fat, but you can substitute vegetable shortening.

1/4 cup fine blue corn masa or cornmeal
3/4 teaspoon salt
7 cups water
1/4 cup cornstarch mixed with 1 cup cold water
2 Tablespoons lard or solid vegetable shortening

In a 3-quart or larger saucepan, combine the masa and salt, then slowly stir in the water. When well mixed, bring to a boil over high heat, stirring constantly, taking care not to let the mixture spatter onto your arms. Reduce heat and simmer, stirring occasionally, 15 minutes. In a bowl stir cornstarch into the water, then stir it into the masa mixture. Return to boiling, using high heat, and cook, stirring, 1 or 2 minutes.

Heat an electric griddle to 350°F (175°C) or a cast-iron griddle over medium heat until a drop of water dances on the surface. The batter tends to spatter while cooking, so if possible, either cook outdoors or place a foil shield around the cooking area. Brush griddle lightly with shortening; when hot, add the batter 1/3 to 1/2 cup at a time. Once the mixture is on the griddle, spread it with a spatula to make a rectangle. Bake until dry, 4 to 5 minutes.

Makes 6 to 8 pieces.

VARIATION
This can be made with any type of cornmeal, but blue cornmeal is traditional.

Texas Corn Bread

Texans like their cornbread simply—not too rich and crumbly, not too sweet, just plain good. This is a typical Texas recipe.

3 Tablespoons butter or bacon drippings
1 large egg, beaten
1 cup milk
1 cup yellow cornmeal
1 cup all-purpose flour
2 Tablespoons sugar
2 teaspoons baking powder
1 teaspoon salt

Preheat oven to 400°F (205°C). Place a heavy ovenproof skillet containing the butter in the oven. Watch carefully so as not to burn. When melted, remove from the oven.

Combine egg and milk in a small bowl. Combine cornmeal, flour, sugar, baking powder, and salt in a medium bowl. Stir egg mixture into cornmeal mixture, stirring just until moistened. Add melted butter from skillet and thoroughly mix. Pour batter into the hot skillet. Bake 30 minutes or until golden brown.

Makes 4 servings.

VARIATION
Add 1/2 cup shredded Cheddar cheese and 2 fresh thinly sliced jalapeño chiles to the batter.

Green-Chile Corn Muffins

These are nice served with almost any meal. They stay moist and do not crumble as badly as some of the corn breads containing corn kernels.

1 (8-ounce) can cream-style corn
3/4 cup milk
1/3 cup melted butter, bacon fat, or vegetable oil
2 large eggs, beaten
1 1/2 cups yellow, white, or blue cornmeal
1 teaspoon baking powder
1/2 teaspoon baking soda
1 teaspoon salt
1 teaspoon sugar
1 1/2 cups mixed shredded Monterey Jack cheese and Cheddar cheese
1 (4-ounce) can chopped green chiles, drained

Preheat oven to 400°F (205°C). Line 18 muffin cups with paper liners, use silicone muffin cups, or grease and flour each cup. In a medium bowl stir together corn, milk, butter, and eggs. In a large bowl whisk together cornmeal, baking powder, baking soda, salt, and sugar. Add corn mixture to the cornmeal mixture and mix just until combined.

Spoon a large spoonful of batter into each prepared muffin cup and top with a little cheese and green chile, dividing evenly and reserving a little for sprinkling on top. Top with remaining batter and reserved chiles and cheese, filling each cup two-thirds full.

Bake 25 to 30 minutes, or until muffins are golden and a wooden pick inserted in the center comes out clean.

Makes 18 muffins.

Hoe Cakes

The origins of this dish are definitely from the Deep South. They were brought west after the Civil War, and are more popular in Texas than farther west. Their name comes from the traditional method of cooking: the batter was placed on a preheated hoe, then cooked in the fire. Hoe cakes are a good and simple addition to a chile-laden meal.

1 1/2 cups coarsely ground cornmeal
1 teaspoon sugar
1 teaspoon salt
1 1/2 Tablespoons half-and-half
1/2 cup boiling water
1/2 cup cold water
1/2 to 1 teaspoon crushed caribe chile (optional)

Combine cornmeal, sugar, and salt in a medium bowl. Stir in half-and-half. Stir in boiling water, then cold water. Stir in crushed chile, if using.

Meanwhile, heat a griddle to medium-hot, or until a drop of water dances on the surface. Oil griddle. To form the cakes, dip your hands in cold water, then form the batter by handfuls into 1/2- to 3/4-inch-thick cakes. Bake the first side until browned, then turn and brown the other side.

Makes 4 to 6 servings.

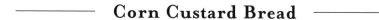

Corn Custard Bread

The custard-like quality of this corn bread makes it special. It has a somewhat marbleized effect, with a custard rippling through it. Save the leftovers; it reheats well.

2 Tablespoons unsalted butter
2 large eggs
1/4 cup sugar
2 cups milk, divided
1 cup buttermilk
1 teaspoon baking soda
1 teaspoon salt
1 2/3 cups coarsely ground cornmeal
1/3 cup all-purpose flour

Preheat oven to 375°F (190°C). Place a large heavy skillet containing the butter in the oven. In a large bowl whisk together eggs and sugar. Stir in 1 cup of the milk, the buttermilk, soda, and salt and mix together. Add the cornmeal and flour, then add the melted butter from the skillet, swirling the butter around the skillet before pouring it out. Stir just to combine.

Pour the mixture into the hot skillet. Pour the remaining 1 cup of milk carefully over the top of the batter but *do not stir*. Bake 30 minutes or until a wooden pick inserted in the center comes out clean.

Makes 6 to 8 servings.

Arizona Spoon Bread

This double-corn, soft-textured bread got its name honestly—it is simply delicious spooned out as a side dish.

    3/4 cup white or yellow cornmeal
    1 Tablespoon baking powder
    1/4 teaspoon baking soda
    1 teaspoon salt
    1 cup boiling water
    1 (17-ounce) can white or yellow cream-style corn
    2 large eggs, beaten
    1 cup milk
    2 Tablespoons butter, melted

Preheat oven to 350°F (175°C). Heat a medium heavy skillet until hot and butter it generously. In a medium bowl combine cornmeal, baking powder, soda, and salt. Stir in boiling water. Mix thoroughly.

Mix in the corn, eggs, milk, and butter. Pour batter into prepared skillet and bake about 30 minutes, or until browned on top and until a wooden pick inserted in the center comes out clean.

Makes 4 servings.

Best Biscuits Ever!

Even though these contain yeast, you can make them without rising. Also, once the dough is made, you can refrigerate it for a few days. These are outrageous with most any spread; we have always loved them with honey or honey butter.

1 package (about 1 Tablespoon) active dry yeast
2 Tablespoons warm water
5 cups all-purpose flour
2 Tablespoons sugar
1 1/2 teaspoons salt
1 teaspoon baking soda
1 teaspoon baking powder
1/2 cup unsalted butter, cut into pieces, chilled
2 cups buttermilk

Preheat oven to 400°F (205°C). Grease a large baking sheet. Dissolve yeast in the warm water in a small bowl and set aside. Combine flour, sugar, salt, and baking powder in a large bowl. Cut in butter with a pastry blender or 2 knives until the mixture resembles coarse cornmeal.

Make a well in the center of flour mixture and add dissolved yeast and buttermilk all at once. Stir to make a soft dough, then place half the dough on a lightly floured board and knead until well combined; repeat with the other half.

When dough is smooth, roll it out to 1/2 inch thickness. Cut into rounds with a 1 1/2- to 2-inch-round cookie cutter. Place on greased baking sheet. Bake 12 to 15 minutes or until lightly browned.

Makes about 48 biscuits.

Note: You can wrap one-half the dough tightly in a plastic bag and bake half the biscuits in up to a week later.

Texas-Style Drop Biscuits

Drop biscuits have always been popular in the South and particularly in Texas, as biscuits are a mainstay with most families. This recipe has been passed down for generations in my husband's family and has very little fat.

    2 cups all-purpose flour
    1 1/2 teaspoons sugar
    1 teaspoon baking powder
    1/2 teaspoon baking soda
    1/2 teaspoon salt
    1 Tablespoon solid vegetable shortening, butter, or lard
    About 3/4 cup buttermilk

Preheat oven to 400°F (205°C). Grease a baking sheet. Combine flour, sugar, baking powder, baking soda, and salt in a medium bowl. Cut in shortening until mixture resembles crumbs. Then stir in the buttermilk to make a dough that holds its shape but is not dry. Add a little more buttermilk, if needed.

Drop by spoonfuls onto greased baking sheet. Bake 12 to 15 minutes or until lightly browned. *Makes 18 to 24 biscuits.*

Grandma Clara's Buttermilk Biscuits

Our family always felt biscuits were more of a special occasion bread and usually served them only for bountiful breakfasts. This was my paternal grandmother's recipe, which she always served with homemade strawberry jam and very fresh sweet butter that she made herself.

2 cups all-purpose flour
2 teaspoons baking powder
1 teaspoon sugar
3/4 teaspoon salt
1/2 teaspoon baking soda
1/4 cup unsalted butter
2/3 cup buttermilk

Preheat oven to 400°F (205°C). Combine flour, baking powder, sugar, salt, and baking soda in a medium bowl. Cut in butter until mixture resembles coarse cornmeal. Stir in the buttermilk to make a soft dough.

Turn out dough onto a floured board and knead lightly 7 or 8 times, just until smooth. Roll to about 3/4 inch thickness and cut into rounds with a 1 1/2-inch-round cutter. Place on an ungreased baking sheet. Bake about 12 minutes, or until light golden. Serve immediately.

Makes about 24 biscuits.

Bolillos (Mexican Hard Rolls)[1]

Once you make these easy-to-do Mexican hard rolls, you will find yourself baking them again and again. They were influenced by the French, who ruled Mexico for a time in the nineteenth century.

1 package (about 1 Tablespoon) active dry yeast
2 teaspoons sugar
1 3/4 cups warm water (110°F, 45°C)
1 teaspoon salt
6 cups sifted all-purpose flour

Stir yeast and sugar together in a large bowl, then stir in warm water. Add salt, then beat in flour, 1 cup at a time, beating well after each addition. After adding the fifth cup of flour, add flour slowly until the dough becomes too stiff to stir.

Turn out onto a lightly floured board and knead 8 to 10 minutes, or until smooth and satiny. Place in a lightly greased bowl, turning to grease the top of the dough, then cover with a sheet of waxed paper and a towel. Let rise in a warm place free of drafts about 1 hour, or until doubled in bulk. When dough is doubled, punch down and allow to double again, checking after 1/2 hour to see if it has doubled.

Cut dough into 36 equal pieces. Shape into long, slender rolls, twisting each end. Or roll the dough into very long ropes about 2 inches in diameter and snip off 3- to 4-inch pieces of dough, twisting each end. For authentic-looking rolls, they should be rather flat with twisted ends. Lay rolls about 2 inches apart on a lightly floured baking sheet. After shaping the rolls, slash the tops with a sharp knife or scissors. Cover with a towel and let rise until doubled in bulk, about 30 minutes.

When nearly doubled, preheat oven to 400°F (205°C) and lightly oil the tops of the rolls with a pastry brush. Bake 20 to 30 minutes or until lightly browned. Serve piping hot with lots of butter.

Makes 36 rolls.

---

1. From *Tex-Mex Cookbook* by Jane Butel. Copyright © 1980 by Jane Butel. Reprinted by permission of Crown Publishers, Inc.

Bear Paw Bread

This pueblo bread originated in the Río Grande area of New Mexico and has always been made in the shape of a bear's paw. It is crusty, easy to make, delicious to eat, and most impressive in appearance! In New Mexico, Native American women sell this bread as a popular treat in and near the pueblos and around the plazas in Albuquerque and Santa Fe. They bake the loaves in hornos (adobe ovens). This recipe can be easily halved; it can also be frozen, well wrapped, for up to three months.

> **2 cups hot water**
> **2 teaspoons solid vegetable shortening, lard, or butter**
> **1 teaspoon honey**
> **1 teaspoon salt**
> **2 packages (about 2 Tablespoons) active dry yeast**
> **1/2 cup warm water (110°F, 45°C)**
> **About 10 cups all-purpose flour, divided**

Place the 2 cups of hot water, shortening, honey, and salt in a large bowl; stir to melt shortening. Dissolve yeast in the warm water in a small bowl. When liquid in the large bowl has cooled to room temperature, stir in yeast mixture.

Add flour 1 cup at a time, beating well after each addition. After 8 cups have been added to the dough, place the remaining 2 cups on a board and turn out dough over flour. Knead dough until smooth and elastic, 10 to 15 minutes.

Place dough in a lightly greased very large bowl, turning to grease top of dough. Cover with a kitchen towel and let rise about 1 1/2 hours, or until doubled in bulk. Turn out on a floured board and knead again for about 3 minutes.

Grease 4 (9-inch) pie pans or 2 baking sheets. Divide dough in quarters and form each piece into a flat circle about 8 inches in diameter. Fold each circle almost in half, allowing the bottom to extend about an inch beyond the top. With a sharp knife, slash the dough twice, cutting through both layers of dough, about halfway back to the fold. This will form three separated sections—the bear's paw. Place each loaf in a greased pie plate or on a baking sheet, curving the folded side in a crescent shape. Separate the slashes. Cover loosely with a towel and let rise until doubled in bulk, about 30 minutes.

Preheat oven to 350°F (175°C) and place a shallow pan of hot water in the center of bottom rack of the oven. Place loaves on the top rack. Bake about 45 minutes, or until lightly browned and bread sounds hollow when tapped.

Makes 4 loaves.

Navajo Fry Bread

The traditional hole in the center of the bread evolved from the Navajo method of frying the pieces of dough on the end of a green piñon twig. To this day, fry bread is considered a very special treat at outdoor festivals, horse shows, and fairs. I can remember waiting in what seemed to be a quarter-mile line just to get a freshly fried disk!

Fry bread is extraordinarily versatile. Native Americans add fresh herbs, like mountain oregano and crushed juniper berries and seeds, to the dough before frying. It can be served as a bread with chile dishes, or used as a basis for Navajo tacos. When freshly fried and drizzled with honey, it becomes a delicious dessert.

4 cups all-purpose flour
4 teaspoons baking powder
1 teaspoon salt
About 1 1/3 cups warm water
Lard or vegetable oil for deep-frying
Cornmeal or flour

Combine flour, baking powder, and salt in a medium bowl. Stir in warm water in small amounts until mixture reaches the consistency of bread dough. Knead thoroughly until smooth and elastic. Cover bowl and let dough rest 10 minutes.

Heat 2 to 3 inches of lard or oil in a deep-fat fryer to 400°F (205°C) or a large 5-quart pot. Pull off pieces of dough and form into 2-inch rounds. Roll out 1/4 inch thick and about 8 to 10 inches in diameter on a board lightly dusted with cornmeal or flour. Make a hole in the center of each piece.

Fry breads, one at a time, on each side until golden, piercing large bubbles with a meat fork as they occur. Serve hot.

Makes about 12 pieces.

Freezing Tip: Wrapped tightly, leftover fry bread can be frozen for up to 3 months. To reheat, wrap bread in foil. Place in a 375°F (190°C) oven 10 to 15 minutes or until hot to the touch. Open foil and heat 5 minutes to crisp slightly.

Sopaipillas (Deep-Fried Breads)

Sopaipillas were first made according to old diaries on a "warm, balmy April Sunday after church at the Old Town Albuquerque San Francisco de Neri church in 1620." This was a treat the Spanish women created to treat the Native Americans who came to church. The Spanish women were forever grateful for all the help the native people had extended them on how to thrive in a very barren empty place such as New Mexico along the Río Grande valley. They have been served with hot, spicy New Mexican meals ever since. Torn open and drizzled with honey, they are wonderful to soften the "bite" of extra hot chiles.

> 4 cups high-gluten bread flour
> 1 teaspoon baking powder
> 11/2 teaspoons salt
> 1 Tablespoon solid vegetable shortening, lard, or butter
> 1 packet (or 1 scant Tablespoon) active dry yeast
> 1/4 cup warm water (110°F, 45°C)
> 1 1/4 cups milk, warmed about 30 seconds in a microwave oven
> Vegetable oil for deep-frying

Combine the flour, baking powder, and salt in a medium bowl, and cut in the shortening until the mixture resembles coarse cornmeal.

Dissolve yeast in warm water in a small bowl and add to warm milk, stirring well. Add yeast mixture all at once to flour mixture and combine to make a soft dough. Turn dough onto a board or other hard surface and knead dough thoroughly about 5 minutes, until smooth, firm, and elastic. Invert a bowl over dough and let rest 10 minutes or until dough is relaxed and when poked with a finger, the finger will go easily all the way to the bottom. Heat 3 to 4 inches of oil in a deep-fat fryer to 375°F (190°C) or a 5-quart pot.

Work with one-fourth of the dough at a time, keeping the balance well covered with the bowl. Roll a section to 1/4 inch thickness or slightly thinner, then cut into triangles or 2 1/2-inch squares; do not reroll any of the dough. Fry sopaipillas, a few at a time, in the hot fat. They should puff and become hollow soon after they are immersed in the oil. If they don't puff up, keep holding each under the surface of the oil with tongs or spoon hot oil over the surface until they puff. Drain on paper towels.

Makes about 24 small puffs.

VARIATION
Dusted with cinnamon sugar while warm, these can double as dessert.

Freezing Tip: See Navajo Fry Bread (recipe on page 257).

DESSERTS

The indigenous ingredients from Mexico made major contributions to the desserts of the Southwest. Pure Mexican vanilla and chocolate are quite popular, pair beautifully, and are a great finish to meals featuring highly spiced foods. Chocolate and chile actually are a wonderful combination in such desserts as the Hot, Hot Chocolate Cake. Also popular are custards, coconut, and fruits in various combinations, which make for lighter desserts that calm and soothe a seared palate.

Flan de Coco (Coconut Flan)

Creamy, coconutty, and delicious. I use an 8-inch cast-iron skillet to caramelize the sugar, then bake the flan right in the same skillet.

- 1 teaspoon butter
- 1 cup sugar, divided
- 1 Tablespoon water
- 1/2 cup shredded coconut
- 1 (12-ounce) can evaporated milk
- 3 large eggs
- 1 teaspoon coconut extract
- 2 cups fresh berries, such as red raspberries (optional)

Preheat the oven to 350°F (175°C). Spread the butter in an 8-inch heavy skillet, then place 1/4 cup of the sugar and water in the buttered skillet over medium-high heat. Stir until the sugar melts and turns light brown or caramel color, then quickly tilt the skillet to get a uniform coating on the bottom and slightly up the side of the skillet. The caramel will harden quickly. Sprinkle caramel with the shredded coconut.

Combine the remaining 3/4 cup sugar, the milk, eggs, and coconut extract in a bowl, beating well, and pour over the coconut. Cover the skillet with foil and place in a large baking pan. Fill baking pan with 1/2 inch of hot water. Bake 30 minutes. Remove foil; bake 30 minutes or until it is slightly puffed and jiggles only slightly.

Cool and refrigerate at least 3 hours. Unmold by running a knife around the side of the custard; place a serving plate over the skillet and invert quickly. The flan should fall out of the pan. If desired, garnish with fresh berries.

Makes 4 to 6 servings.

Classic Flan

Make this early in the day or even the day before. The caramelized sugar forms a sauce when the flan is turned out on serving dishes. This recipe is very versatile. It can be halved, evaporated skim milk can be substituted for the whole milk, and egg beaters can be used instead of whole eggs. It is nearly fool proof if you follow the instructions carefully.

2 Tablespoons unsalted sweet butter for buttering cups
1 1/2 cups sugar, divided
6 large eggs
3 1/2 cups whole milk
1 cinnamon stick
1 teaspoon pure Mexican vanilla extract

Preheat oven to 350°F (175°C). Butter 12 4-ounce custard cups very generously. Cook 1/2 cup of the sugar in a small, heavy dry skillet over medium heat, stirring constantly, until sugar is melted and caramelized. Pour immediately into the bottoms of prepared custard cups. (If you get too much in one, the caramel cools quickly and you can crack off some to more evenly distribute.)

Using a simple whisk, beat eggs in a large bowl only until light and lemon colored. (Do not use an electric mixer as too much air will be incorporated and will not go away.) Gradually beat in the remaining 1 cup of sugar, beating well after each addition.

Heat milk with the cinnamon stick in a medium heavy saucepan over medium heat to just below boiling. Add hot milk to egg mixture, slowly tempering it in at first, so as to not cook the eggs. Add vanilla.

Pour custard mixture into the caramel-lined custard cups. Set cups in a baking pan on a towel, then fill baking pan with 1 inch water. Bake 35 minutes, or until they are slightly puffed and only barely jiggle. Refrigerate at least 3 hours. To serve, if cold, warm slightly in the microwave (about 30 seconds each) if desired. Unmold by running a knife close to the outer edge of each cup. Invert on a serving plate and serve as desired.

Jenny's Cheesecake Flan

Jenny Candelaria, who worked with me for ten years while I was at Public Service Company of New Mexico, was very fond of this hybrid cheesecake flan. It's wonderful with any kind of berries or chocolate sauce.

3/4 cup sugar
2 teaspoons butter
2 (8-ounce) packages cream cheese, softened
1 (14-ounce) can sweetened condensed milk
4 large eggs, lightly beaten
2 teaspoons pure Mexican vanilla extract
1/2 teaspoon salt
1 cup water

Preheat oven to 350°F (175°C). Cook sugar, stirring constantly, in a heavy dry skillet over medium heat until melted and caramelized. Pour the caramel into a well-buttered deep 9-inch round cake pan, tilting to coat the bottom completely.

Beat cream cheese in a large bowl until fluffy. Gradually beat in sweetened condensed milk until smooth. Add eggs, vanilla, and salt and mix well. Stir in water. Pour cheese mixture into caramelized pan; set in a large baking pan with a towel in the bottom. Fill baking pan with 1 inch of hot water. Bake 55 to 60 minutes, or until the top springs back when lightly touched. Cool and refrigerate until chilled.

Loosen side of flan with a knife. Invert onto a serving plate and shake to loosen. Garnish as desired. Refrigerate leftovers.

Makes 10 to 12 servings.

Adobe Bars

Resembling adobe blocks, New Mexico's most traditional building material, these cookies are made with a rich combination of layered butterscotch, chocolate, marshmallow, and pecans. The bars are good travelers, and thus terrific for picnics. Ice cream goes especially well with them.

1/2 pound cold unsalted butter
2 cups granulated sugar
6 large eggs, divided
3 cups all-purpose flour
2 teaspoons baking powder
1/2 teaspoon salt
2 cups chopped pecans
1 cup semisweet chocolate chips
2 cups miniature marshmallows
2 cups firmly packed light brown sugar

Preheat oven to 350°F (175°C). Grease 2 (9-inch-square) baking pans. Beat butter in a large bowl with an electric mixer until fluffy. Add granulated sugar, 2 whole eggs, and 4 egg yolks, reserving the whites. Beat until combined. Combine flour, baking powder, and salt in a bowl. Add flour mixture to egg mixture, 1 cup at a time, beating first on low speed until the dry ingredients are incorporated, then on medium speed to combine well.

Spread half the batter in each greased pan. Evenly sprinkle half the pecans, chocolate chips, and marshmallows over the batter in each pan.

Beat reserved egg whites in a medium bowl until stiff. Sprinkle brown sugar over the whites, a small amount at a time, and carefully fold in, without breaking down the egg whites, until well combined. Spread over the top of each pan, dividing the meringue evenly.

Bake 15 to 20 minutes or until a wooden pick inserted in the middle of the cookie mixture comes out clean. Cool slightly, then carefully cut while warm into rectangular bars. Serve slightly warm or at room temperature.

Makes about 60 bars.

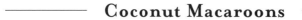

Coconut Macaroons

Coconut was always a favorite with my Mexican aunt and cousins. The sweetened condensed milk makes these cookies moist. This recipe is very versatile—you can make the traditional macaroons or try one of the many variations.

> **2 (7-ounce) packages flaked coconut (5 1/3 cups)***
> **1 (14-ounce) can sweetened condensed milk**
> **2 teaspoons pure Mexican vanilla extract**
> **1 1/2 teaspoons almond extract**

Preheat oven to 350°F (175°C). Line a baking sheet with foil and grease the foil generously. Combine coconut, sweetened condensed milk, and extracts in a large bowl and mix well. Drop by rounded teaspoonfuls onto prepared baking sheet. Bake 8 to 10 minutes or until lightly browned around the edges. Remove from baking sheet immediately (macaroons will stick if allowed to cool on baking sheets). Store loosely covered at room temperature.
Makes about 48 cookies.

*To reduce cost, and if you don't care too much for coconut, omit 1 (7-ounce) package of coconut and substitute 2 cups fresh bread crumbs (4 bread slices whirred in a blender).

VARIATIONS:
Macaroon Kisses: Prepare and bake as above. Press solid milk chocolate candy drops in center of each macaroon immediately after baking.

Chocolate Macaroons: Omit almond extract. Add 4 (1-ounce) squares unsweetened chocolate, melted.

Chocolate Chip Macaroons: Omit almond extract. Add 1 cup mini chocolate chips.

Cherry Nut Macaroons: Omit almond extract. Add 1 cup chopped nuts and 2 Tablespoons maraschino cherry syrup. Press maraschino cherry half into center of each macaroon before baking.

Rum Raisin Macaroons: Omit almond extract. Add 1 cup raisins and 1 teaspoon rum flavoring.

Almond Brickle Macaroons: Add 1/2 cup almond brickle chips. Proceed as above. Bake 10 to 12 minutes. Cool 3 minutes; remove from baking sheets.

Maple Walnut Macaroons: Omit almond extract. Add 1/2 cup finely chopped walnuts and 1/2 teaspoon maple flavoring.

Nutty Oatmeal Macaroons: Omit almond extract. Add 1 cup rolled oats and 1 cup chopped nuts.

Bizcochitos (Anise Sugar Cookies)

These spicy, anise-flavored cookies from New Mexico are rich, crisp, and very easy to make. They are wonderful in ice cream sandwiches—a chocolate-glazed cookie on the bottom, vanilla ice cream in the middle, and another cookie on top—and they are also my holiday favorite. Stored in a tightly sealed container, they can be frozen up to six months.

And they have quite a history—the cookies were developed as a celebration treat for the victorious Mexican army who defeated Napoleon's army on May 5, 1856, sometimes known as the Battle of Pueblo where the fight took place, thus creating the Cinco de Mayo holiday. Lard must be used for a moist, flaky texture.

This cookie has been legislated as the state cookie of New Mexico.

1 1/2 cups cold lard
1 cup sugar
2 large eggs
2 teaspoons anise seeds
4 cups all-purpose flour
2 teaspoons baking powder
1/2 teaspoon salt
About 3 Tablespoons brandy, apple juice, or milk
3 Tablespoons sugar
2 teaspoons ground cinnamon
Chocolate Glaze (recipe follows) (optional)

Preheat oven to 350°F (175°C). Whip lard at highest speed of the electric mixer until fluffy and looks like whipped cream, then add the sugar in a large bowl until fluffy. Add eggs and anise seeds, and beat until very light and fluffy. In a large bowl sift together flour, baking powder, and salt. Add to creamed mixture along with the brandy. Mix thoroughly to make a stiff dough. Place a long piece of waxed paper about 40 inches long on a flat baking sheet. Place the dough on one-half of the paper and double the waxed paper over the top and flatten dough to about one inch thick. Refrigerate or freeze for a few minutes to chill dough until it is stiff.

Roll out dough between the layers of waxed paper to about 3/8 inch thickness. Cut with well-floured cutters into cookie designs or into 3-inch rounds. (Because these cookies were made to celebrate defeating the French Army, the traditional cookie shape is the fleur de lis—the stylized iris on the French flag.)

Combine the 3 Tablespoons sugar and the cinnamon in a shallow bowl; dip unbaked cookie tops into the cinnamon sugar before placing on an ungreased cookie sheet. Bake 10 to 12 minutes or until firm when pressed.

Cool cookies on wire racks. If desired, prepare glaze. Cool slightly and dip part of each cookie into the glaze.

Makes about 4 dozen cookies.

Chocolate Glaze

  1 (6-ounce) package semisweet chocolate pieces (about 1 cup)
  1 1/2 Tablespoons solid vegetable shortening or butter
  1 teaspoon pure Mexican vanilla extract

Combine chocolate chips, shortening, and vanilla in a saucepan. Heat gently over low heat until melted and smooth, stirring constantly.

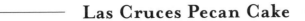

Las Cruces Pecan Cake

Pecans grow well in the sandy soil of New Mexico and are a favorite for desserts. This rich pound cake is excellent topped with the Lemon-Butter Glaze or with Mexican Fudge Sauce (recipe on page 288). It can be frozen for up to six months.

1 1/2 cups sugar
1 cup cold butter
2/3 cup ground pecans
1 Tablespoon lemon juice
1/4 teaspoon salt
5 large eggs
1 3/4 cups sifted all-purpose flour
Lemon-Butter Glaze (recipe follows)

Preheat oven to 325°F (165°C). Generously grease and flour a 10-inch springform pan. Place sugar, butter, ground pecans, lemon juice, and salt in the large bowl of an electric mixer. Beat until creamy and fluffy. Add eggs one at a time and beat thoroughly until the mixture is very light. Add flour and beat until smooth.

Spoon batter into prepared pan and bake about 1 hour or until a wooden pick inserted in the center of the cake comes out clean. Cool in pan 10 minutes. Turn out cake on a wire rack. Prepare glaze. Serve with warm glaze.

Makes 10 to 12 servings.

Lemon-Butter Glaze

1/4 cup butter
1 cup honey
5 teaspoons lemon juice
1/4 cup coarsely chopped pecans

Combine butter, honey, and lemon juice in a small pan over low heat, turning to medium-high after the ingredients are well mixed. Boil gently 2 minutes and remove from heat. Cool 10 minutes; stir in the pecans.

Note: Other nuts can be substituted for the pecans.

Hot, Hot Chocolate Cake

Once I shared this recipe with the listeners of Sam Arnold's Saturday morning radio show on station WKOA in Denver and we got thousands of requests for it. At the time, it was our birthday cake for celebrants at our New York City Pecos River Café.

1/4 cup crushed caribe chiles
1 cup boiling water
6 Tablespoons unsweetened cocoa powder
1 teaspoon baking soda
1 teaspoon pure Mexican vanilla extract
1/2 cup cold unsalted butter or vegetable shortening
2 cups sugar
3 large eggs
2 cups cake flour
1/2 teaspoon salt
1/2 cup buttermilk
Hot Fudge Frosting (recipe follows)

Preheat oven to 350°F (175°C). Grease and flour 1 (13 x 9-inch) pan, 2 (9-inch) cake pans, or 3 (8-inch) cake pans. Boil chiles in the water 10 minutes, then let set about 20 minutes. This can be done early in the day or ahead of time. Strain the chiles, rubbing with a wooden spoon or rubber spatula to remove as much pulp as possible. Pour the chile water in a measuring cup. Add enough hot tap water to make 1 cup. Stir cocoa powder into chile water to make a smooth paste. Add baking soda and vanilla, stir, and set aside while preparing the cake batter.

Beat butter until very fluffy with an electric mixer in a large bowl. Then add the sugar and beat until fluffy again. Add the eggs, one at a time, beating vigorously after each addition. Sift flour and salt into a small bowl. Add alternately with the buttermilk, using low mixer speed. Beat on medium speed until smooth, then add the cocoa mixture and mix well.

If baking in layers, evenly divide the batter among the pans. Smooth batter to edges. Bake 35 minutes or until cake springs back when lightly pressed. (Bake rounds 20 to 25 minutes.) Cool in pan 10 minutes, then turn out cake on wire racks to cool completely.

Prepare frosting. Frost cake while frosting is still warm. If the frosting starts to crease, stir in more half and half. Then sprinkle with nuts and/or crushed chile.

Makes 3 (8-inch) or 2 (9-inch) layers or 1 (13 x 9-inch) cake.

Hot Fudge Frosting

2 cups granualted sugar
1 cup firmly packed brown sugar
3 Tablespoons unsweetened cocoa powder
3 Tablespoons corn syrup
1 1/2 cups half-and-half, plus extra if needed
Chopped pecans and/or crushed caribe chile

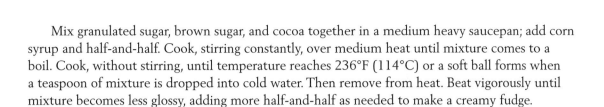

Mix granulated sugar, brown sugar, and cocoa together in a medium heavy saucepan; add corn syrup and half-and-half. Cook, stirring constantly, over medium heat until mixture comes to a boil. Cook, without stirring, until temperature reaches 236°F (114°C) or a soft ball forms when a teaspoon of mixture is dropped into cold water. Then remove from heat. Beat vigorously until mixture becomes less glossy, adding more half-and-half as needed to make a creamy fudge.

Chocolate Zucchini Cake

A deliciously moist cake, this recipe was developed in New Mexico, where zucchini grow literally like weeds.

1/2 cup cold unsalted butter or vegetable shortening
1/2 cup vegetable oil
1 3/4 cups sugar
2 large eggs
1/2 cup buttermilk
1 teaspoon pure Mexican vanilla extract
1 1/2 cups all-purpose flour
1/4 cup unsweetened cocoa powder
1 teaspoon baking soda
1/2 teaspoon baking powder
1/2 teaspoon ground cinnamon
1/2 teaspoon ground cloves
2 cups finely shredded zucchini
1/2 cup chocolate chips

Preheat oven to 325°F (165°C). Grease and flour a 13 x 9-inch baking pan. Beat butter and oil together until fluffy using an electric mixer. Gradually mix in the sugar, a little at a time, and beat until very light and fluffy.

Add eggs, buttermilk, and vanilla. Beat until very well mixed. Combine flour, cocoa, baking soda, baking powder, cinnamon, and cloves in a small bowl. Add to egg mixture and beat until smooth. Then, using low speed of the mixer, mix in zucchini.

Pour batter into prepared baking pan. Top with the chocolate chips, spreading them uniformly across the top. Bake 40 to 45 minutes or until a wooden pick inserted in the center comes out clean. Cool on a wire rack.

Makes 1 (13 x 9-inch) cake.

VARIATION
Add 1/2 cup nuts, raisins, or coconut with zucchini for added flavor.

Apricot Sherried Trifle

Soft custard topping on a sponge cake and garnished with fruit is a popular dessert after a spicy Southwestern meal.

     1 sponge cake, 10 inches in diameter
     1/2 cup plus 2 teaspoons cream sherry, divided
     2 cups milk
     1/3 cup sugar
     Pinch of salt
     1/4 cup all-purpose flour
     2 large eggs, separated
     1 large egg white
     1/8 teaspoon freshly grated nutmeg
     1/4 cup apricot jam
     2 Tablespoons toasted slivered almonds
     12 large, extra-fancy dried apricots, cooked in 1/2 cup water and cooled

Place the sponge cake on a large serving platter. Sprinkle with the 1/2 cup sherry and let stand while the custard is being prepared.

Pour the milk into a heavy 2-quart saucepan. Stir in the sugar and salt. Cook over low heat, stirring until sugar dissolves. Remove from heat. Spoon out about 1/2 cup of the warm milk mixture into a small bowl and let cool. Sprinkle flour over the cooled mixture. Stir until smooth. Add egg yolks and stir well. Add this to the remaining milk mixture. Cook, stirring constantly, until custard thickens and coats the back of a spoon. Cool slightly.

Meanwhile, beat the 3 egg whites until they are stiff but not dry, adding the 2 teaspoons sherry and the nutmeg while beating. Fold beaten whites into custard.

Spread sponge cake with apricot jam. Scatter the slivered almonds evenly on top. Pour the custard over the cake. Garnish with the cooked apricots, placing 4 in the center and the remaining 8 evenly around the edge. To serve, slice into 8 wedges, centering an apricot on each wedge.

Makes 8 servings.

Lady Baltimore Cake

More coconut! This recipe was my father's favorite birthday cake. He particularly loved fresh coconut. Fill this with either the Coconut Filling or Lemon Cream Filling—the choice is yours. Originally the filling was a rich fig and nut filling.

White Layer Cake (recipe follows)
Coconut Filling or Lemon Cream Filling (recipes follow)
Lady Baltimore Fluffy Frosting (recipe follows)
1 cup or more shredded fresh coconut, toasted until lightly browned

Prepare cake. Prepare desired filling. Prepare frosting. Place 1 cake layer on a cake plate. Spread with filling. Top with remaining layer. Spread frosting over the top and side. Sprinkle with toasted fresh coconut.
Makes 1 (9-inch) layer cake.

White Layer Cake
1/2 cup cold butter or solid vegetable shortening
1 1/2 cups sugar
2 1/2 cups sifted cake flour
2 1/2 teaspoons baking powder
1/4 teaspoon salt
1 cup milk*
1/4 teaspoon almond extract
1 teaspoon pure Mexican vanilla extract
4 large egg whites

Preheat oven to 375°F (190°C). Grease and flour 2 (9-inch) cake pans. Beat butter in a large bowl with an electric mixer until very light; add sugar gradually, and beat until light and fluffy. Sift cake flour, baking powder, and salt together into a bowl. Add flour mixture to butter-sugar mixture, alternately with milk, using low mixer speed. Beat after each addition until smooth. Add almond and vanilla extracts.

Beat egg whites in a large bowl until stiff but not dry. Fold egg whites into batter. Divide batter between prepared pans. Bake 20 minutes or until cake springs back when lightly pressed in center and cakes have pulled away from the sides of the pans. Cool in pans 10 minutes, then turn out cakes on wire racks to cool completely.

*Can substitute 1 cup fresh coconut milk.

Coconut Filling

1 cup milk
2 Tablespoons sugar
1 1/2 Tablespoons cornstarch
Pinch of salt
1/4 to 1/2 cup shredded fresh coconut
1/2 teaspoon pure Mexican vanilla extract

Scald 3/4 cup of the milk in a small saucepan, using medium-high heat, stirring constantly. Mix sugar, cornstarch, and salt in the top of a double boiler. Stir in the remaining 1/4 cup cold milk. Add hot milk gradually and cook over hot water, stirring until thickened. Cook about 10 minutes longer, stirring occasionally. Cool slightly, and add coconut and vanilla. As soon as it becomes thick from cooling, immediately spread between the layers of the cake.

Lemon Cream Filling

3/4 cup sugar
3 Tablespoons cornstarch
3 large egg yolks, slightly beaten
1 cup water
6 Tablespoons fresh lemon juice
1/4 teaspoon salt
Grated peel of 1 lemon

In a small bowl mix together sugar and cornstarch. In another small bowl combine egg yolks and water. Add egg mixture to the top of a double boiler, then gradually stir in the sugar mixture. Cook over hot water, stirring constantly, until thickened. Add lemon juice, salt and grated lemon peel and mix well. As soon as it becomes thick from cooling, immediately spread between the layers of the cake.

Lady Baltimore Fluffy Frosting

1 1/2 cups sugar
2/3 cup boiling water
1/2 teaspoon light corn syrup
2 large egg whites
1 teaspoon pure Mexican vanilla extract

Combine sugar, boiling water, and corn syrup in a medium heavy saucepan. Bring quickly to a boil using high heat, stirring only until sugar is dissolved. Boil rapidly without stirring until a small amount of syrup forms a soft ball in cold water, or spins a long thread when dropped from the tip of a spoon (240°F, 115°C).

Meanwhile, beat egg whites in a medium bowl until stiff but not dry. Pour hot syrup in a fine stream over egg whites, beating constantly with an electric mixer. Add vanilla. Beat 10 to 15 minutes, or until the frosting is cool and of the right consistency for spreading.

VARIATION

For a large party, double the recipe to make 3 (10-inch) layers.

Margarita Pie

No cooking required to prepare a dessert that will get you compliments. It is quick, attractive, and yummy!

- 1 1/4 cups finely crushed pretzels
- 1/2 cup butter, melted
- 1/4 cup sugar
- 1 (14-ounce) can sweetened condensed milk
- 1/3 cup fresh lime juice
- 2 Tablespoons tequila
- 2 Tablespoons Triple Sec
- 1 cup whipping cream, whipped
- Lime slices for decoration

Lightly butter a 9-inch pie plate. Combine crushed pretzels, melted butter, and sugar in a small bowl; press firmly on bottom and up the side to the rim of the buttered pie plate. Refrigerate while making filling.

Combine sweetened condensed milk, lime juice, tequila, and Triple Sec in a large bowl and mix well. Fold in whipped cream. Pour into prepared crust.

Cover and freeze 2 to 4 hours. If frozen, soften in refrigerator slightly before serving. Decorate with thinly sliced lime slices sliced in half, then twisted together. Freeze or refrigerate leftovers.

Makes 1 (9-inch) pie.

Strawberry Margarita Pie

All the same flavors of a strawberry margarita in a sweet crust—yummy!

Graham Cracker Crust (recipe follows)
1 envelope (1 Tablespoon) unflavored gelatin powder
1/4 cup fresh lime juice
1/2 cup sugar, divided
2 large eggs, separated
2 Tablespoons tequila
1/4 cup frozen sweetened strawberries
1 cup whipped cream
Fresh strawberries for decoration (optional)

Prepare graham cracker crust.

Sprinkle gelatin over lime juice in a small pan. Add 1/4 cup of the sugar and the egg yolks. Stir to blend. Cook over very low heat, stirring constantly, until gelatin dissolves and mixture thickens. Do not boil.

Remove from heat, and stir in tequila and strawberries. Refrigerate, stirring occasionally, until mixture is thick enough to mound on a spoon. Beat egg whites until stiff; gradually beat in remaining 1/4 cup sugar to make a glossy meringue. Fold into the gelatin mixture. Whip cream until stiff, then fold whipped cream into gelatin mixture.

Spoon gelatin mixture into crust. Cover and refrigerate until firm. Decorate with fresh strawberries, if desired.

Makes 1 (9-inch) pie.

Graham Cracker Crust

1 teaspoon butter for preparing pan
1 1/2 cups graham cracker crumbs
1/4 cup sugar
1/2 cup butter, melted

Preheat oven to 350°F (175°C). Butter a 9-inch pie plate, then mix together the graham cracker crumbs with the sugar and melted butter and press into the pie plate, making sure the crumb crust comes up above the rim of the pie plate. Bake 10 minutes or until firm, then cool on a wire rack.

Kahlúa Cream Pie

Kahlúa, the liqueur of Mexico, combines with cream to make a heavenly dessert.

1 envelope (1 Tablespoon) unflavored gelatin powder
1/2 cup cold water
1/2 cup sugar, divided
3 large eggs, separated
1/8 teaspoon salt
1/2 cup Kahlúa liqueur
1 1/2 cups whipped cream
1 (9-inch) baked pie crust
Chocolate Glaze (recipe on page 266)
1/4 cup toasted, sliced almonds

Sprinkle gelatin over cold water in a small pan. Add 1/4 cup of the sugar, the egg yolks, and salt. Stir to blend. Cook over very low heat, stirring constantly, until gelatin dissolves and mixture thickens. Do not boil.

Remove from heat and stir in liqueur. Refrigerate, stirring occasionally, until mixture is thick enough to mound on a spoon.

Whip the cream in a medium bowl until stiff. Beat egg whites in another large bowl with clean beaters until stiff. Gradually beat the remaining 1/4 cup sugar into the whites to form a glossy meringue. Fold meringue into the gelatin mixture along with half the whipped cream. Refrigerate the remaining whipped cream.

Turn the filling into the pie crust. Refrigerate 2 hours or until chilled. Drizzle Chocolate Glaze over top of pie and decorate with reserved whipped cream and almonds.

Makes 6 to 8 servings.

Mississippi Mud Pie

This rather trendy dessert has become popular in Southwestern family-style restaurants in the South and East. It's almost like a baked pudding and is sometimes called a cake.

1 cup butter, softened
2 cups granulated sugar
4 large eggs
1 1/2 cups all-purpose flour
3 Tablespoons unsweetened cocoa powder
1 1/2 cups flaked coconut (optional)
1 1/2 cups pecans, finely chopped
1 (7-ounce) jar marshmallow creme
1 teaspoon pure Mexican vanilla extract
Powdered sugar or whipped cream

Preheat oven to 350°F (175°C). Grease a 9-inch cake pan. Whip butter until fluffy, then add granulated sugar in the large bowl of an electric mixer until fluffy again. Add eggs one at a time and beat well after each addition. Add flour, cocoa powder, coconut if desired, pecans, marshmallow creme, and vanilla, and beat at low speed just to combine.

Pour into prepared cake pan. Bake 35 minutes or until a wooden pick inserted in the center comes out clean. Cool slightly on a wire rack. Cut into wedges. Serve warm with a sprinkle of powdered sugar or a dollop of whipped cream.

Makes 1 (9-inch) cake.

Manzana Empanadas
(Apple Turnovers with Cinnamon-Sugar Crust)

These empanadas are baked rather than deep-fried. Make them large or small and use other dried fruits for variety. Serve warm with ice cream, pack for picnics and lunch box desserts, or have ready for mid-afternoon snacks or tea. I have also served them with turkey and pork entrées. They can be frozen, baked or unbaked, for up to six months.

> 1/2 pound (2 cups) dried apples, other dried fruits, or a combination
> 2 cups water
> 1 cup sugar, divided
> 1/2 cup raisins soaked in 1 cup hot water, drained
> 1 teaspoon plus 1 Tablespoon ground cinnamon (Tablespoon optional)
> 1/2 teaspoon grated nutmeg
> 1/4 teaspoon salt
> Pastry Dough (recipe follows)
> Powdered sugar (optional)
> Milk (optional)

Place dried apples, water, and 3/4 cup of the sugar in a saucepan. Bring to a boil using high heat. Reduce heat, cover, and simmer until very soft, about 15 minutes, adding a little more water as needed. Drain apples, reserving the syrup, and cool. Chop cooked apples and place in bowl. Add raisins, the 1 teaspoon cinnamon, the nutmeg, and salt, adding reserved apple syrup, if needed, and mix together to make a moist filling.

Preheat oven to 425°F (20°C). Prepare pastry.

Roll out dough on a floured surface to a thickness of about 1/8 inch. Cut out 3-inch rounds for small empanadas and about 4 1/2-inch rounds for larger empanadas. Place a little filling in the center of each, moisten edges of pastry, and fold over. Crimp the edges or press with the tines of a fork to seal. Pierce the center of each empanada to allow steam to escape.

The tops of the empanadas can be thickly covered with sifted powdered sugar or with milk and cinnamon sugar.

For the powdered sugar version, place empanadas on ungreased baking sheets and bake until the edges are lightly browned. Place on a serving platter and generously dust with powdered sugar by placing the sugar in a sieve and rubbing it with a spoon.

For the cinnamon sugar version, combine the remaining 1/4 cup sugar and the 1 Tablespoon cinnamon in a shallow bowl, brush tops with milk, and gently dip in the cinnamon-sugar mixture. Arrange empanadas on a baking sheet and bake 8 to 10 minutes, or until golden. Cool on wire racks.

Serve warm or at room temperature.

Makes about 36 large or 54 small empanadas.

Pastry Dough

4 cups all-purpose flour
2 teaspoons baking powder
1 teaspoon salt
1/4 teaspoon ground coriander (optional)
1 cup solid vegetable shortening, lard, or butter
About 2/3 cup milk or water

Combine flour, baking powder, salt, and coriander, if using, in the bowl of a food processor or a large bowl. Cut in shortening until mixture resembles coarse crumbs. If using the food processor, mix in the milk until a soft pastry results. Otherwise, stir in milk gradually until a soft dough results. Chill while making the filling. Then roll half of the dough at a time to a thickness of just under 1/8 inch.

Nectarine Crisp

An all-time favorite at our house. Prepare this when nectarines are in season. You may substitute other fresh or frozen fruits such as peaches, cherries, or apples.

1 cup firmly packed brown sugar
1 cup all-purpose flour or a mixture of oatmeal, bran cereal, and flour
1/4 teaspoon ground cinnamon
1/8 teaspoon grated nutmeg
1/2 cup butter
2 cups peeled and thickly sliced fresh nectarines

Preheat oven to 375°F (190°C). Butter an 8-inch square baking dish. Mix together sugar, flour, cinnamon, and nutmeg in a medium bowl, and cut in the butter until mixture resembles coarse crumbs.

Spread nectarines in prepared baking dish. Sprinkle with crumb mixture.

Bake 35 to 40 minutes or until fruit is soft and crumbs are browned. Or cook in a microwave oven 8 minutes on High, turning once.

Makes 6 servings.

VARIATION

Substitute 2 cups of fresh or frozen fruit of your choice, such as strawberries, rhubarb, or Italian prune plums.

Cinnamon-Almond Dessert Tamales

These have a wonderful combination of flavors and are indeed a treat from Old Mexico. Before steaming, they can be frozen for up to six months. Remove from freezer, and steam 11/2 hours.

1/2 recipe (2 1/2 cups) prepared Tamale Masa (recipe on page 180)
1/2 cup sugar
1 teaspoon ground cinnamon
1/2 cup ground almonds
12 to 16 corn husks, soaked in hot water to soften, drained, and patted dry
3/4 cup raisins (can be soaked in rum or brandy)

Combine the prepared masa, sugar, cinnamon, and ground almonds in a bowl.

Spread about 3 Tablespoons of the sweet masa mixture in a line down the center of each soaked corn husk. Top the mixture with a few raisins. Fold and tie corn husks (see instructions on page 179). Steam, covered, over boiling water, 45 to 50 minutes.

Makes 12 to 16 tamales.

VARIATION

Omit the raisins and spread masa mixture with 2 teaspoons of raspberry or strawberry preserves. Continue as above.

Christmas Tamales

Pink and pretty, sweet, and bursting with flavor.

1/2 recipe (2 1/2 cups) prepared Tamale Masa (recipe on page 180)
1/2 cup sugar
1 Tablespoon grenadine syrup
3/4 cup golden raisins
1/4 cup candied citron, finely chopped
1/4 cup piñon nuts (pine nuts)
12 to 16 corn husks, soaked in hot water to soften, drained, and patted dry

Sweeten the prepared masa with the sugar and grenadine syrup. Add the raisins, citron, and nuts and mix.

Spread about 3 Tablespoons masa mixture in a line down the center of each softened corn husk. Fold and tie corn husks (see page 179). Steam, covered, over boiling water, 45 to 50 minutes.

Makes 12 to 16 tamales.

Buñuelos (Fritters in Syrup) New Mexico Style

This is northern New Mexico's version of buñuelos. Local cooks often make this out of leftover sopaipillas, if there ever is such a thing. Or you can make a half recipe of sopaipilla dough just for these. Traditionally they are made into rounds, about two to three inches across.

> 2/3 cup firmly packed brown sugar
> 1/2 cup sherry
> 1/2 cup water
> 1/2 cup raisins
> 1 teaspoon ground cinnamon
> 1/8 teaspoon anise seeds (optional)
> 1/2 recipe Sopaipilla dough (recipe on page 258) or leftover sopaipillas

Combine brown sugar, sherry, water, raisins, cinnamon, and anise seeds, if desired, in a small saucepan. Bring to a boil using high heat and cook until slightly thickened.

Break off walnut-size pieces of dough and roll them into rounds on a floured surface about 1/4 inch thick or slightly thinner. Deep-fry and drain according to directions for Sopaipillas (recipe on page 258).

Dip the warm fritters in the warm sauce and place them in a bowl. Serve warm and pass extra syrup.

Makes about 24 fritters.

Isleta Bread Pudding (Capiratada)

Rich and satisfying, this bread pudding is a good way to use not-so-fresh bread and is a Lenten favorite.

1/4 cup butter, softened
1/2 pound firm white bread, sliced*
1 1/2 cups firmly packed dark brown sugar
3 cups water
2 whole cloves
1 (3-inch) piece cinnamon stick or 1 teaspoon ground cinnamon
2 large eggs
1/2 cup milk or half-and-half
1 teaspoon pure Mexican vanilla extract
1/2 cup slivered almonds
1/2 cup piñon nuts (pine nuts)
1 apple, peeled and sliced in thin wedges
1 cup raisins
1 cup shredded Monterey Jack cheese
Whipped cream or ice cream

Preheat oven to 350°F (175°C). Butter a 1 1/2-quart casserole and set aside. Butter the bread slices, place on a baking sheet, and bake 15 minutes or until toasted. When cool, cut into cubes.

Boil brown sugar, water, cloves, and cinnamon stick in a saucepan until slightly thickened using high heat, about 5 minutes. Remove from heat, remove and discard cloves and cinnamon stick, and set the syrup aside.

Beat together eggs, milk, and vanilla in a medium bowl. Stir in almonds, piñon nuts, apple slices, and raisins. Place half the bread cubes in the prepared casserole. Spoon half the egg mixture over bread, then top with half the shredded cheese. Repeat, ending with a layer of shredded cheese.

Pour reserved syrup over pudding. Bake 35 to 45 minutes or until the liquid is absorbed and the pudding is firm. Serve warm, topped with whipped cream or ice cream.

Makes 6 to 8 servings.

VARIATIONS

If a moist texture is desired, bake, covered, 30 minutes. Remove cover and bake another 5 minutes.
*Substitute leftover cinnamon rolls for bread.

Eugenia's Creamy Rice Pudding

Eugenia Giles, an Alabama native transplanted many years ago to Albuquerque, gave me this recipe. She started making it after her husband, Glyn, had heart surgery. Even made with skim or low-fat milk, it's creamy and delicious.

    1/2 cup rice (arborio or regular)
    1/3 cup sugar
    1/2 teaspoon salt
    1/8 teaspoon ground cinnamon
    1/8 teaspoon ground mace
    1/8 teaspoon ground nutmeg
    4 cups milk
    1/2 cup raisins
    Ground cinnamon (optional)
    Ground nutmeg (optional)

Preheat oven to 300°F (150°C). Rinse rice; then mix sugar, salt, cinnamon, mace, nutmeg, milk, and raisins together in a 1 1/2-quart baking dish.

Bake 2 1/2 hours, stirring about every 30 minutes to fold in the brown skin that forms over the top. The pudding is done when the rice is tender and the milk is creamy. Serve warm or cold with cinnamon and nutmeg, if desired.

Makes 6 to 8 servings.

Deep-Fried Ice Cream

After a spicy meal, this is a deliciously cooling dessert. We have made this for many years in our weeklong cooking classes to everyone's delight. The students always make the Cajeta Sauce (recipe on page 290) and the Mexican Fudge Sauce (recipe on page 288) and make different patterns using toothpicks or squirt bottles, such as spider webs, chains of hearts, and zigzags.

> 1 quart vanilla, strawberry, or other flavor ice cream
> 1 large egg
> 1/2 teaspoon pure Mexican vanilla extract
> 1/2 cup graham cracker crumbs
> 1/4 cup granulated sugar
> 1/4 cup firmly packed brown sugar
> 1/2 teaspoon each ground cinnamon and grated nutmeg

Slice ice cream into 8 equal portions with a hot knife. If ice cream is frozen too solid, soften slightly before slicing. (Or you may soften ice cream and form into balls.) Freeze ice cream slices until firm.

Beat egg in a shallow bowl and add vanilla. Combine crumbs and sugars in a shallow bowl. Dip each ice cream slice into the egg mixture. Roll in the crumb mixture. Dip again in egg mixture, then again into crumbs. Freeze ice cream until solid, dipping again into crumbs if not well coated. Ice cream must be frozen hard before frying.

Heat oil in a deep-fat fryer to 350°F (175°C) or pan. Lower each slice, using a slotted spoon, into the oil for 2 seconds or until slightly golden, remove immediately and serve.

Makes 8 servings.

VARIATION

If a lighter taste is preferred, use a combination of crushed cereal with the graham cracker crumbs. For added flavor, serve with a chocolate sauce, cajeta sauce, or fruit sauce.

Chile Chocolate Ice Cream

The accent of chile in chocolate was created by Aztec warriors as their favored drink before going into battle. Their first choice was cinnamon, but it had to come all the way from China, so chile was a more popular one. Here, just for good measure, we are combining *both* chile and cinnamon with the chocolate—a definite pleasure!

1/2 cup water
1/4 cup crushed caribe chiles
2/3 cup sugar, divided
2 (3-inch) cinnamon sticks
3/4 pound dark semisweet chocolate, broken into pieces
1/4 cup unsalted butter, cut into pieces
3 cups whipping cream
6 large egg yolks

Boil the water and crushed chile together in a small saucepan using medium high heat until the chile flesh is softened. Strain, rubbing with a wooden spoon or rubber spatula to remove as much pulp as possible. Return the chile water and pulp to the saucepan and add 1/3 cup of the sugar and the cinnamon sticks. Bring to a boil using high heat, stirring; boil 1 minute. Remove from heat and let stand 1 minute. Discard cinnamon sticks. Add chocolate and butter. Let stand several minutes until chocolate is melted. Stir until mixture is smooth. (If necessary, place over low heat until chocolate melts.)

Scald cream in a large saucepan using medium heat. Beat yolks with remaining 1/3 cup of sugar in a bowl until thick and lemon-colored. Beat in a little of the cream and return to saucepan. Cook using medium heat, stirring, until mixture is hot. Remove from heat. Beat in chocolate mixture. Pour into a heatproof bowl. Refrigerate until chilled, stirring occasionally.

Transfer to an ice cream maker and freeze according to manufacturer's directions.
Makes 1 1/2 quarts.

Oreo Smush

This overly simple but yummy and filling dessert has been very popular in barbecue and Southwest restaurants, particularly in the southern United States.

1 pound Oreo cookies, crushed and divided
1 quart vanilla ice cream
Mexican Chocolate Fudge Sauce I (recipe on page 288) or a purchased fudge sauce
1 cup whipping cream, whipped

Butter a 9-inch square or similar-size dish. Press a uniform layer of cookie crumbs in the bottom of the dish, making it at least 1/4 inch thick.

Spoon enough ice cream over the crumbs to make a 1-inch-deep layer. Spoon a thin layer of fudge sauce over the ice cream. Then sprinkle half of the remaining crumbs over the sauce.

Repeat ice cream layer and fudge sauce layer, then sprinkle with remaining crumbs. Top with a layer of whipped cream, swirling cream with a spatula. Cover and freeze until firm. Cut into squares to serve. If too firm to slice easily, let soften slightly.

Makes 6 to 8 servings.

Hot Fudge Taco

I developed this recipe for the Pecos River Café (a restaurant of which I was an owner in New York City) and it really became a hit. You do need a round, special cone baker for this. You are making your own sugar cone for the "taco."

4 Belgian waffle cones, made in a U shape*
1/2 pound dipping chocolate
Small scoops of three flavors of ice cream
Mexican Fudge Sauce I (see below)
Whipped cream (optional)
Maraschino cherries (optional)

Make waffle cones according to manufacturer's directions, but form waffles into U shapes while still warm to make taco shells. Let cool.

Melt dipping chocolate in a small skillet over low heat. Dip waffle shells into melted chocolate to coat. Place dipped shells on waxed paper and allow to harden.

Place each shell on a serving plate, put scoops of ice cream in shells, and drizzle with fudge sauce. Decorate each taco with a dollop of whipped cream and a maraschino cherry, if desired.

Makes 4 servings.

*This cone mix and baker are available for mail order.

Mexican Fudge Sauce I

Sold in most Mexican specialty shops, Mexican chocolate has a unique flavor and consistency. It is already sweetened, and contains ground almonds and spices. Keep a batch on hand in the refrigerator; it will keep up to two months.

1 (about 3-ounce) round Mexican chocolate (such as Ibarra), broken into pieces
2/3 cup half-and-half or low-fat evaporated milk

Place chocolate in a small heavy saucepan and stir over low heat until it melts. Add the half-and-half very slowly, stirring constantly to mix evenly. Heat, but do not boil. Serve the sauce warm over ice cream or drizzle over Las Cruces Pecan Cake (recipe on page 267).

Makes about 1 cup.

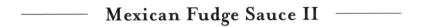

Mexican Fudge Sauce II

If Mexican chocolate is unavailable, try this fudge sauce. Store leftover sauce in a covered container in the refrigerator. If the sauce becomes too thick, thin it slightly by adding a little boiling water.

1 (12-ounce) can evaporated milk
1 3/4 cups sugar
4 (1-ounce) squares unsweetened chocolate, broken into pieces
1/4 cup butter
1 teaspoon pure Mexican vanilla extract
1/2 teaspoon salt
1 teaspoon ground cinnamon
1/4 teaspoon ground cloves
1/8 teaspoon grated nutmeg

Heat milk and sugar in a medium heavy saucepan, using medium heat and stirring constantly, until mixture simmers. Add chocolate and stir until melted. Beat until smooth. (If sauce has a slightly curdled appearance, beat vigorously; it will become creamy smooth.) Remove from heat and stir in the butter, vanilla, salt, cinnamon, cloves, and nutmeg. Serve warm.

Makes 3 cups.

Cajeta Sauce

This sauce is very popular in Mexico and has a wonderful caramel flavor. It is not overly sweet as some of our caramel toppings are. It's easy to make and will last several weeks, covered, in the refrigerator. Use as a sauce under Deep-Fried Ice Cream (recipe on page 285), swirling it together with the Mexican Fudge Sauce I (recipe on page 288).

3/4 cup sugar
2 Tablespoons water
1 (12-ounce) can evaporated goat's milk*

Put the sugar and water in a heavy skillet. Place over medium heat and cook, stirring constantly, until the sugar turns to liquid and then continue stirring until it turns a medium-brown color.

Remove from heat and gradually stir in some of the milk. Continue to stir and add milk until all the milk is added. Cook, stirring frequently, until the sauce thickens. This takes about 1 hour for thick sauce; less time is needed for a thinner sauce.

Makes 1 1/2 cups.

*Evaporated goat's milk is quite available most anywhere in the world. A popular American brand is Meyenberg.

Spiced Pecans

I learned this recipe from my Swedish grandmother. The pecans are wonderful with coffee and dessert or sprinkled over ice cream with Mexican Fudge Sauce I (recipe on page 288) for a super sundae.

2 Tablespoons cold water
1 large egg white
1/2 cup sugar
1/2 teaspoon salt
1/4 teaspoon ground cloves
1/2 teaspoon ground cinnamon
1/4 teaspoon ground allspice
2 1/2 cups whole pecan halves or most any nut

Preheat oven to 300°F (150°C). Add water to egg white and beat until foamy. Add sugar, salt, cloves, cinnamon, and allspice and stir well. Let stand until sugar dissolves, about 15 minutes; then stir. Add nuts and stir until well mixed. Spread the nuts out on a large ungreased baking sheet.

Bake 20 minutes. Stir, then bake 15 minutes and stir again. Bake 5 to 10 minutes longer, or until the nuts just glaze. They should not be sugary or overbrowned.

Makes 2 cups.

VARIATION
Substitute almonds, walnuts, or peanuts for pecans.

New Mexican Pralines[2]

Pecans are abundant in Texas and New Mexico, and they are wonderful in these creamy pralines.

> 1 cup firmly packed brown sugar
> 2 cups granulated sugar
> 3 Tablespoons light corn syrup
> 1/4 teaspoon salt
> 1 cup half-and-half
> 4 Tablespoons (1/2 stick) butter
> 2 teaspoons maple flavoring
> 1 1/2 cups pecan halves

Butter a 3-quart heavy saucepan. Combine the brown sugar, granulated sugar, corn syrup, salt, half-and-half, and butter in the saucepan. Cook slowly over medium heat until the mixture reaches the medium firm ball stage when dropped into cold water (246°F/120°C). Remove from heat.

Let the candy stand undisturbed until cool, then add the maple flavoring and pecans and beat until creamy. Drop by spoonfuls onto waxed paper. If the candy begins to harden, add a few drops of half-and-half, place over the lowest heat, and stir until creamy. The mixture should drop smoothly from the spoon.

Makes 36 candies.

---

2. From *Tex-Mex Cookbook* by Jane Butel. Copyright © 1980 by Jane Butel. Reprinted by permission of Crown Publishers, Inc.

Natillas with Fresh Pineapple

This light, traditional, yet very soothing soft custard is just what's called for at the end of a spicy, somewhat filling meal. If at all possible, obtain a very ripe Mexican pineapple, as they tend to be sweeter than other varieties. Do not add the custard to the pineapple until just before serving. For the prettiest presentation, use parfait or sherbet glasses and layer the pineapple with the natillas.

1 cup milk
3 Tablespoons sugar
Pinch of salt
1 large egg, separated
1 Tablespoon all-purpose flour
Freshly grated nutmeg
1/4 fresh pineapple, peeled and cubed

Scald milk with sugar and salt in a medium heavy saucepan over medium-low heat. Remove from heat and cool slightly.

Add about 2 Tablespoons of the warm milk to egg yolk, then gradually add flour and whisk until well blended. Add flour mixture to the warm milk mixture. Cook, stirring constantly, until thickened and mixture coats the back of a spoon. Remove the custard from heat.

Beat egg white in a small bowl until stiff but not dry. Fold beaten egg white into custard. Place in a serving bowl and grate some nutmeg over the top. Refrigerate until serving time.

To serve, place 3 or 4 pieces of pineapple in the bottom of each sherbet or parfait glass and add a layer of custard, then another layer of pineapple followed by a topping of custard. Grate more nutmeg over the top.

Makes 4 servings.

Note: You can omit the pineapple or substitute any other fruit.

Naranjas a la Mexicana (Oranges Mexican Style)

3 seedless oranges or blood oranges
2 Tablespoons powdered sugar
1/4 cup fresh lime juice
2 Tablespoons Cointreau or Triple Sec (optional)
1/4 cup shredded coconut (optional)

Remove peels and pith from oranges and cut into rounds if the membranes are tender, or cut out segments; sprinkle with sugar. Drizzle lime juice over oranges, add Cointreau, and gently mix until all pieces are well coated. Refrigerate until chilled. Serve in goblets and garnish with coconut, if desired.

Makes 4 to 6 servings.

Tropical Cream

1 envelope (1 Tablespoon) unflavored gelatin
1/4 cup orange juice or liquid from canned mango
2 cups fresh or canned mango pieces
1 (14-ounce) can sweetened condensed milk
1/4 cup dark rum
1 1/2 Tablespoons lime juice

Sprinkle gelatin over orange juice in a small bowl and stir until gelatin is softened. Set the bowl in a saucepan of simmering water and stir until gelatin is dissolved.

Place mango pieces, sweetened condensed milk, rum, and lime juice in a blender or food processor. Add the gelatin mixture and process until pureed. Pour into a 5- or 6-cup ring mold or individual molds, and refrigerate until set. To serve, dip each mold briefly in hot water to unmold.

Makes 4 to 6 servings.

Fruit Tostados

A beautiful and innovative way to serve fresh summer fruits, these tostado baskets are always a big hit. The crisp bites of tostado are an ideal complement to the meltingly soft fruits. The tostados can be made up to four weeks in advance.

2 quarts vegetable oil
4 (10-inch) flour tortillas
4 cups fresh summer fruits (use a variety of colors, shapes, and sizes, such as melon balls, strawberries, blueberries, and pineapple wedges or banana rounds)
1 Tablespoon cactus honey or strong-flavored blossom honey
1 Tablespoon fresh lime juice

Heat oil to 375°F (190°C) in deep fryer or in a deep heavy pot, using a thermometer to maintain the correct temperature. Fry the tortillas using the tostado technique on page 343. Drain the fried tostado shells on layers of paper towels.

Place fruit in a large bowl. Combine the honey and lime juice in small bowl. Pour over the fruit and carefully stir to coat the fruit; do not bruise it. Refrigerate until ready to serve, up to 2 hours but not more than that as the fruits will start to weep.

Warm the tostado baskets in a 250°F (120°C) oven 15 to 20 minutes, or until warm and crisp if fried ahead. To serve, arrange macerated fruits in the tostado baskets. Evenly distribute the juice. Serve immediately.

Makes 4 servings.

VARIATION
Sprinkle warm tostado baskets with cinnamon sugar before filling.

BEVERAGES

The beverages of the Southwest developed alongside the often fiery foods, and so became either strong-flavored enough or sweet enough to prevent their being overshadowed by the spices. The lime-laden margaritas and other beverages really serve to soften the bite of spicy chiles. Even teas and coffees will have the benefit of added citrus or cinnamon touches, which make them a better complement for Southwestern foods.

Sangría

Brought over from Spain, this wine-based drink has become quite popular with Mexican foods.

1 lime
1 orange
1 lemon
2/3 cup water
1 cup sugar
1 (3-inch) cinnamon stick
Ice cubes
1 (1 1/2-liter) bottle dry red wine, such as a Merlot, Malbec, or Rioja

Thinly slice lime, orange, and lemon, adding notches to the edge of the peel for a decorative touch, if desired, and place in a medium heatproof bowl.

Put the water, sugar, and cinnamon stick in a saucepan and bring to a boil using high heat, stirring to dissolve the sugar. Pour hot syrup over the fruit, allow to cool, and refrigerate to chill thoroughly.

Put ice into a punch bowl or large pitcher, and pour in the chilled fruit in syrup. Add the wine. Stir to combine and serve, placing at least 1 slice of each fruit in each glass.

Makes about 2 quarts.

Blonde Sangría

Similar to the more common red sangría, this one is based on white wine and is much lighter in flavor.

2/3 cup water
3/4 cup sugar
1 apple
1 lemon
1 orange
1 pint fresh whole strawberries, stems removed
Ice cubes
1 (1 1/2-liter) bottle dry white wine such as a Sauvignon Blanc or Pinot Grigio
Mint sprigs

Put water and sugar in a small saucepan and bring to a boil using high heat, stirring to dissolve sugar. Cool to room temperature.

Slice the apple, lemon, and orange and place in a medium bowl with the strawberries. Pour the cooled syrup over the fruit and refrigerate to chill thoroughly.

Put ice into a large pitcher or punch bowl and add the chilled fruit in syrup. Add the wine. Stir to combine. Garnish with mint and serve.

Makes about 2 quarts.

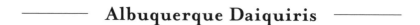

Albuquerque Daiquiris

These have become a favorite since we started testing them with the apricots from the tree in our backyard.

1/2 (6-ounce) can frozen limeade concentrate
3 medium-size ripe apricots or 2 peaches
1 cup light rum
8 to 10 ice cubes

Place frozen limeade, apricots, rum, and ice in a blender and blend until mixture is slushy, adding more ice cubes if necessary.

Pour into chilled long-stemmed goblets or old-fashioned glasses and serve immediately.
Makes 4 drinks.

VARIATION
Substitute 1/2 cup sweetened frozen strawberries, 1 banana, or 1/2 cup fresh pineapple chunks for the apricots. Use frozen or well-drained canned fruit if fresh fruit is unavailable.

Border Daiquiris

These are my favorite daiquiris.

1 cup light rum
3/4 (6-ounce) can frozen limeade concentrate
8 to 10 ice cubes
4 thin slices lime

Place rum, frozen limeade, and ice in a blender. Blend until slushy, adding a little more ice if necessary. Pour into glasses, garnish with lime slices, and serve immediately.
Makes 4 drinks.

VARIATION
If a blender is not available, crush the ice cubes and shake well with the rum and limeade concentrate.

Tequila Sour

Here the Southwest favorite—tequila—is substituted for whiskey.

    1/3 cup fresh lemon juice
    2 ounces tequila
    2 teaspoons sugar
    Ice cubes
    Half slice orange
    1 maraschino cherry

Combine the lemon juice, tequila, sugar, and ice in a shaker; shake well and pour into a glass. Garnish with orange slice and cherry.
Makes 1 drink.

Tequila Sunrise

Refreshing and thirst-quenching on a hot afternoon.

Crushed ice
1 Tablespoon fresh lime juice
2 ounces tequila
1 1/2 teaspoons grenadine syrup
1/3 cup fresh orange juice

Place ice in a tall glass. Add lime juice, tequila, grenadine, and orange juice; then serve.
Makes 1 drink.

Perfect Margaritas

The national drink of Mexico. They are definitely the best when made with freshly squeezed lime juice and good-quality silver tequila and Triple Sec or Cointreau. These margaritas are strong, so be careful! The little bit of egg white makes a beautiful, foamy head on each drink.

Coarse or kosher salt (optional)
2 ounces lime juice (juice of 4 or 5 limes) (save halves after juicing for rimming the glasses)
6 ounces tequila
2 ounces Triple Sec
1 teaspoon fresh egg white (can be frozen) (optional)
Ice cubes

If salted rims are desired, place salt in a small, dry saucer. About an hour before serving, squeeze limes; then rub the rims of each of 4 goblets with a squeezed lime half to moisten; then dip into the salt to lightly coat the rims. Place glasses in freezer to frost.

Combine lime juice, tequila, Triple Sec, egg white, and ice in a blender or cocktail shaker. Blend or shake well. Taste and add more lime juice or Triple Sec, if desired. Place 3 to 4 ice cubes in each glass or goblet. Pour margaritas into the frosted goblets and serve.

VARIATIONS

Combine fresh lemon juice and lime juice for a delicious, if unconventional, margarita.

Imperfect Margaritas: For less strong margaritas, reduce tequila to 3 ounces.

Frozen Margaritas: Keep adding ice and blending until mixture is slushy and firm.

Fruited Margaritas

2 ounces lime juice (juice of 4 limes)
4 ounces frozen strawberries, raspberries, pineapple, banana, or other favorite fruit
6 ounces tequila
1 ounce Triple Sec
1 teaspoon egg white (can be frozen) (optional)
3 cups ice cubes or more

Prepare salt-rimmed goblets as directed on page 302, if desired. Place lime juice, frozen strawberries, tequila, Triple Sec, egg white, and ice in a blender, and blend until slushy. Serve in goblets.

Makes 4 drinks.

Margarita Punch

For big parties, prepare this easy-to-do, delicious punch.

2 fresh limes, thinly sliced, for ice rings
3 liters all-natural agave silver tequila
3 (12-ounce) cans frozen limeade concentrate
About 3 cups ice cubes

Prepare an ice ring, using sliced limes (see tip).

Process remaining ingredients in batches of about 2 cups tequila, 1/2 can limeade concentrate, and 1/2 cup ice cubes each. Process until slushy and serve in a punch bowl with ice ring.
Makes 48 (4-ounce) drinks.

Tip: To make an ice ring, pour 2 or 3 inches of water into a ring mold. Freeze until firm. Add lime slices, other fruit slices, or mint leaves and a little more water. Freeze until firm. Fill mold with water. Freeze until firm.

Virgin Margaritas

These refreshing drinks can be served either frozen or over ice.

1 (12-ounce) can frozen limeade concentrate
1/4 cup frozen orange juice concentrate, pulpy variety (1/3 of a 6-ounce can)
1/4 cup frozen grapefruit juice concentrate (1/3 of a 6-ounce can)
8 ounces ginger ale
Ice cubes
1 lime, cut into 8 thin rounds

Place frozen concentrates in a blender and process until combined. Pour half the mixture into a pitcher. Add half of the ginger ale and some ice cubes to the blender and process on high speed, adding ice until desired consistency is reached. Repeat with remaining ingredients. Serve in large goblets with a lime slice as a garnish.
Makes 8 servings.

Coyote Punch

Originally from Texas via the Deep South, this is an excellent hearty punch. You can vary the juices.

Maraschino cherries and 1 thinly sliced orange for ice ring (optional)
5 black tea bags
3 cups boiling water
2 1/2 cups sugar
1 quart ice water
1 (12-ounce) can frozen orange juice concentrate
1 (12-ounce) can frozen lemonade concentrate
1/2 liter good-quality bourbon
Ice cubes

Prepare an ice ring using cherries and orange, if desired (see page 304).

Steep tea bags in the boiling water in a teapot or heatproof bowl about 10 minutes to make strong tea. Add sugar, stirring until dissolved.

Add tea mixture to the iced water, then add frozen concentrates and stir until well mixed. Pour into a punch bowl. Add the ice ring, if using, then the bourbon and serve over ice.

Makes 25 servings.

VARIATION
For a south-of-the-border twist, substitute rum for the bourbon.

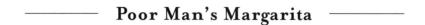

Poor Man's Margarita

Begin with a can of ice cold beer as made popular by Tecate. Drink from the can for a true Guadalajara effect.

Fresh limes, cut into wedges
Canned beer
Coarse or kosher salt

Rub lime wedges around the rims of beer cans to wet them, then rub generously with salt. Place remaining lime wedges and a dish of salt in the middle of the table for those who wish more.

Bloody María

The perfect drink before a Southwestern brunch.

1/4 cup fresh tomato juice
2 ounces tequila
1 teaspoon Worcestershire sauce
Dash of celery salt
Few drops hot pepper sauce
Ice cubes

If desired, salt rim of a large stemmed glass (see page 302). If time permits, place in the freezer. Combine tomato juice, tequila, Worcestershire, celery salt, and hot pepper sauce in a shaker; pour into an ice-filled glass.
Makes 1 drink.

Iced Herb Blossom Tea

Bright red and refreshing, this tea is somewhat like a sangría without the alcohol, especially if you add the spirals and slices of fruit.

6 hibiscus blossom tea bags or equivalent in loose tea
Water
3 oranges, with the peel cut off into about 4-inch spirals
2 lemons, cut into thin rounds
2 limes, cut into thin wedges
Ice cubes

Early in the day, put tea bags in a 2- to 3-quart glass jar or pitcher of water. Cover and set in the sun. Or 2 or more hours before serving time, bring 2 1/2 quarts water to a boil, then pour the water into a heatproof pitcher. Immediately add the tea bags and set aside.

When the tea has become a bright red and the flavor has developed, remove tea bags and add the orange peel strips and lemon slices. Let set until serving time.

Serve in tall glasses over ice, adding an orange peel spiral and a lemon slice to each glass. Place a lime wedge over the rim of each glass.

Makes 12 servings.

Good Old-Fashioned Sun Tea

Especially in the Southwest with its bright blue skies and solar warmth year-round, the very best teas are made in the sun. To get the best flavor, you'll need to determine the exact spot to place the glass jar and for how long. The tea is fresh tasting, never bitter. The tea gets darker as it stays in the refrigerator, yet still has good flavor.

Water
4 tea bags or 1/4 cup loose tea leaves
Ice cubes

Fill a 1-gallon glass jar or a glass pitcher with cold tap water to within 2 inches or so of the top. Add tea bags or loose tea in a tea ball.

Then place jar in the sun, either indoors or outdoors. In 3 to 4 hours, the tea should be steeped. Remove the bags or loose tea. Serve immediately over ice or refrigerate up to 4 days.

Makes 1 gallon tea.

Cactus Tea

The chilled version of this drink without the spices is sometimes served in Mexican restaurants.

1 (12-ounce) bag whole cranberries, 12 prickly pear fruit, or 1 cup dried Mexican red hibiscus
1/2 gallon apple cider
5 cinnamon sticks
8 whole cloves
5 oranges, sliced into rounds
4 lemons, sliced into rounds
6 black tea bags
Sugar or honey to taste

Combine cranberries, cider, cinnamon sticks, cloves, and fruit slices in a large stainless or enamel saucepan. Simmer, covered, 3 hours over low heat. Strain through a sieve lined with several layers of cheesecloth into a large heatproof bowl.

Add tea bags and steep 10 minutes. Remove tea bags and add sugar to taste.

Makes 16 (5-ounce) servings.

Cocoa, New Mexican Style

This tastes almost the same as Mexican hot chocolate made from commercial Mexican chocolate rounds such as Ibarra.

1/4 cup sugar
2 teaspoons all-purpose flour
3 Tablespoons unsweetened cocoa powder
Dash of salt
1/4 teaspoon ground cinnamon
Pinch ground cloves
1/2 cup water
2 cups milk
1 teaspoon pure Mexican vanilla extract
Whipped cream
4 cinnamon sticks

Combine sugar, flour, cocoa powder, salt, cinnamon, and gloves in a medium saucepan and bring to a simmer over medium heat. Stir in the water and simmer 3 minutes.

Gradually add milk and heat until hot, but do not boil. Using a molinillo (a Mexican chocolate stirrer), a fork, or a whisk, whip cocoa until frothy. Pour hot cocoa into mugs or stemmed glasses and serve immediately with dollops of whipped cream and cinnamon sticks.

Makes 4 servings.

VARIATION
Grate a little nutmeg onto the whipped cream.

New Mexican Coffee

Use a rich, dark-roasted coffee. Add the sugar to the ground coffee or serve with the brewed coffee.

3/4 teaspoon ground cinnamon or 1 cinnamon stick
1/3 cup piloncillo (unrefined Mexican sugar) (optional)
About 10 Tablespoons freshly ground coffee
Water

Add cinnamon and sugar, if using, to ground coffee, then add water and brew coffee as usual.
Makes about 8 servings.

VARIATION
Brown sugar may be substituted if piloncillo is unavailable.

Smith & Currans

These were supposedly developed in the oil fields.

Crushed ice
1 jigger crème de cacao
1 jigger milk
Club soda

Fill a tall glass with crushed ice. Add the crème de cacao and milk. Fill the glass with club soda, stir, and serve.
Makes 1 drink.

Gifts from a Southwestern Kitchen

The flavors of chiles, cacti, fruits, and flowers blend and accent both savory and sweet delights that make for mealtime pleasure and prized presents. There are many choices here from which to choose, depending on what is available, your time, and your skills.

Some gifts, such as the specialty vinegars and oils, are quick and easy to do, and when presented in pretty or unusual bottles please even the most discerning. Other recipes, such as those for the butters and pickles, require more time, but will inspire many compliments. Plan to make these gifts when the ingredients are at their best and most plentiful.

Jalapeños en Escabeche

This recipe from Janet Pugh, a close friend, is one of the best I know. It is especially suited to small-batch preparation, but you can certainly double the recipe if you wish. The only tedious part is the preparation of the chiles, but the sautéing in sesame oil adds excellent flavor, and serves to tame their heat a bit. You can use these as a relish or as an ingredient in sauces, salsas, and guacamole.

3 medium-size carrots, sliced into 1/4-inch rounds
1 cup cider vinegar
1 cup distilled water
2 medium-size Spanish onions, very thinly sliced and separated into rings
6 garlic cloves, peeled
1 teaspoon coarse salt
2 teaspoons ground Mexican oregano
3 large whole bay leaves
1/2 cup sesame oil
2 pounds jalapeño chiles

Cook carrots in a saucepan in a small amount of salted water over medium heat until crisp-tender. Drain, cool, and set aside.

Combine vinegar, water, onions, garlic, and salt in a large nonreactive saucepan. Cook using a medium-high heat until onions are slightly tender. Add oregano and bay leaves. Bring just to a boil.

Heat sesame oil in a large skillet over medium-low heat. Add jalapeño chiles, adjusting the heat so that they blister. Using tongs, turn the chiles in the hot oil until the skins blister. If desired, peel chiles. Add with carrots to the vinegar mixture. Cool and refrigerate 24 hours before serving.

Makes 3 to 4 pints.

Note: When preparing the chiles, either wear rubber gloves or very generously butter your fingertips and palms to prevent a chile burn, which lasts up to 24 hours. If you wish to remove the seeds and veins of the chiles, cut chiles in half and scoop out with a melon baller or a grapefruit knife.

Pear Honey

Mother's very favorite! She always used the windfalls and less than perfect pears, discarding the soft and blemished portions.

6 cups pear puree*
3 cups sugar
Grated peel and juice of 2 oranges
1/2 teaspoon grated nutmeg
1/2 teaspoon ground cinnamon

Combine pear puree, sugar, orange peel and juice, nutmeg, and cinnamon in a large saucepan over low heat. Cook, stirring frequently, until mixture is thick. While it is still hot, pour it into sterilized jars and seal. Process 15 minutes in a simmering hot water bath that is bubbling hot (see page 314).
Makes about 2 pints.

*To make pear puree: Wash, slice, and core 6 or 7 pears (1 1/2 pounds) and cook them over low heat with a little water to prevent them from sticking until they are very soft. Press the pears through a sieve or puree them in a blender.

Hot, Hot Honey

This spicy honey has recently become popular in northern New Mexico and is really terrific on sopaipillas, biscuits, and as a glaze for meats.

1/4 cup crushed caribe chiles or to taste
Water
2 cups honey

Simmer chiles with a small amount of water in a small saucepan over medium heat until the chile pulp becomes soft and slides off the peel, about 30 minutes. Strain and stir the pulp into the honey that has been placed in a heavy saucepan. Bring to a simmer, using medium-low heat, and pour into a sterilized jar and seal. Process 10 minutes in a simmering hot water bath (see page 314). Store in a cool place.
Makes 1 pint.

Piñon Peppered Jam

3 large bell peppers, finely chopped
3 to 6 medium-size jalapeño chiles, seeded and finely chopped
1 1/2 cups cider vinegar
6 1/2 cups sugar
1 (6-ounce) bottle liquid pectin
1/2 cup piñon nuts (pine nuts)

Combine bell peppers, jalapeño chiles, vinegar, and sugar in a large, heavy nonreactive saucepan. Bring to a boil and cook, uncovered, over medium heat, stirring frequently, until the mixture becomes transparent, about 30 minutes.

Remove from heat and cool about 10 minutes, then stir in the pectin. Return to heat and boil over high heat, stirring constantly, 2 minutes or until jelly falls off spoon in a sheet test or is 9°F (4°C) above the boiling temperature of water in your area. Remove from heat, skim, stir in piñon nuts, and cool about 10 minutes. Stir well to distribute the nuts. Ladle into hot sterilized jars and seal.

Process jars in a simmering hot water bath* for 15 minutes. Remove and cool.
Makes 5 (1/2-pint) jars.

*Hot water bath: place jars on a trivet in a large pot that will hold all the jars with space for water to circulate. Add water to reach 1 inch over the tops of the lids. Cover the pot and boil for the time required in the recipe.

VARIATION
For a Christmas look that is great for gifts, prepare some recipes with red bell peppers and chile peppers and some with green bell peppers and chiles.

Prickly Pear Jam

Prickly pears are the fruit of the Opuntia cactus. The rosy red juice they produce is quite flavorful and can be combined with other fruits such as plums, nectarines, or other firm fruit.

4 pounds of red ripe prickly pears
2 cups orange juice
Water
3 cups sugar

Cut the stickers off the prickly pears, using tongs to hold them and scissors to cut off the thorns. Cut the prickly pears into pieces and place them in a pot with the orange juice and enough water to cover the fruit. Cook over medium heat until the fruit is tender, then run through a blender, food processor, or food mill to puree.

Measure 4 cups fruit pulp into a heavy, flat-bottomed saucepan. Stir in sugar. Bring to a boil over high heat, stirring constantly. Reduce heat and simmer until jam falls off spoon in a sheet test or is 9°F (4°C) above the boiling temperature of water in your area. Pour into sterilized jars and seal. Process in a simmering hot water bath (see page 314) for 10 minutes.

Makes 4 pints.

Note: To do the sheet test for jelly or jam, dip a cool metal spoon in boiling liquid, then pour mixture from spoon into a saucer. The liquid should come off the spoon in a sheet.

Pear Chutney

Serve with roasted meats or chicken.

7 pounds firm pears, peeled, cored, and chopped.
3/4 pound apples, peeled, cored, and sliced
2 pounds onions, chopped
1 1/2 pounds raisins, chopped
1/2 pound crystallized ginger, sliced
Grated peel and juice of 1 lemon
1 teaspoon salt
8 whole cloves
8 cups wine vinegar
4 cups firmly packed dark brown sugar
8 small dried hot red chiles or 2 teaspoons pequin quebrado
5 garlic cloves, minced

Put pears and apples in a large earthenware crock or nonreactive bowl. Add onions, raisins, ginger, garlic, lemon peel, lemon juice, and salt. Tie chiles and cloves in a cheesecloth bag. Put vinegar, sugar, hot chiles, and cloves in a large enameled saucepan and simmer for 5 minutes.

Pour the hot mixture over the fruit in the crock and let it stand 12 hours. Transfer the mixture to a large preserving pot and simmer 3 or 4 hours or until the chutney is rich and dark. Stir frequently near the end of cooking to prevent scorching. Remove spice bag halfway through the cooking. Pour hot chutney into hot sterilized jars and seal. Process in simmering hot water bath (see page 314) for 15 minutes.

Makes 14 pints.

Apricot Chutney

I first made this when I lived in Albuquerque in 1964, and I have been making it ever since.

- 1 1/4 pounds fresh apricots
- 1 1/4 pounds fresh peaches
- 1/4 pound raisins
- 1/2 lemon, quartered and thinly sliced
- 1 cup cider vinegar
- 2 Tablespoons fresh lime juice
- 1 1/2 cups sugar
- 1/4 cup crystalized ginger, coarsely cut
- 2 small hot red chiles, finely chopped, or 1 teaspoon pequin quebrado
- Ground ginger to taste (optional)

Cut apricots into quarters. Peel and chop peaches. Place fruit in a 5 quart pan. Add raisins, lemon, vinegar, and lime juice. Cook, stirring, over low heat until fruit is tender.

Add sugar and cook over low heat until chutney thickens, about 1 1/2 hours. Stir frequently near the end of cooking to avoid scorching. Stir in hot chiles and ground ginger, if using. Process in a simmering hot water bath (see page 314) for 15 minutes.

Makes 3 pints.

VARIATION
If you'd like a darker color, use dark brown sugar instead of granulated sugar.

Ethel's Chile Sauce

When I worked at Public Service Co. of New Mexico, a retired officer's wife gave me this recipe for tomato chutney that she called chile sauce. It's a very, very old recipe that is more Anglo than Hispanic—yet it is wonderful. Ethel told me this recipe came to her from one of her mother's bridesmaids. She said she simmered hers much longer (probably due to Albuquerque's high altitude), until it was the consistency she liked. She loved getting Deming, New Mexico, (southern New Mexico) tomatoes for this because they were sun-ripened and not watery.

2 large onions, chopped
2 hot red chiles, chopped
12 large tomatoes, peeled and diced
2 cups cider vinegar
1 heaping Tablespoon salt
2 cups firmly packed dark brown sugar
1 teaspoon ground allspice
1 teaspoon grated nutmeg
1 teaspoon ground cloves

Place onions, chiles, tomatoes, vinegar, salt, brown sugar, allspice, nutmeg, and cloves in a large nonreactive pan and simmer together at least 1 hour or until thickened to desired texture. Pour hot chutney into hot sterilized jars and seal. Process in a simmering hot water bath (see page 314) for 15 minutes.

Makes 4 pints.

Mesquite Marmalade

A wonderfully spicy, slightly smoky condiment to serve with seafood, poultry, or meats or over cream cheese. It's even great on fresh bread. I discovered this when I once had a leftover pint of mesquite juice from soaking mesquite chips for barbecuing.

    2 dried chipotle chiles
    1 Tablespoon cider vinegar
    4 1/4 cups water, divided
    1 orange, ends cut off, quartered and thinly sliced
    1 lemon, ends cut off, quartered and thinly sliced
    1 1/2 cups chopped white onions
    2 cups strained mesquite liquid made from soaking 1/4 cup
        mesquite chips in 2 cups of water overnight
    6 cups sugar
    1 (1 3/4-ounce) package powdered pectin

Simmer chipotle chiles in vinegar and 1/4 cup of the water in a small nonreactive saucepan over medium heat for 5 minutes. The liquid should be spicy and dark colored. Drain, reserving liquid. Finely chop chiles.

Combine orange, lemon, onions, chiles and their liquid, mesquite liquid, the remaining 4 cups of water, and sugar in a large 5 quart stock pot. Stir and place over high heat, stirring frequently. Boil 5 to 10 minutes or until fruit and onions are translucent. Remove from heat and skim off any white foam.

Return to high heat and stir in pectin. Cook and stir until the marmalade falls off spoon in a sheet test or is 9°F (4°C) above boiling temperature in your area. Pour into sterilized jars and seal. Process in a simmering hot water bath (see page 314) for 15 minutes.

Makes 3 pints.

Mary Eunice's Tomato Marmalade

This recipe came to me from West Texas and is pretty and delicious. Plum or Roma tomatoes are preferred; however, regular tomatoes can be substituted. This marmalade makes a wonderful gift.

8 pounds ripe plum tomatoes
3 oranges, peel and pulp chopped finely
3 lemons, peel and pulp chopped finely
8 cinnamon sticks
1 Tablespoon whole cloves, tied in a cheesecloth bag
16 cups sugar (about 7 pounds)

Dip tomatoes briefly, a few at a time, in a saucepan of boiling water to loosen skins. Slip off skins, chop tomatoes roughly, and measure 4 quarts. Set aside. Put chopped oranges and lemons, removing all seeds, in a large nonreactive stockpot. Tie cinnamon sticks and cloves in a cheesecloth bag. Add to pot along with the chopped tomatoes. Pour off and discard most of the tomato liquid (all that is watery looking). Add sugar.

Bring to a boil over high heat, stirring, until sugar has dissolved. Boil, stirring to prevent sticking, until marmalade falls off spoon in a sheet test or is 9°F (4°C) above boiling. Remove spice bag. Ladle the marmalade into sterilized jars. Process in a simmering hot water bath (see page 314) for 15 minutes. Cool. Store in a cool, dark place.

Makes 8 pints.

Note: I have also made this with a combination of yellow pear, green zebra, and red tomatoes, which was quite attractive.

Tomato Conserve

When tomatoes are abundant, you may wish to try this conserve. It's good with poultry and lamb or as a spread on toast.

4 pounds tomatoes
2 lemons
1 orange
1 (5-inch) cinnamon stick
10 whole cloves
6 3/4 cups sugar
1/3 cup crystallized ginger, finely chopped
1/2 (1 3/4-ounce) package powdered pectin

Dip tomatoes briefly, a few at a time, in a saucepan of boiling water to loosen skins. Quickly transfer tomatoes to ice water afterward. Slip off skins, chop tomatoes roughly, and measure 4 1/2 cups. Let stand in a nonreactive stockpot overnight or at least a few hours before cooking.

Thinly slice unpeeled lemons and oranges and cut into quarters or sixths depending on size, removing all seeds. Add to tomatoes. Tie cinnamon and cloves in a cheesecloth bag and add to pot.

Bring to a boil over high heat. Add sugar and ginger. Cook until sugar dissolves, then add the pectin, stirring, until mixture falls off spoon in a sheet test or is 9°F (4°C) above boiling. Remove spices. Cool at least 7 minutes and skim off foam. Stir well and ladle into sterilized jars and seal. Process in a hot water bath (see page 314) for 15 minutes.

Makes about 13 (6-ounce) jars.

Eugenia's Pickled Green Tomatoes

Eugenia came to Albuquerque from Alabama several years ago. This recipe for her special sweet tomato pickles is typically Southern and is wonderful with Southwestern dishes. The recipe takes several days to complete, but it is worth the effort.

- 2 cups pickling salt
- 8 gallons distilled water
- 7 pounds green tomatoes, sliced 1/2 to 3/4 inch thick
- 1/2 pound alum
- 1/4 cup ground ginger
- 3 cinnamon sticks
- 6 whole cloves
- 6 whole allspice
- 5 pounds sugar
- 6 cups (5-percent-acidity) cider vinegar

Day 1: Dissolve the salt in 2 gallons of distilled water in a large nonreactive container. Add tomatoes and refrigerate overnight.

Day 2: Drain and rinse tomatoes. Place tomatoes and 2 gallons of distilled water in a large nonreactive container and refrigerate overnight.

Day 3: Drain and rinse tomatoes. Dissolve alum in 2 gallons of distilled water in a large nonreactive container. Add tomatoes and refrigerate overnight.

Day 4: Drain and rinse tomatoes early in the day. Place tomatoes, 2 gallons of distilled water, and ginger in a large nonreactive container. Let stand 6 hours. Drain tomatoes. Place cinnamon sticks, cloves, and allspice in a cheesecloth and tie. Put sugar, vinegar, and spices in a large nonreactive stockpot and boil over high heat, stirring, until sugar is dissolved. Remove from heat. Add tomatoes. Let stand 3 hours. Bring to a boil over high heat, reduce heat, and simmer 1 hour. Discard spice bag. Pack the hot mixture into sterilized jars and seal. Process in a simmering water bath (see page 314) for 15 minutes.

Makes 10 pints.

Cider Apple Butter

All sorts of apples and cider were abundant in the Catskills, so I bought several different kinds of apples and created this apple butter using fresh cider and gave jars as Christmas gifts. We really liked it. My goddaughter even said she liked it on ice cream.

1 gallon fresh sweet apple cider
10 1/4 pounds tart apples, peeled and quartered, seed sacks removed
2 teaspoons ground cinnamon
1/4 teaspoon ground cloves
1 1/4 teaspoons ground ginger
Freshly grated nutmeg

Boil cider in a large stockpot until it is reduced to 2 quarts. Add apples and cook until very tender. Press through a colander or process in a food processor, in batches, until pureed. Return puree to the pot. Add cinnamon, cloves, ginger, and nutmeg and cook over low heat until thick, stirring to prevent burning. Remove from heat. To test thickness, spread a small spoonful on a cool plate, allow it to cool to room temperature, and check thickness. Continue cooking if needed. Pour hot apple butter into sterilized jars and seal. Process in a simmering hot water bath (see page 314) for 15 minutes.

Makes 8 pints.

Rosy Santa Rosa Honey Butter

Honey gives this "butter" a rich, subtle flavor, making it equally good for toast as for pancakes and waffles.

5 pounds ripe plums, pitted and sliced
3 cups light, mild-flavored honey
1/2 teaspoon ground cinnamon or to taste
1/4 teaspoon grated nutmeg

Process plums, a few at a time, in a blender or food processor until smooth to make 2 quarts of puree. Pour the puree into a large stockpot.

Stir in honey and simmer, uncovered, stirring more frequently as the mixture thickens, to the desired texture, 1 1/2 to 2 hours. Remove from heat. To test thickness, spread a small spoonful on a cool plate and cool it to room temperature. If not thick enough, continue cooking. Pour the hot honey butter into hot sterilized jars and seal. Process in a simmering hot water bath (see page 314) for 15 minutes.

Makes 3 pints.

Sweet Tomatillo Relish

Tomatillos (the Mexican green husk tomatoes) are quite prolific. They just keep on bearing, and the fruit freezes so well. All you have to do is peel off the husk, rinse, and freeze. To use them, just simmer them in a small amount of water about 5 to 8 minutes or until cooked to your satisfaction.

    1 3/4 pounds tomatillos (about 25 large)
    5 large ripe tomatoes, chopped
    2 large green bell peppers, chopped
    3 large onions, chopped
    1 1/2 cups sugar
    1 1/2 cups cider vinegar
    1 1/2 Tablespoons pickling salt
    1 1/2 teaspoons ground cinnamon
    1/4 teaspoon ground allspice
    1/4 teaspoon ground cloves

Remove husks and stems from tomatillos. Rinse and chop fruit, and combine in a 6-quart nonreactive pot with tomatoes, bell peppers, onions, sugar, vinegar, salt, cinnamon, allspice, and cloves. Boil gently over medium-high heat, uncovered, 1 to 1 1/2 hours, or until the mixture reaches the desired consistency; stir frequently as it thickens.

Ladle relish into sterilized jars and seal. Process in a simmering boiling water bath (see page 314) for 15 minutes.

Makes about 10 (6-ounce) jars.

VARIATION
Cool relish, pack into freezer containers, and freeze up to three months.

Bobbie's Watermelon Pickles

A woman who attended some of my cooking classes shared this recipe with me, and it's a winner.

10 pounds peeled watermelon rind, cut into 1 1/2 x 2-inch pieces
7 cups sugar
2 cups white distilled vinegar
Dash of salt
1 teaspoon whole cloves
3 (3-inch) cinnamon sticks, broken

Cover watermelon rind with water and boil over high heat until tender, 20 to 30 minutes. Drain. Boil sugar and vinegar in a large nonreactive pot for 5 minutes. Add the cooked rind, salt, cloves, and cinnamon sticks and bring to a boil over high heat. Remove from heat and let stand overnight. The next morning, bring mixture to a boil, ladle into sterilized jars, and seal. Process in a simmering water bath (see page 314) for 15 minutes.

Makes 10 pints.

— Sweet Sandia Watermelon Pickles —

The mountains behind Albuquerque were called the Sandias by the Pueblo Indians and the name stuck. *Sandia* is the Spanish word for watermelon, and the mountains from afar look like a watermelon on its side. Distilled water and five-percent-acidity vinegar is critical to making these successfully.

1/2 cup pickling salt
About 1 gallon distilled water, divided
4 pounds watermelon rind, peeled and cut into 1-inch cubes (8 cups)
8 cups sugar
1 quart (5-percent-acidity) white distilled vinegar
2 lemons, thinly sliced
4 cinnamon sticks
2 Tablespoons whole cloves

Dissolve salt in 2 quarts of distilled water in a nonreactive container. Add watermelon rind and refrigerate overnight.

Drain the next morning. Put watermelon rind into a large pot. Add enough distilled water just to cover watermelon rind. Cook until barely tender over high heat reduced to a low heat to maintain a simmer, then drain.

Prepare a syrup by boiling together over high heat the sugar, vinegar, lemons, and cinnamon stick and cloves tied in a cheesecloth bag until the sugar dissolves. Add cooked watermelon rind. Bring to a boil over high heat, reduce heat to low, and simmer 1 hour. Discard spice bag. Pack pickles into sterilized jars and seal. Process in a boiling water bath (see page 314) for 15 minutes.

Makes 6 pints.

Valley Mincemeat

This is an old Albuquerque recipe with a well-balanced flavor. It is equally good made with venison or antelope.

  2 1/2 pounds beef stew meat, cooked until tender
  5 pounds tart apples, coarsely chopped
  2 pounds seedless dark raisins
  1/2 pound dried currants
  1/2 teaspoon ground allspice
  1/2 teaspoon freshly ground black pepper
  1 teaspoon ground cloves
  1 Tablespoon ground cinnamon
  2 teaspoons salt
  2/3 cup red currant jelly
  2/3 cup apple jelly
  2 (1-pound) cans tart cherries, undrained
  1 quart apple cider
  3/4 cup apple cider vinegar

Process beef in a food processor until finely chopped, in batches if necessary.

Combine the apples, raisins, currants, allspice, pepper, cloves, cinnamon, salt, currant jelly, apple jelly, cherries, cider, and vinegar in a large nonreactive pot and bring to a boil, stirring frequently. Add chopped beef and boil 30 minutes, stirring frequently. Cool quickly and pack into freezer containers. Mincemeat can be frozen up to 4 months. Thaw in refrigerator before using.

Makes 8 to 10 cups, enough for 3 pies.

Note: When making mince pies, add 3 tablespoons of brandy or rum to the filling for each pie. Bake double-crusted pies at 425°f (220°c) about 40 minutes or until crust is browned and filling is bubbly.

VARIATION
If using game instead of beef, add 1 pound chopped beef suet to ingredients.

A Range of Rubs

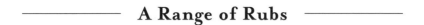

Texans swear by rubs! Use them to rub on beef before barbecuing. This amount is enough for about twenty pounds of meat. Any leftover rub should be frozen.

1/4 cup salt
1/4 cup freshly ground black pepper
1/4 cup ground mild dried chiles
1 Tablespoon granulated (dried) garlic

Combine salt, pepper, dried chiles, and garlic in a small bowl.
Makes about 3/4 cup.

VARIATIONS
Pork Rub: Add 1/4 cup sugar. After rubbing pork ribs with rub, top them with thinly sliced lemon slices.

Chicken Rub: Add 2 Tablespoons dry mustard and 1 teaspoon ground thyme.

Fruit Vinegar

Any combination of fruits and spices can be used with a compatible type of vinegar.

1 cup red raspberries or other fruit
1 quart red wine vinegar

Place raspberries in a sterilized jar. Warm vinegar in a stainless steel saucepan over high heat and pour over raspberries. Seal jar. Let stand 1 month before using. Strain out raspberries and bottle in sterilized jars.
Makes 1 quart.

Chile Vinegar

A spicy vinegar for meats, salads, and vegetable dishes.

1 quart small red ripe chiles, such as jalapeños or serranos, finely chopped*
1 quart (5-percent-acidity) vinegar
1 Tablespoon salt
Whole red chiles (optional)

Put chopped chiles into a sterilized large glass jar. Add vinegar and salt. Seal jar. Let stand for a week in indirect sunlight. Turn upside down daily. Strain and bottle in sterilized jars. Add whole chiles, if desired.

Makes 1 quart.

*Dried red chiles can be substituted.

Mexican Sage Vinegar

This vinegar is excellent in sauces for poultry, in salads, or over vegetable combinations. For gift giving, buy attractively shaped bottles with lids or corks.

3 large Mexican (black) sage sprigs for each jar
1 Mexican oregano sprig for each jar
1 quart (5-percent-acidity) cider vinegar

Place sage and oregano in one or more sterilized jars. Warm vinegar in a stainless steel pan using high heat. Pour vinegar over herbs and seal. Let stand one month before using.
Makes 1 quart.

VARIATION
For added flavor and color, place 1 long peeling of a red apple in each jar along with the sage and oregano.

Chile Oil

For flavoring foods quickly at the table, a dash of chile oil will always do the trick. You can also use it in salad dressings and for flavoring meats. Chile oil is a very efficient way to get hotness. The oils from the hottest part of the chiles combine with the fats in the olive oil, creating a very hot oil.

3 cups extra-virgin olive oil, preferably Spanish
2 cups crushed caribe chiles

Place oil and chiles in a heavy saucepan and bring almost to a simmer over medium-low heat. Remove from heat to prevent chiles from turning black.

Cover and cool overnight, then strain to remove the chile flakes. For safest keeping, refrigerate between uses and warm to room temperature before using.
Makes 2 cups.

Lyn's Rose Potpourri

Have fun making your own potpourri from your garden. You can substitute different flowers.

1 quart dried rose petals
3 dried rose hips
6 dried mint leaves
4 dried rose geranium leaves
1 dried fern leaf
1 Tablespoon powdered orris root*
1 dried orange peel
3/4 teaspoon ground ginger
3/4 teaspoon ground allspice
3/4 teaspoon ground cloves
3/4 teaspoon ground cinnamon
1/2 cup salt
3 drops oil of jasmine**
3 drops oil of eucalyptus**

In a large bowl combine rose petals, rose hips, mint, geranium leaves, and fern leaf. Add orris root. Blend in peel, ginger, allspice, cloves, and cinnamon and mix so that they are well blended. Add salt, oil of jasmine, and oil of eucalyptus and shake or stir gently.

Pack in jars and seal tightly at least 2 to 3 days. Then place in a potpourri jar or shallow dish. *Makes 4 cups.*

*Orris root is available at most pharmacies.
**Oils such as these are available at health food stores.

Lavender Rose Potpourri

Just like a Victorian essence, this blend is really my favorite.

1 pound dried rose petals
1 pound dried lavender
1/4 pound powdered orris root (see note on page 332)
1 ounce ground allspice
1 ounce ground cinnamon
1 ounce ground cloves
1 ounce tonka*

Combine rose petals, lavender, orris root, allspice, cinnamon, cloves, and tonka in a large bowl. Pack ingredients into an ornamental bowl or lidded jar and cover tightly. Let sit several days or until the aroma is uniformly pungent.
Makes 4 cups.

*Tonka is an aromatic bean from South America and is available at most pharmacies, natural food stores, or craft stores.

VARIATIONS
Ground nutmeg, mace, cassia, cardamom, or coriander can be added.
To enhance the floral fragrance, add dried lemon and orange blossoms.
To add color, add nasturtium and mimosa.

GLOSSARY

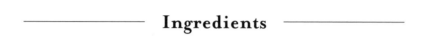

Ingredients

The entire Southwestern cuisine, and New Mexico's in particular, is made up of very few unusual ingredients. Following is a description of the major ingredients used in the recipes in this book.

AVOCADOS

The very finest are the Haas, or old-fashioned Mexican avocados, which are pear-shaped and have a black, textured skin. They have the richest, most buttery texture and flavor, and are the best base for guacamole and garnishes. The second best is the freckled, dark-green, pear-shaped Fuertes, which has a smaller neck than the Haas. The ones to avoid are the shiny green, smooth-skinned, round varieties, which are too sweet and watery. For ripening avocados, see page 12.

BEANS

The true Southwestern bean is the pinto, a brown-speckled, grayish legume that cooks up to a firm, flavorful, almost nutlike taste. (The pinto is rated as the healthiest of all beans.) Cooked and mashed, pintos become refritos, or refried beans. Black beans are becoming more popular because of the increasing Cuban and South American influence. Also, a whole range of unusual new hybrid beans are now starting to become available.

CHEESES

In Tex-Mex cooking throughout the Southwest, Monterey Jack cheese, or Jack cheese, blended equally with yellow Cheddar cheese, is the cheese most often used. Monterey Jack cheese was developed in Monterey, California, where the best Jack is still produced. Wisconsin Jack and most other commercial Jack cheeses are much firmer textured and less creamy and flavorful. They do shred better, but the tradeoff is generally not worth it if the Monterey Jack cheese is available.

Queso Fresco or Queso Blanco is the traditional Mexican cheese. It is white, somewhat dry, and salty—a bit reminiscent of feta, which can be used as a substitute.

CHILES

Chiles are the one major ingredient that singlehandedly determines both the temper and the taste of the dishes in this cuisine. I've always used the Spanish spelling for chile, ending with an *e*, rather than the Anglicized or chili spelling; I spell the cooked dish *chili*.

Chiles are native to this hemisphere. They are capsicums and members of the nightshade family along with potatoes, tomatoes, and eggplant. The source of heat in chile is capsaicin, an oil-borne substance that can run from relatively tame to fiery hot. This substance is most prevalent in the seeds and ribs, and if you remove these, a chile will be milder. You can also make them milder by soaking them in lime juice for at least 2 hours or overnight.

Chiles are used both green, before ripening, and red, when ripe. To preserve the green ones for use, they must first be parched and then frozen. Commercially they are canned, but canned ones are not as flavorful, as the process turns them a more olive green and reduces flavor. Freezing green chiles works well; they just lose their crisp texture.

The flavor of red chiles is fragile; after drying they should be kept chilled or frozen. Many people do not realize this and hence lose most of the pungency and flavor of the chiles.

Pure ground chiles are not to be confused with chili powder, which is an ingredient that was created for the marching Texas Confederate armies so they could re-create the practical dish of the cowboys—chili con carne. The formula for chili powder is approximately 40 percent ground chiles, 40 percent salt, and the remaining 20 percent flavorings and preservatives. This compound, when found on the home spice shelf, is generally darkened from years of being stored at room temperature, which destroys the freshness of the chiles. The recipes in this book require pure ground dried chiles to achieve the intended flavors.

Chiles do not need to be confusing. A great deal of the confusion comes from the fact that as various new chiles have been hybridized or developed, they have been called different names in different locations and still different names when they are red or ripened.

Chiles are rather crazy genetically; up to thirty-five piquancies can be found on the same plant. Therefore, the visual test of recognizing heat in a chile is critical to know. In a green or unripe chile, the easiest way to determine hotness in a group of the same type of chiles is to look for the broadest shoulders and the most blunt tips for milder flavor, and, conversely, narrower shoulders and more pointed tips for hotter flavor.

As with most growing fruits and vegetables, the flavor of chile is totally dependent on soil, water, and geographic location. The same seeds produce different results in different locations around the world.

For red chile, I do believe in pure ground chiles instead of working with whole pods. Why? Because whole pods cannot be tested for uniformity of flavor, heat, and pungency and generally do not have as fresh a flavor; they also require at least 30 minutes more work with less sure results.

Mild Chiles Formerly these were called California chiles or Anaheim chiles. Recently, this notation was changed to mild New Mexico chiles. Rather than specify a certain variety of chile, I just call them mild or green chiles. They have very low heat and act as a flavor base for chile-laden dishes. When green, these chiles will generally be large, relatively light green with broad shoulders and blunt tips.

Hot Chiles These are the basic New Mexico chiles and are about twice as hot as the mild ones I call for, yet they are not overwhelmingly hot. They will generally be as hot as many people like their spicy foods.

Caribe Chiles These are from northern New Mexico and are known for their sweet, hot taste. They are a third hotter than the hot New Mexico chiles. Originating in the Caribbean and brought into northern New Mexico by the Spanish conquistadors, caribe chiles are among my personal favorites. I keep crushed dried caribe chiles on the dining table in a little hand-painted clay pot. The combination of caribe chile and fresh lime satisfies the desire for salt and pepper and is much healthier. Also, I use crushed caribe chiles a great deal for garnishing.

Pequin Chiles The original chile, which still grows in the border states. I've often called it the fairy godmother of chiles. It is very hot, about four times hotter than the New Mexico hot chile mentioned above. It is sold either crushed or ground and is used as a condiment—rarely in very large quantity because of its heat.

Jalapeño Chiles These are one of the most popular relish chiles, and they grow easily almost everywhere. They are usually dark green in color with thick flesh, having a hot to very hot chile flavor. They are generally one of the most available fresh nationwide. They are also available pickled.

Serrano Chiles These are generally dark green with very slender shoulders and a pointed tip and are about one or two inches long. They are very hot, having less flavor than a jalapeño chile and less thick flesh.

Mexican Chiles Because of the range of names for the same variety of chile, I do wish to point out some of the more popular types.

Poblano or Ancho Chiles This large-hipped chile looks like a first cousin to a bell pepper and can be quite mild. It is usually called a poblano when green and an ancho when red and/or dried.

Pasilla Chiles This chile is very similar to the New Mexico and Poblano and Ancho hot chiles and is generally sold both as fresh red chiles and dried chiles.

Guajillo Chiles These are long, pointed chiles and are brownish-red in color. They are sometimes referred to as cascabels, which are a different chile; they are rounder and often rattle due to their seeds inside. They are hot, but not as hot as the pasilla.

Chipotle Chiles These should have a brownish-red color and a smoky aroma. They are red, ripe jalapeño chiles that have been smoked in banana leaves.

Habanero Chiles Sometimes called Scotch bonnets or Jamaican chiles, they are extremely hot and are generally used only in salsas or as a condiment.

CORN

For centuries corn has held its position as a magical food. Ancient Native Americans worshiped the goddess of corn and believed that man was created from corn dough, or masa. With this favored status, corn received much special care. Lacking modern refrigeration, the Aztecs learned that once it was dried, corn could be stored almost indefinitely without spoiling, if generously sprinkled with lime. Their corn was not only cured with lime, it was also often stored in the web of limestone caves honeycombing the isthmus of Mexico. The taste so ubiquitous in multitudes of Mexican corn dishes originated in this method of preservation.

Dried corn is traditionally white. Blue corn is popular in New Mexico, however, and has a quite different, richer flavor as a result of its curing. After it is smoked in adobe ovens with piñon wood, it is lava-wheel-ground to a fine powder or flour, which is used in dishes like blue corn bread, rellenos batter, tamales, and tortillas. (Blue corn has been found to be the only food that has all the vitamins, minerals, and essential amino acids to support healthy life.) Yellow corn, the most popular color used in the United States, is more American than Mexican.

Masa Masa is the dough made from masa harina, the flour made by grinding dried lime-treated kernels of corn or posole, which is the mother process. Masa is also the term for the ground lime-treated corn that has been made into a dough by adding warm water.

Posole Made from lime-treated whole kernels of corn, posole is available fresh or often in the meat section of the supermarket in New Mexico. Posole is also the name of the stew containing the kernels of posole. Posole is *not* hominy, which is made from treating the corn with harsh chemicals, removing the cellulosic coating.

FATS

Lard The mainstay of New Mexican and American-Mexican cooking. It has a greater ability to hold air and is moister than any other shortening, making it the favorite for pie pastry and tamales. Solid vegetable shortening or butter will not achieve the same results. Bacon drippings can be substituted for in the same way; however, the flavor will be lacking.

Olive Oils For salad dressings, salsas, bastes, or marinades, I prefer extra-virgin olive oil, preferably Spanish. The Spanish oils have a fruity essence that is particularly pleasant in Southwestern foods.

Vegetable Oils Corn, soy, or any combination of the two is best for deep-frying. I do not recommend canola oil as it can impart a shellac-like or strong flavor.

SPICES & SEASONINGS

New Mexico, where many of the early culinary traditions for Southwestern foods began, was always landlocked, so the traditional recipes called for very few spices and herbs. For authentic flavors, do not add herbs and spices from other cuisines. The easiest obtainable herb was Mexican oregano, and it was the one most often used. Comino or cumin was harder to come by and was introduced by the Spanish. Following is a list of the most often used seasonings.

Anise The seeds are favored in desserts such as bizcochitos and are licorice-flavored. These seeds seem to last almost forever without staling.

Azafran This is not to be confused with true saffron, which is harvested from crocus stamens in Spain and India. This wild variety completely lacks flavor and is basically used for color, much as annatto is.

Bay Leaves These are popular for flavoring meat and vegetable dishes. Always remove from the dish before serving.

Cilantro The green leaves of the coriander plant are a relatively recent addition to Southwest cooking. The plant is a close relative of the parsley family and is often called Chinese parsley. It possesses a special clean, clear, almost a stringent flavor that makes either close friends or adamant enemies. For those who appreciate its taste, the leaves of this aggressive herb are an invaluable addition to soups, salads, and relishes. When adding cilantro to dishes, be sure to *only* coarsely chop—never mince as it will develop an undesirable flavor and odor. Many like the seed form, or coriander, to flavor baked goods.

Comino or Cumin This originated in the Middle East, where most of it is still grown. It is available as whole seeds or ground. It is what gives the familiar taste to chili.

Garlic Use the large, purplish heads of Mexican garlic for the most pungent flavor. If you use other types of fresh garlic with smaller cloves, you should probably double the quantity called for in the recipes in this book. Figure that each clove should fill a generous 1/2 teaspoon or more.

Mexican Oregano This is a closer relative to the mint family than Mediterranean oregano. Possessing lavender blossoms and big leaves, it grows native all over the hills of northern New Mexico. Native cooks almost always add a pinch to the pot of any chile dish. A word of caution: If you cannot get this musky flavored mint-like oregano, do not use the Italian or Greek types if you want authentic flavors. If the real Mexican type is not available, it is best left out.

Mexican Vanilla Vanilla has been made in Mexico from beans of the vanilla orchid for ages and was originally discovered by the Aztecs. Mexican vanilla is special because it is stronger and more aromatic than other types. However, one must be careful to purchase only pure vanilla, and can only be assured that it is pure vanilla if approved by the United States Food and Drug Administration.

Mint Often locally called yerba buena, or good herb, mint is freely used in sauces, desserts, and beverages. Like Mexican oregano, it grows wild and has been used for centuries.

Pickled Jalapeño Chile Juice The juice from pickled jalapeño chiles is very versatile and is never discarded. Cooks reserve it even after the chiles are gone to use in seasoning soups, stews, and other dishes. Substitute cider or white vinegar and crushed or ground hot chiles, about a pinch of chiles per Tablespoon of vinegar.

Sage Mexican sage is the local variety of the well-known herb for dressings or stuffings. It is popular in many meat and poultry dishes. It gains a deep color at high altitudes and is often labeled black sage.

Tips & Techniques

PARCHING GREEN CHILES

Green chiles freshly parched, or parched and frozen, are far superior to their canned equivalents. Canning always seems to impart a metallic taste and changes the texture and flavor. Although freezing does soften the crisp texture, it does not impair the taste. Because chiles are perishable and seasonal, freezing is often the only alternative. Green chiles are generally available from late June, when the first of the crop comes in, to late September, when they ripen and become red, signaling the end of the season.

Parching is necessary to remove the very leathery peel of fresh chiles. The process is easy, but be sure to wear rubber gloves or generously butter your hands to prevent a burn from the chile's irritating oils. Intense direct heat is needed to parch the peel, but take care to leave the flesh itself uncooked. Immediate chilling of the parched chile halts the cooking process and causes the skin to blister away from the uncooked flesh. If you are freezing chiles, freeze them after parching but with the peel on for greatest flexibility of use. Parched green chiles freeze well for one year. With a double-oven range, you can parch a bushel of chiles in one and a half to two hours.

To parch chiles, first wash them, removing all sand and dirt. Leave the stem on, then pierce each one with a sharp knife, about one inch down from the stem. For large quantities, cover the entire top rack of an electric oven with heavy foil; if yours is a gas stove, cover the broiler rack. For smaller quantities, cover a baking sheet. Outdoor grills work especially well for parching. Then place the rack under an electric broiler four inches from the broiler unit; if using gas, place the rack in the highest position. Preheat the broiler, then place a single layer of chiles on the foil. Allow each side to blister before turning. Allow each chile to uniformly blister for easy removal of the peel. As soon as each chile is parched, remove to the sink, a large bowl, or a tub of ice water. Immerse each chile in water. Allow to cool, then either peel or package in plastic freezer bags. To peel, always start at the stem and pull off strips of the peel.

Blot dry between layers of paper towels before using. For rellenos, keep the stem on, but for other uses, remove. For a milder taste, once the chile is parched, strip out the seeds and veins with the back side of a knife. To freeze, place the chiles on baking sheets and flash freeze before bagging in freezer weight bags for greatest flexibility of use.

If you are parching only a few chiles, place each directly on a medium-hot electric surface unit, or hold it with tongs or a meat fork over a gas burner. If parching outdoors on a gas, electric, or charcoal grill, place the rack about four inches above white-hot coals. Watch carefully—the chiles parch quickly.

PREPARATION OF WHOLE RED PODS OR CRUSHED CHILES

Clean any dust or dirt from the whole pods, and place on a large shallow pan such as a baking sheet. Then heat in a 300°F (150°C) oven until the color heightens and a pungency is noted, about 10 to 15 minutes. Do not allow to burn! Transfer the chiles to a large saucepan. For every one cup of crushed or whole chile pods, add four cups of water; simmer thirty minutes, or until the skin slips from the flesh. Strain out the pods, rubbing the skin with a spoon to get the greatest amount of flesh.

Quantities of this can be made ahead and then frozen in one-recipe amounts in freezer containers or even in ice cube trays and removed, then stored in a plastic bag.

PREPARATION OF CHIPOTLE & SMOKED CHILES

Rinse and clean the chiles, then cover with warm water to which about 1/2 teaspoon red wine vinegar or cider vinegar has been added for each chile. Soak for about thirty minutes or simmer five to eight minutes in a microwave oven or on top of the stove.

GENERAL INFORMATION ON FRYING & HEATING TORTILLAS

In general, tortillas gain about 50 calories each when fried. To eliminate this, they can be warmed on a griddle or comal or in a plastic bag or plastic wrap for 10 to 15 seconds each in a microwave oven. Or wrap a stack of them in foil and heat in a moderate oven (350°F, 175°C). When making enchiladas, the corn tortillas are normally soft or lightly fried. For flat enchiladas, you do not need to fry them. For rolled enchiladas, the tortilla must be lightly fried and drained.

CRISP-FRIED TORTILLAS

Special fryers and holders are now available for making both the U-shaped taco shells and the fried tortilla bowls (tostado shells) that are used for tostados and salads. When using shaped shells for tostados, depending on their size, you may want to serve two per person, since they don't hold as much as a flat tostado. These shells fry beautifully when using either corn or flour tortillas. You may dust the fried flour tortillas in cinnamon sugar for dessert. Packed carefully and sealed airtight, these shells can be frozen. They will keep for one month at room temperature.

——— Woods for Grilling ———

MESQUITE

Mesquite is the wood of choice, especially for Texans, and it has become quite popular outside of Texas. Mesquite is a bush that grows throughout the Southwest and used to be considered a weed, such as dandelions in pastures. When mesquite burns, it imparts a strong oil-based aroma to meats and vegetables and whatever is grilled. When selecting mesquite, always check to be sure the wood or chips have been heat treated—some call it pasteurization—to rid the wood of vermin.

Fruit Woods and Others

Cherry, apple, grape cuttings, hickory, and other fruit and nut woods are popular for adding to charcoal fires for added aroma. These can be bought at stores that feature barbecue grills and supplies. Or they can be gotten as cuttings or trimmings from orchards and growers.

Equipment

Southwestern cooking requires very little special equipment. You can become a master of the cuisine with a modest investment. Traditional tools, such as the tortilla press, a taco fryer, tostado fryer, and a bolillo, are relatively inexpensive and fun to use. Appliances such as food processors, blenders, and mixers are an added convenience; and microwave ovens or convection ovens are terrific for speeding up such cooking processes as baking and melting cheese. You might consider investing in an electric deep-fat fryer. The thermostatic control assures even browning of temperature-delicate foods such as sopaipillas and taco shells, which makes the expense totally worthwhile. Lacking this appliance, an accurate frying thermometer is critical.

Tortilla Press

This is a real boon to making smooth, even corn tortillas. Recently, American gourmet equipment manufacturers have begun designing and marketing more convenient and efficient models. Look for smooth interior surfaces, a diameter of six to seven inches, and a strong, well-designed lever to pull down for flattening the tortillas. A heavy metal one such as cast iron is generally preferred as their weight makes it easier to make the tortillas.

Bolillo

A short rolling pin that is a uniform two inches in diameter and eight or more inches long. (Coincidentally the bread rolls in Mexico bear the same name.) It fits ideally in the palm and rolls flour tortillas to a uniform thinness. I find the rustic type with no handles the easiest to work with. The bolillo is also perfect for rolling empanada and bizcochito dough.

Tapa or Comal

This is a griddle used for baking tortillas over high heat for rapid browning. In New Mexico, the traditional tapas are former cast-iron stove inserts. A cast-iron griddle, or other dark, heat-absorbing surface is best. Do not allow a fast-talking salesperson to sell you a shiny model . . . they are useless! Comal is the Mexican/Spanish name for a tapa.

Taco Fryer

Look for a model that will hold the tortillas in a U shape while immersed in deep, hot fat. For home use, the most practical type will have a double taco holder at the end of a long handle. Some multiple taco fryer models simply do not work—the holders for the tortillas float away, allowing the tortillas to release from the bottom of the frying mechanism.

Tostado Fryer

Tostados are the bowls made by frying corn and flour tortillas in a tostado fryer. Tostado fryers are available in specialty shops and by mail order. If you cannot find a tostado fryer or want to make different sizes of tostados, you can make your own from an unpainted, opened, clean steel can.

Start by making four openings at equal intervals with a beverage opener around the flat bottom of the can near the rim. Then make an opening between each of the openings on the bottom but on the side of the can near the middle. The openings allow the oil to drain from the can when it is immersed in the hot oil. Choose a can size that will allow the edges of the tortillas to come up around the can to form the side of the bowl.

To fry tortillas, preheat oil to 375°F (190°C). Carefully place a tortilla flat on the hot oil with tongs. Using tongs, immediately press the can (opened end down) into the center of the tortilla, pressing the tortilla down into the hot oil but not to the bottom on the pan. The hot oil will come out of the openings at the top and cook the inside of the tortilla. Cook until the rapid bubbling subsides, or 22 seconds on average, then drain on paper towels.

Molinillo

A long-handled, wooden utensil with rather intricate interlocking circles on the end. When the handle is rubbed between the palms, the circles create a very effective whipping action that is ideal for blending and foaming hot Mexican chocolate or soft custards as they cook.

Metate

This is the Mexican or Southwestern version of a mortar and pestle. A blender or a food processor will also do the job.

INDEX